FURTHER INDIA

A General View from Mandalay Hill

THE STORY OF EXPLORATION

FURTHER INDIA

BEING

THE STORY OF EXPLORATION FROM THE
EARLIEST TIMES IN BURMA, MALAYA
SIAM AND INDO-CHINA

BY

HUGH CLIFFORD, C.M.G.

AUTHOR OF
"IN COURT AND KAMPONG," "STUDIES IN BROWN HUMANITY,"
"BUSHWACKING," "A FREE-LANCE OF TO-DAY," ETC.

WITH ILLUSTRATIONS FROM DRAWINGS, PHOTOGRAPHS
AND MAPS

AND WITH MAP IN COLOURS
BY J. G. BARTHOLOMEW

NEW YORK
FREDERICK A. STOKES COMPANY
PUBLISHERS

TO

DÊMS

THIS BOOK IS LOVINGLY DEDICATED
IN MEMORY OF
THE DAYS DURING WHICH
IT WAS WRITTEN

CONTENTS

LIST OF ILLUSTRATIONS

v

LIST OF ILLUSTRATIONS vii

FURTHER INDIA

CHAPTER I

CHRYSE THE GOLDEN AND THE CHERSONESUS AUREA

THE great peninsula which forms the south-eastern corner of the Asiatic continent, comprising, as we know it to-day, Burma, Siam, French Indo-China and the Malay Peninsula, will be found, in comparison with other regions of the East, to have suffered at the hands of Europeans from a wholly unmerited neglect. Latterly, it is true, the Powers of the West have been busy here, as in other quarters of the world; but in spite of their new-born political importance only a languid interest has, for the most part, been excited in the countries themselves and in the problems to which their affairs have given rise. The failure of the lands of southeastern Asia to make a strong appeal to the imagination of the peoples of Europe is to be ascribed, however, not to their intrinsic unimportance, nor yet to any lack of wealth, of beauty, of charm, or of the interest that springs from a mysterious and mighty past. The reason is to be sought solely in the mere accident of their geographical position. Lying as they do midway upon the great sea-route which leads from India to China, it has been the fate of these countries to be overshadowed from the beginning by the immensity and the surpassing fascination of their mighty neighbours. Thus, even when India and Cathay had emerged at last from the nebulous haze of myth, superstition and conjecture with which the imaginations of Europeans had early enshrouded them, southeastern Asia continued to be wrapped in obscurity, such knowledge of it as was possessed being practically confined to a bare acquaintance with its coast-lines, with a few ports of call, and with the seas traversed by ships in their passage from the shores of Malabar to the southern provinces of China. Similarly, in our own time, while every schoolboy can point out Canton or Peking, Delhi or Peshwur, as a matter of course, not one educated man in fifty can put his finger unhesitatingly upon the spot on the map which represents Chieng Tong or Bhamo, Pahang or Pnom-Penh. The real exploration of this region, beyond the limits of a narrow zone of coastlands, was not accomplished until during the latter half of the nineteenth century, while the work done in this direction by Francis Garnier and a host of smaller men is even less known in these islands than are the localities in which their labours were performed.

It is not easy to realise to how late a period in their history the Greeks remained in almost total ignorance of the Eastern world, or indeed of any inhabited lands lying at a distance from the seaboard of the Mediterranean. It was not until the invasion of Xerxes forced the fact upon their attention in uncompromising wise that they completely grasped the proximity of Persia. Hecatæus of Miletus, who wrote between 520 and 500 B. C., is the first of the ancients to make mention of India and the Indus by name, and Megasthenes, who was in the service of the Syrian King, Seleucus Nicanor, during the third century B. C., was the earliest writer to extend the western acquaintance with the East to the banks of the Ganges. He traversed the great peninsula from the Indus to the former river by means of what he describes as "the royal road"—probably the first of the grand trunk-roads of India—crossed successively the Sutlej and the Jumna, and descended the Ganges to Palibothra, a town at the mouth of the Sone which was the capital of a king called Sandracottus (Chandra-gupta). He brought back with him much detailed information concerning the country, its people and its products, and he speaks of cinnamon and other spices as being imported from the southern parts of India, which may possibly be an indication of the existence, even in his time, of the spice-trade of the Malayan Archipelago.

It was not, however, until after the beginning of our era that the first, faintest hint reached Europe concerning the existence of lands lying to the east of the Ganges. It is found in the writings of Pomponius Mela, whose date can be fixed from internal evidence at A. D. 43, which make mention of a headland named Tabis, described by the author as the most easterly extremity of Asia, and of another, apparently further to the south, called Tamus. Off the latter lay Chryse, or the Golden

Isle, while Argyre, the Isle of Silver, was opposite to the
mouth of the Ganges. Pomponius Mela places the land
of the Seres—the name by which the inhabitants of
northern China were known—south of Tabis and between that headland and India. These statements,
though they represent nothing more than a vague groping after the truth, are interesting because they mark the
dawn of a perception that beyond the Ganges there lay
further to the east certain inhabited lands, and because
they show that in Pomponius Mela's time the Seres were
recognised as occupying country at the extreme east of the
Asiatic continent. Concerning Chryse itself Pomponius
Mela, it is probable, entertained no very definite ideas,
but his mention of the mythical isle indicates that a new
geographical conception had come into being. Hence-
forth the Ganges was no longer to be regarded as the
eastern limit of the habitable world. The map of the
earth according to Pomponius Mela, here reproduced
from Mr. E. H. Bunbury's admirable *History of Ancient
Geography*, shows the distorted character of his notions
concerning the configuration of the seas and continents ;
but in the insignificant island of Chryse, there seen lying
off the promontory of Tamus, we must recognise the
earliest attempt ever made by a European to locate the
lands of southeastern Asia.

It was about this time, as we learn from the works of
Pliny the Elder and from that of the anonymous author
of the Periplus of the Erythræan Sea, both of which belong to the latter half of the first century, that a great
revolution was worked in Asiatic navigation. Pliny tells

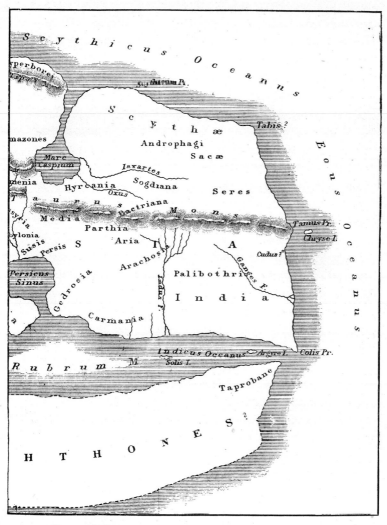

Part of the World according to Pomponius Mela

From Bunbury's "History of Ancient Geography"

island sent to the Court of the Emperor Claudius. He states, among other things, that trade was carried on by the natives of Taprobane (Ceylon) with the Seres of northern China, though doubt is cast upon the matter by the fact that the Chinese are described as fair-haired, blue-eyed giants. On the other hand it is significant that no mention is made of any commercial relations subsisting between the peoples of Ceylon and those of south-eastern Asia. This is, at the best, but negative evidence, yet it is noteworthy as seeming to indicate that the sea-route between India and China was not even then in general use, despite the fact that commercial intercourse between the two empires had been carried on overland from a period of remote antiquity.

Of Chryse, the Golden, Pliny, in fact, has nothing to tell us, and the author of the Periplus, whose personal knowledge did not extend beyond Nelkynda, probably Melisseram, on the Malabar coast, says of it only that it was situated opposite to the mouths of the Ganges and that it produced the best tortoise-shell found in all the Erythræan Sea. He speaks, however, of Thina, the land of silk, situated " where the seacoast ends externally," whence we may gather that Chryse was conceived by him as an island lying not only to the east of the Ganges, but also to the southward of the Chinese Empire. This indicates a distinct advance in knowledge, for the isle of Chryse, albeit still enveloped in a golden haze, was to the author of the Periplus a real country, and no mere mythical fairy-land. Rumours, it would seem, must have reached him concerning it—rumours upon which he be-

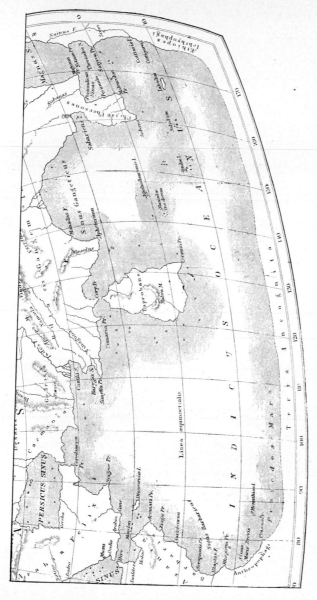

Part of the World according to Ptolemy

From Bunbury's "History of Ancient Geography"

lieved he could rely—and this would tend to prove that the sea-route to China *via* the Straits of Malacca, even though it was not yet in general use, was no longer unknown to the mariners of the East. We know that less than a century later the sailor Alexander, from whom Marinus of Tyre derived the knowledge subsequently utilised by Ptolemy, had himself sailed to the Malay Peninsula and beyond, and it may safely be concluded that the feasibility of this southeastern passage had become known to the seafarers of China long before an adventurer from the West was enabled to test the fact of its existence through the means of an actual voyage.

Ptolemy's views concerning the geography of southeastern Asia, derived mainly from the works of his predecessor Marinus of Tyre, may best be appreciated by a glance at the map here reproduced from Mr. Bunbury's *History of Ancient Geography*. His primary misconception of the Indian Ocean as another and vaster Mediterranean was responsible for many of his geographical distortions, yet if this preconceived notion, and the bias which it imparted to his ideas, be borne in mind, it will be found that there is good reason to believe that the information supplied to him was derived originally from a man who had first-hand knowledge of the sea-route to China. Marinus had quoted the sailor Alexander as journeying from the Golden Chersonese along a coastline which " faced south "—that is to say, ran from west to east,—for a period of twenty days, until a port called Zabæ was reached. From this point, he declared, ships sailed eastward of *south* for a still longer period until the town of Cattigara was reached. The exact locality of Cattigara has been much disputed, Mannert placing it in Borneo, while Bunbury inclines to the belief that some point on the coast of Cochin China is indicated. On the other hand Marinus and Ptolemy both expressly state that Cattigara was a city of the Sinæ, or in other words a port of southern China, and a study of the route followed at a later period by Arabian and European travellers alike reveals the fact that few ever passed on a long voyage to the eastward of the Golden Chersonese unless they were bound for the Celestial Empire. Furthermore, it will be found that it is only by taking some port of southern China as our starting point—*viz.*, as being the town of Cattigara—that Ptolemy's itinerary can be made to have any sequence or meaning. The Sinus Magnus, which is described as the first sea crossed after leaving Cattigara, would then be the China Sea ; the Promontorium Magnum, dividing it from the Sinus Perimulicus, which is perhaps identical with Marinus's Zabæ, would be some point upon the shores of Indo-China, corresponding with Champa, the kingdom which at a later period was an invariable port of call for vessels making the China voyage. Similarly, the Sinus Perimulicus itself, which is described as washing the eastern shores of the Golden Chersonese, would be the Gulf of Siam ; the Golden Chersonese would be, as it is usually agreed that it is, the Malay Peninsula ; and the Sinus Sabaricus, on the western shores of the Chersonese, would correspond to the Straits of Malacca from their southern portals to the Gulf of

Martaban. The island of Iabadius, or Sabadius—the
reading of the name is doubtful—has generally been
taken to represent Java, though there appears to be
slight reason for the assumption, Java lying at a considerable distance from the sea-route to China, and being to
a much later time visited with comparative infrequency
by travellers from the west. On the other hand, Sumatra
lay close to the track of ships plying between India and
the Far East; was a regular port of call from the period
to which belongs the first authentic records of the China
voyages; and could not fail to be sighted by ships running up the Straits of Malacca. It will be seen from the
above that it is only by starting from southern China,
that is by recognising Cattigara as a port of the Celestial
Empire, possibly the Zayton of the medieval wanderers,
or a town which preceded Zayton, as Zayton itself preceded Canton, that Ptolemy's descriptive outline can be
applied to the true geographical facts of the region dealt
with. No straining of probabilities becomes necessary;
no statements have to be elaborately explained away;
and it may be stated without fear of refutation that this
ceases to be the case if any other point be taken as the
site of Cattigara.

To the account of the distances said to have been supplied to Marinus by the sailor Alexander, no real importance can be attached. It was the rough estimate of a
man who was probably very ignorant, and it was given
to a geographer who was not averse to making a bold
guess if thereby the reported facts could be forced to fit
in with ideas previously conceived. The same qualifying

consideration must be held to apply to the direction in which ships making the voyage to Cattigara are said to have sailed after passing the Golden Chersonese. The brief examination of Ptolemy's itinerary already attempted will suffice to establish the probability that Marinus's informant had actually travelled over the sea-route to southern China, and that the geographical confusions shown in the map of the world according to Ptolemy were due less to error in the information supplied than to the faulty reasoning occasioned by misconceptions on the part of the philosophers themselves.

Although, as we have seen, the earliest indication of any conception of lands lying far to the east and south of the valley of the Ganges on the part of the learned of the West belongs to the year A. D. 43, and the first mention of the *Chersonesus Aurea* occurs in the works of Marinus of Tyre about a century later, it would appear that the name which the latter was the first to attach to a definite locality had become familiarly known to *savants* in Europe at a somewhat earlier period. This came about, it is probable, through the accounts brought back by mariners who had themselves made the voyage to this distant quarter of the earth, of whom there is no particular reason to believe that Marinus's Alexander was the first. The name itself would be suggestive of great wealth; distance would lend to it its customary enchantment; the vague information current concerning it would serve to deck it with a halo of mystery, with the glamour of romance; whence it would naturally arise that the Golden Chersonese would come to be regarded

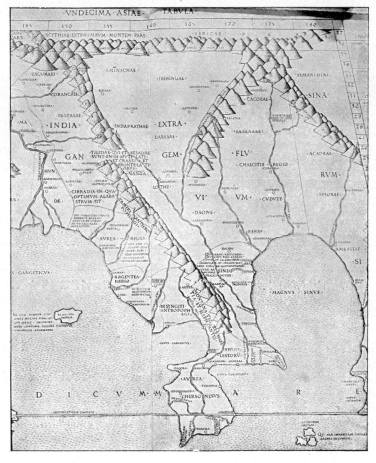

Ptolemy's Further India, as interpreted in the XVth
Century

From the Roman Ptolemy of 1490

as the source whence was drawn the almost fabulous riches of which history held the record.

In this connection a curious passage may be cited from Josephus's *Antiquities of the Jews*, which was written during the latter half of the first century, at a period, it will be noted, prior to the date of the works of Marinus of Tyre. Here, in speaking of the pilots furnished to Solomon by Hiram of Tyre, he writes:

"To whom Solomon gave this command that they should go along with his stewards to the land that of old was called Ophir, but now the *Aurea Chersonesus*, which belongs to India, to fetch gold."

Here, it will be remarked, Josephus speaks of the Chersonese with a certain familiarity, as of a region with the existence of which his readers would be in some sort acquainted, but apart from this he makes two very definite statements—that Ophir and the *Chersonesus Aurea* are one, and that Ophir belonged to India. The second of these would seem to imply that he recognised that the Chersonese was not an integral portion of India, and since the name had never been borne by any country of the West, he must have intended to convey the meaning that it lay beyond the valley of the Ganges, which in his day was recognised as the eastern boundary of Hindustan.

It is now generally held that Ophir itself was, in all probability, a mere distributing centre situated somewhere in the neighbourhood of the entrance to the Red Sea, and that the pilots of Hiram of Tyre did not guide the Stewards of Solomon to the actual source of the gold which went to deck the temple of Jehovah in Jerusalem. The discovery of vast mines in southern Africa, which are believed to date from an immense antiquity, has led of late years to the conclusion that this was the region whence Solomon in his glory drew his stores of gold.

M. Auguste Pavie in the second volume of his monumental work on Indo-China contends that ancient Kambodia is the original Ophir, and that to the whole of the vast peninsula, rather than to its southern portion of Malaya, was applied in ancient days the name of the *Chersonesus Aurea*. The wonderful civilisation of the Khmers which brought into being the splendid buildings of Angkor, of which more will be said in a later chapter, testifies to the existence of a mighty empire in Indo-China which must once have been a centre of wealth and commerce. The vast siltage, borne down from the remote interior by the floods of the Mekong, has changed the face of the country within historical times, and Angkor Thom itself, now distant nearly two hundred miles from the coast, was once a seaport. That the Khmer Empire must in its day have played an important part in the history of eastern Asia cannot be doubted, but M. Pavie's arguments, plausible though they often are, fail to carry conviction when he seeks to prove the identity of Kambodia with Ophir. Also, as regards his contention that the whole of Indo-China was included in the term the Golden Chersonese, it is difficult to believe that what is in fact an immense peninsula was ever recognised as such by the early mariners and geographers. Its bulk is too

great for its peninsular character to be easily or immediately appreciated, while the Malay Peninsula, that long
and slender tongue of land projecting to the south of the
continent of Asia, forces an understanding of its nature
upon the least scientific and observant traveller.

In these circumstances M. Pavie's arguments seem to
be impossible of acceptance, and the recent discovery in
the Malayan State of Pahang—the home of apes and
ivory and peafowl—of immense gold mines of very
ancient date and of a workmanship that has no counterpart in southeastern Asia, supplies an ample reason for
the designation of "golden" so long applied to the
Chersonese.   Here, hidden away under the shade of the
primeval forest, are excavations which must have yielded
in their time tons of the precious metal, and if Josephus
spoke truly, and did not, as is more probable, merely
hazard a bold conjecture, here perhaps are to be found
in the heart of the *Chersonesus Aurea* the mines of
Solomon the King.   Of the race that worked them, of
the slaves who toiled and suffered and died therein, we
to-day possess no clue, for this, the story of the earliest
exploration of a portion of southeastern Asia, is lost to
us forever.   Here, however, at the very outset of our
enquiry, we obtain a glimpse of one of those pregnant
suggestions wherewith Asia impresses our imaginations
by virtue of her antiquity, her wonder and her mystery.
Hers is the land of buried story, of hidden records, of
forgotten romance.   The East baffles while she fascinates
us : fascinates because she baffles.   Sphinx-like she pro-
pounds riddles which few can answer, luring us onward

with illusive hopes of inspiring revelations, yet hiding ever in her splendid, tattered bosom the secrets of the oldest and least amply recorded of human histories.

After the time of Ptolemy there follows a long and barren period during which little advance in geographical knowledge was made by the nations of the West, nor is it until the sixth century that anything resembling new light is thrown by a European upon the topography of southeastern Asia. Moreover the shedder of that light is himself a grotesque figure, an angry theologian bent upon proving the impossible, and moved to intense fury by the impiety of those who, touching more nearly the skirts of truth, have not the advantage of agreeing with him. This is Cosmas Indicopleustes, a monk and an Alexandrian Greek, who between 530 and 550 A. D. set himself the task of proving that the universe was fashioned after the model of the Ark made by the Children of Israel in the desert. It is not necessary to follow him through the mazes of his argument, all of which he supported by texts culled from the Scriptures, but out of the tissue of absurdities to which he pinned his faith two facts emerge. While inveighing in season and out of season against those who clung to the belief that the world was globular, and against the unspeakable naughtiness of the adherents to the poisonous doctrine of the antipodes, he displays a sound knowledge of the sea-route to China, stating that a ship after travelling sufficiently far to the east, must turn to the *north*, and must sail in that direction " at least as far as a vessel bound for Chaldea would have to run up the Straits of Hormuz to the mouths of the Euphrates" in order to reach the Celestial Empire, thus disposing once for all of Ptolemy's theory of a great southern continent enclosing the Indian Ocean upon which the land of the Sinæ, or southern Chinese, was formerly supposed to be situated. Cosmas, too, as Yule remarks, "was the earliest writer to speak of China in a matter-of-fact way, and not as a country enveloped in a half-mythical haze." In his work, therefore, we find the first written record of an appreciation on the part of a European of the true relative positions of China and of the lands of south-eastern Asia. The advance in knowledge thus indicated is not great, but it is considerably ahead of that possessed by Ptolemy, and for the sake of the truth which he was the earliest to disseminate we may forgive Cosmas the monk the farrago of nonsense with which he surrounded it, and also much of his bigotry and rage.

Meanwhile inter-Asiatic intercourse by means of the sea-routes had been steadily on the increase. It was the energy and the enterprise of Hippalus, a Greek,—or so we are led to believe by the classical writers who are on this point our only authorities—which showed the way to the Arabs and the Persians across the Indian Ocean, but during the centuries which followed upon his discovery, though an immense trade was in the hands of the merchants of Alexandria, the greatest sea-power in this quarter of the world, after the decline of the Roman Empire, was that of the Persians. As early as the middle of the second century the Romans had es-

tablished trading-stations at Aden, on the shores of
Arabia and in Socotra, while during the same period the
commerical relations between the Persians and India had
undergone a great expansion. Before the first half of
the fifth century had ended this commerce had been
considerably extended while the Roman trade had declined, and according to Masudi and Hamza of Ispahan
the port of Hira was visited at this time by numbers of
vessels, not only from the mainland of India, but also
from distant China. The rise of the Muhammadan
power, while it closed the portals of the East to the
nations of Europe, gave to the Muslims the practical
monopoly of Asiatic trade with the West, and during
their prime the Khalifs of Baghdad were well-nigh
supreme in the Indian Ocean. Muhammadan colonies
were scattered broadcast over the eastern world, and in
758 the followers of the Prophet in China were sufficiently numerous to be able to cause serious disturbances
in that country. The existence of these colonies too
made it possible for a Muslim to travel with ease in
almost any quarter of the East, and the excellent Ibn
Batuta, the professional religious man who preyed upon
the Faithful with such satisfaction to himself and to his
victims, though he was one of the earliest to give to us a
detailed account of his wanderings, was certainly not
among the first Muhammadans to take advantage of the
opportunities which the accident of their religion
afforded to them.

It has already been noted that no mention of the sea-
route to China occurs in any work prior to that of Mari-

nus of Tyre, despite the fact that the overland route from
India to the Celestial Empire had been in general use
from a very remote period. It is certain, however, that
the existence of the former means of communication
must have been known to the mariners of the Far East
long before any rumour concerning it filtered through to
the geographers of Europe. The overland route was
still much frequented as late as the thirteenth century,
when the Polos passed over it on their journey to China,
and its greater antiquity would suffice to account for the
fact that it was familiarly known to traders from the
West who visited India long before the sea-passage had
been heard of by them. It is none the less impossible
to believe that the latter highway was unknown, at any
rate to the natives of Southern China, some time before
the beginning of our era. The Chinese civilisation is one
of the most ancient in existence, presenting as it does
the twin marvel of an immense antiquity and of a pre-
cocious development inexplicably arrested. The Chinese
are said to have understood the use of the mariner's
compass as early as B. C. 2634, and though there is reason
to question the accuracy of this statement, their written
records concerning the properties of the lodestone date
from early in the second century of our era, and it is
thought that the compass was in practical use long before the earliest treatise of this kind which has come
down to us. If this were so, it is at least possible that
Chinese seamen were accustomed to venture out of sight
of land before ever Hippalus made his way across the
Indian Ocean, and a glance at the map will show that

few opportunities for doing so would occur unless voyages from the point of Kambodia to the Malay Peninsula and the islands of the Archipelago, or again from the Straits of Malacca to Ceylon and India had become habitual.

We may conclude with a fair show of probability that the littorals of the China Sea, the Gulf of Siam and the Straits of Malacca were explored by the seamen of China not earlier than the coast-line between the mouths of the Indus and the Straits of Hormuz was skirted by the fleet of Alexander under Nearchus in the fourth century B. C.

Again, the unmistakable impress of Hindu influence which is to be detected in the architecture of the Khmers of Kambodia, several of whose buildings date from 200 B. C., demonstrates the fact that intercourse between India and Indo-China must have been frequent at a very early period, and such intercourse would almost certainly have been conducted by sea. It has even been accepted by many as a fact that Gauthama Buddha himself visited Kambodia, and if this were so—the matter is one which is hardly susceptible of mathematical proof—it would presuppose communication between India and Indo-China as early as 500 B. C.

Owing to the fact, already noted, that after the rise of the Muhammadan power the sea-borne trade between western and eastern Asia passed almost exclusively into the hands of Muslims, the first detailed accounts of the sea-route to China come to us from the Arabian and Persian geographers. The earliest Arabic manuscript of this kind belongs to the year A. D. 851, and has been edited and translated by M. Reinaud, the French Ori-

entalist. The first few pages of this work are lost, but
its earlier portion was obviously written by one who had
himself made the China voyage. The second part of
the book dates from the year 916, and is the work of a
certain Abu Zaid Hassan, a native of Siraf on the Persian Gulf, who, though he does not appear to have had
any personal experience of the trade-route dealt with,
must have enjoyed opportunities of obtaining first-hand
information from those who had themselves made the
voyage. The portion of the book written by the mer-
chant-mariner is in the nature of sailing directions, and
the Arab's genius for mispronouncing foreign tongues,
which is second only to that of the Englishman, causes
the proper names given in the manuscript to present a
series of puzzles to the enquirer. M. Reinaud himself
would appear to have completely misunderstood the
route indicated, and by far the best identification which
has yet been suggested is to be found in an article from
the pen of M. Alfred Maury in the *Bulletin de Géographie*
for the year 1846.

It would be tedious to examine in detail the grounds
for the identification of the various seas and lands there
set forth, but the facts to be gathered from an examination
of the somewhat wearisome itinerary laid down in the manuscript are that ships sailing from India for China took,
during the ninth century, approximately the following
course. After touching at Ceylon and the Nicobars,
they came to anchor in a port near the northeastern extremity of Sumatra. Thence, after occasionally touching at a State on the western coast of the Malay Penin-

sula, they made their way to the southern outlet of the
Straits of Malacca, halted at the island of Bentan to take
in fuel and water, or for similar purposes at an island of
the Natuna group, came to port once more at some harbour either of the eastern shores of the Malay Peninsula,
Siam or Kambodia, passed on to Champa, and thence to
Zayton or some other port of the southern provinces of
China. It will be noted that the route thus traced is
practically identical with that over which we have supposed the sailor Alexander to have journeyed, and in a
later chapter we shall find that a precisely similar course
was followed by all the medieval travellers to and from
China of whose wanderings we have a record. The sea-
route *via* southeastern Asia had by this time become a
well-beaten track, but certain ports of call were used to
the exclusion of all others, and the primary value of this
great highway was as a means of getting to and from
China, few wanderers being tempted to stray from the
appointed path which custom had marked out for ships
plying in these waters.

The establishment of important commercial colonies
in China by the Arabs and the Persians, concerning
which Abu Zaid Hassan's portion of the manuscript
furnishes some interesting particulars, presupposes that
the passage to the Celestial Empire *via* the Straits of
Malacca and the China Sea was now made by these people with great frequency, and the ports of call along that
route, which seem to have been practically the same from
the time of Marinus of Tyre to that of Ibn Batuta who
returned from his wanderings in 1347, were also to some

extent used by the Arabs as settlements and trade
depôts. It is obvious from internal evidence furnished
by the works of Abu Zaid, of Masudi, Edrisi and
Abulfeda that a few Arab mariners turned aside from the
beaten track sufficiently far for Java to become a country
which was comparatively well-known, but this was the
exception, not the rule, and nowhere do we find reason
for thinking that the Arabs ever ventured far inland, save
only in China itself. In spite of a wider and surer
knowledge of Malaya and Indo-China than any which
at this time was possessed by Europeans, the notions entertained concerning these regions by the Arabian
geographers were still very vague and imperfect.
Ptolemy's misapprehension concerning the Mediterranean
character of the Indian Ocean was endorsed and per-
petuated by successive Arabian geographers, many of
whom doubtless arrived at this false conclusion independently of their great predecessor. Some held with him
that the African continent was prolonged in such fashion
that it lay to the south of Malaya, while others were of
opinion that the great southern *terra incognita*, whose
existence they had deduced from unknown premises,
was divided from Africa by a narrow strait. For the
rest, in spite of persistent attempts to treat geographical
questions in a scientific manner, and to divide the
habitable world into climates, or latitudes and longitudes,
the general ideas at which they arrived concerning the
comparative sizes and the relative positions of various
countries were extraordinarily inexact.

This is well illustrated by the two maps showing the

world according to Masudi and Edrisi respectively, here reproduced from M. Reinaud's excellent edition of *La Géographie d' Aboulféda*. Masudi, who wrote during the first half of the tenth century and who was a contemporary of Abu Zaid Hassan, had not only travelled extensively, but was also well versed in the literature of his subject and had had access to older Arabic works which have since been lost to us. His book therefore represented the widest and soundest geographical knowledge of his time, yet a glance at the chart which puts his conception of the universe before us in a convenient form suffices to demonstrate how radical were many of his misconceptions concerning the form and nature of the earth's surface, and how great was his confusion in matters of detail. For him Indo-China and Malaya consisted of one lozenge-shaped peninsula to the south of which lay Sumatra in the same latitude as Ceylon, while Java was situated further to the eastward almost on the same parallel. China itself was also a peninsula, separated from that of Indo-China by a great gulf, while far to the south of all lay a vast *terra incognita* which had its beginning near the south of the Sudan.

Edrisi's chart is even more confusing, although its author who lived and wrote under King Roger II of Sicily, completed his work in 1153–54. He fills almost the whole of the southern hemisphere with the African continent, makes the Mediterranean occupy an altogether disproportionate space in the universe, vastly exaggerates the size of Sicily and of Ceylon, while to neither India nor China does he give the prominence which rightly

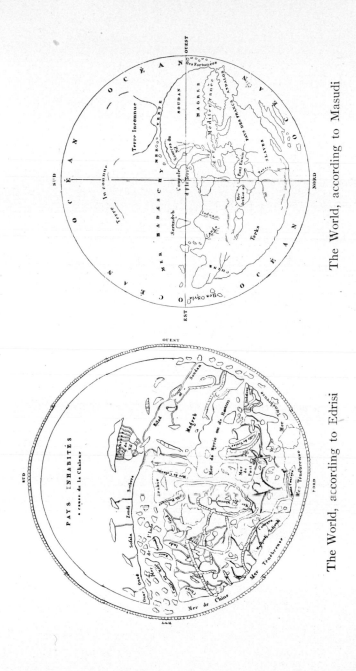

The World, according to Masudi

The World, according to Edrisi

belongs to it. When he passes to the eastward of Al Rami, or Sumatra, he becomes involved in inextricable confusion.

An examination of these two charts will serve better than aught else to bring home to the reader the exceedingly rudimentary state of geographical knowledge even as late as the twelfth century, yet it must be remembered that at this period the geographers of Arab nationality were far in advance of Europeans, and that, notwithstanding their many errors, substantial progress is shown by their work if it be compared with the shadowy surmises and guesses of Marinus and Ptolemy, more especially with regard to southeastern Asia.

CHAPTER II

THE first of the European wanderers in the Far East, the personal narrative of whose adventures has come down to us, is Messer Marco Polo, the Venetian. The wonderful story of the great overland journey made by this traveller in the company of his father and uncle when they set out from Constantinople " to traverse the world," will be dealt with in a separate volume, and need not here be recapitulated in detail. For us the travels of Marco Polo begin and end with his passage across the seas and amidst the islands of southeastern Asia on his return journey from Cathay to Europe. And once again the fate, which we have noted as dooming the Indo-Chinese peninsula to obscurity, causes this portion of Marco Polo's narrative to be more tangled and more destitute of detail than almost any other chapters in his book. The slovenliness of his descriptions of the countries between Champa, or Chamba, as he calls it, and Ceylon, and the scant measure of reliable fact which is to be extracted from his account of his journey, moved the late Mr. John Crawfurd to contemptuous indignation. " The information communicated," he declares, " is more like what might be expected from a Chinese than a European traveller, and the author who had gone to China at eighteen, and lived there for twenty

24

Marco Polo, from a painting in the Gallery of
Monsignore Badia at Rome

From the book of Ser Marco Polo (by permission of Mr. John Murray)

years, was probably in his turn of thinking as much a Chinese as a European." What hampered Marco Polo in his observations of southeastern Asia far more materially than any accident of training, however, was that after traversing the entire continent, and living for a score of years in the land of the Great Kaan, the comparative insignificance of the countries of the Malay Archipelago must have struck him with peculiar force. There is internal evidence of some such attitude of mind in many of his references to these regions. In several passages Polo is constantly to be detected comparing everything he saw with that greater world of Cathay in which so large a portion of his life had been spent, and it is not wonderful, therefore, if he dismissed with a bare mention lands and peoples which fell so far short of the standard whereby he scaled them.

Setting out from the port of Zayton in the province of Fokien, Marco relates that " after sailing for some three months " he and his shipmates arrived " at a certain island towards the south which is called Java. . . . Quitting this island they continued to navigate the Sea of India for eighteen months before they arrived whither they were bound," *viz.*, at Hormuz. The journey was made in immense Chinese junks, several of which carried crews of 250 or 260 men. The Java of which Marco Polo here speaks is not Java proper, but " Java the Less," as he elsewhere names it, or in other words, Sumatra. To the voyage to the mouth of the Straits of Malacca, therefore, must be added the run up the coast of Sumatra to a point near its northeastern extremity, an insignificant

distance it is true, but one which a sailing vessel may
take a long time in covering, since in these sheltered
waters navigation is not aided by the constant winds of
the monsoon. When every allowance has been made,
however, it must be confessed that Marco Polo's journey
from China to Sumatra occupied a prodigious time.

When, therefore, Sumatra was at last reached the force
of the northeast monsoon was spent, and Marco Polo
and his comrades had to make up their minds to a five
months' stay upon the island while they awaited the
return of a favourable wind.

Concerning the lands of southeastern Asia he has no
very illuminating information to supply. Champa, or
Chamba, was to him remarkable chiefly because it was a
" very rich region, having a King of its own," whose
children numbered 326 souls! He notes the vast
quantity of tame elephants in use in this country, the
" abundance " of lignaloes, and the existence of extensive
forests of a jet-black timber, called *bonús*, but his account
of Kublai Kaan's attempts to subdue the country is
startlingly inaccurate. His description of Java—not
" Java the Less," but the smaller and richer island over
which the Dutch flag flies to-day—is hardly more exact,
and it is plain that, lying as it does far from the highway
between China and the West, he never personally visited
it. He greatly overestimates its size, mentions that its
king had no over-lord, and credits it with many vegetable
products which it does not produce, the fact being that
Java was at this period the great emporium of the trade
of the Malayan Archipelago, the produce of the islands

being brought thither and thence distributed to the markets of the world. The islands of Sondur and Condur, 700 miles from Champa, at which Marco's ship would appear to have touched, are the Pûlau Kondor of to-day, once the site of a factory of the British East India Company, and now a penal settlement to which convicts are sent from Saigon, the capital of French Indo-China. Locac—" a good country and a rich; (it is on the mainland); and it has a king of its own. The people are idolaters and have a peculiar language, and pay tribute to nobody, for their country is so situated that no one can enter it to do them ill,"—is also described as yielding brasil " in great plenty; and they also have gold in incredible quantity." " They also," he adds, " have elephants and much game. In this kingdom too are gathered all the porcelain shells which are used for small change in all these regions." The identity of Locac has been much disputed, but the strongest case is made out by Sir Henry Yule, who places it in the Malay Peninsula, somewhere in what is now called Lower Siam.

Marco Polo's Pentam, " a very wild place," 500 miles towards the south, is almost certainly the island of Bentan near the entrance to the Straits of Malacca, " and when you have gone these sixty miles and again about thirty more, you come to an island which forms a kingdom, and is called Malaiur. The people have a king of their own and a peculiar language. The city is a fine and noble one, and there is great trade carried on there, and all other necessaries of life." It is impossible to disregard Polo's distinct assertion that Malaiur was an island, and

further the fact that it is not included in his list of
Sumatran kingdoms, wherefore it seems probable that in
his day there existed a Malayan state of considerable
importance, possibly upon the island on which the town
of Singapore now stands.

Sumatra, or " Java the Less," is dealt with in somewhat greater detail. In speaking of Ferlec (Pĕrlak) he
says :

" This kingdom, you must know, is so much frequented by the Saracen merchants that they have con-
verted the natives to the Law of Mahommet—I mean the
townspeople only, for the hill-people live for all the world
like beasts, and eat human flesh, clean or unclean. And
they worship this, that, and the other thing; for in fact
the first thing they see on rising in the morning, that
they do worship for the rest of the day."

We have here yet another proof of the frequency with
which the Arab merchants resorted to Malaya, and a
hint at the length of that intercourse, for even the more
civilised sections of a community do not become con-
verted to an alien faith save after long and intimate asso-
ciation with its professors.

Basma (Pâsei), another Sumatran State, declared itself,
Marco Polo tells us, to be subject to the Great Kaan, though
it paid him no regular tribute, only sending him presents
from time to time. Ibn Batuta, the Arab traveller, when
he returned from China some fifty years later, made the
voyage in a ship which belonged to " the King of Sumatra " who had been to pay homage to the Emperor,
and it is possible that this Muhammadan potentate may

have been no other than the then Râja of Pâsei. It is in writing of this State that Polo tells us of wild elephants and of " numerous unicorns, which are very nearly as big." His description of these latter monsters is delightful :

" They have hair like that of a buffalo, feet like those of an elephant, and a horn in the middle of the forehead, which is black and very thick. They do no mischief, however, with the horn, but with the tongue alone ; for this is covered all over with long and strong prickles (and when savage with any one they crush him under their knees and then rasp him with their tongue). The head resembles that of a wild boar, and they carry it ever bent towards the ground. They delight much to abide in mire and mud. 'Tis a passing ugly beast to look upon, and it is not in the least like that which our stories tell us of as being caught in the lap of a virgin : in fact 'tis altogether different from what we fancied."

Here, in spite of some flowers of fancy, we have no sort of difficulty in recognising the rhinoceros, a truly different creature to the graceful unicorn of our legends; but it is curious that the Sumatran species is *two* horned, and that while it has hair like that of a water-buffalo, it carries its head far more erect than does the one-horned variety commonly met with on the other side of the Straits of Malacca. One cannot help fancying that Polo had actually seen a specimen of the one-horned rhinoceros, and that he subsequently heard of the existence of the creature in Sumatra, for on the whole he describes the animal with wonderful accuracy.

Another interesting passage about Basma is as follows:
" I may tell you moreover that when people bring home pigmies which they allege come from India, 't is all a lie and a cheat. For these little men, as they call them, are manufactured on this Island, and I will tell you how. You see there is on this Island a kind of monkey which is very small and hath a face like a man's. They take these, and pluck out all the hair, except the hair of the beard and on the breast, and then they dry them and stuff them and daub them with saffron and other things until they look like men. But you see it is all a cheat; for nowhere in India nor anywhere else in the world were there ever men seen so small as these pretended pigmies."

The creature here referred to is obviously the yellow gibbon, found in great numbers in the Malay Peninsula and in Sumatra, an ape of peculiarly human aspect, tailless, and though of a purely arborial habit unable to walk save upon its hind legs. If Polo is right, the manufacture of " freaks " would seem to be by no means a modern or an American invention!

Of Dagroian, which would seem to have occupied the position of the little State now known as Pêdir, Polo tells us that the natives were in the habit of devouring their ailing relatives, whose death they caused by suffocation as soon as their recovery had been declared to be impossible by the medicine-men. The reason of this custom, as given by Polo, is curious:

" And I assure you," he says, " they do suck the very bones till not a particle of marrow remains in them; for

they say that if any nourishment remained in the bones
this would breed worms, and then the worms would die
for want of food, and the death of these worms would be
laid to the charge of the deceased man's soul. And so
they eat him up stump and rump. And when they have
eaten him they collect his bones and put them in fine
chests, and carry them away, and place them in caverns
among the mountains where no beast nor other creature
can get at them. And you must know also that if they
take prisoner a man of another country, and he cannot
pay ransom in coin, they kill and eat him straightway.
It is a very evil custom and a parlous."

As every one has learned from experience, who has
himself made some attempt to collect versions of local
superstitions, to examine quaint customs, and to seek for
their explanations from the people among whom they
prevail, it is fatally easy to misconceive and misinterpret
if long and familiar intercourse has not given to the enquirer a very thorough understanding of and sympathy
with the native point of view. One and the same practice, regarded from the standpoint of those to whom immemorial usage has made it a matter of course, and from
that of the stranger who lights upon it unexpectedly,
assumes wholly different aspects and proportions, and to
this fact is due more than half the cock-and-bull stories
and patently absurd explanations which to this day travellers bring back with them from their sojourns among
peoples whom they have imperfectly comprehended.

Of Lambri—the Lambrij of de Barros, the Al Ramni
of the Arabs—a State which seems to have been situated

upon the northern borders of the modern Acheh, Polo
tells us that the natives called themselves the subjects of
the Great Kaan, that they cultivated brasil, and had
" plenty of camphor and all sorts of spices." He also
relates that there were here men with tails, " a palm in
length," hairless, and " about the thickness of a dog's,"—
a very popular fable of the Archipelago which is still
current among the natives in many places even in our
own time.

Polo's remarks on the subject of the Sumatran States
have been examined in some detail, not because they
have much intrinsic importance, but because they can
claim a certain interest as being the first notes ever made
by a European upon the condition of an island of the
Malayan Archipelago. Of geographical data little indeed is to be won from a perusal of Messer Marco's
book, his itinerary showing, what we already knew, that
the sea-route from China *via* southeastern Asia had become a great highway of commerce, and that certain
ports of call, known to the Arabs centuries earlier, were
still used to the exclusion of all others at the end of the
thirteenth century. For the rest we learn that the trade
in the distinctive products of the Malayan Archipelago
was flourishing in 1296, as it had been, in all probability,
before the days of Ptolemy; that the ubiquitous Arab
merchants had already established colonies and begun
the conversion of the Malays to Muhammadanism on
the east coast of Sumatra; and that cannibalism was a
marked feature in the customs of the pagan people of
the island. All this adds little to the story of explora-

tion in southeastern Asia, yet we have felt constrained to follow Marco Polo closely because the figure of this early European wanderer is at once so interesting, so picturesque and so romantic, and the imagination is tempted to dwell and linger over the story of the three lonely white men who so far as we have any record, were the first of their kind to sojourn for a season amid the mysterious forests of Malaya—the lands which were fated to become at a later period the heritage of the nations of the West.

The impossibility of fixing even approximately the date which first saw the opening-up of the sea-route to China has already been noted, and though Messer Marco Polo is the earliest European wanderer in the Far East who has become for us articulate, it is possible that many before him penetrated to Cathay or traversed the seas of which he wrote. The wide dissemination of Nestorian Christianity from Jerusalem eastward to Peking, which had taken place by the fourteenth century, argues a closer intercourse between the West and the East *via* the overland route than is generally recognised, while the celebrated inscription disinterred at Sing-an-fu proves that the heretical doctrine was publicly preached in China, and received sanction and encouragement from the authorities, as early as the seventh century. That the intercourse which is thus implied was carried on wholly by land seems the reverse of probable, yet the fact remains that no authentic record of Europeans having travelled through southeastern Asia is to be found earlier than the date of the Polo manuscripts.

Of later wanderers, however, there are not a few, though for the most part their references to Malaya and Indo-China are merely incidental, and it is curious to note the impunity with which, during the Middle Ages, solitary white men were able to travel unmolested through Asiatic lands. This forces upon us a recognition of the fact that the European invasion of Asia, which began with the rounding of the Cape by Vasco da Gama in 1497, has had a very injurious effect upon the character of the Oriental peoples. Prior to the coming of the white men an extraordinary measure of tolerance, even of hospitality, was extended to strangers without distinction of race or creed. All the early travellers combine in bearing testimony to the care which was taken of aliens by, for example, the authorities in China, the people who before all others are to-day a byword for their suspicious dislike of foreigners. The reason of this change of attitude is to be sought for, not in the naughtiness of the Oriental, nor in his moral degeneracy, but in the misconduct of the early European filibusters which put the East forever on the defensive, and caused the name of the white man to stink in the nostrils of the brown peoples.

The only medieval wanderers with whose passage through southeastern Asia we need concern ourselves are Blessed Odoric of Pordone in Friuli, a friar of the Order of St. Francis, Abu Abd Allah Muhammad Ibn Abd Allah El Lawâti, commonly called Ibn Batuta, "the traveller without peer of the whole Arab nation," as he is affectionately called by a holy man of

Odoric

From the Cittadino Italiano

his own faith, and Friar John de' Marignolli, who in 1338 was sent by the Pope on a mission to the Great Kaan.

Odoric is supposed to have been born in 1286, to have begun his Oriental travels about 1318, to have returned to Europe in 1330 or thereabouts, and to have dictated his reminiscences to a brother Franciscan at Padua ere he crept home to the House of his Order at Udine, where he died in January, 1331. He made his way to Constantinople, thence overland to the Persian Gulf, eventually reaching the coast of Malabar, where he visited the shrine of St. Thomas the Apostle at Mailapur, the modern Madras.

" Departing from this region towards the south across the ocean sea," he tells us, " I came in fifty days to a certain country called Lamori (the State in Sumatra called Al Ramni by the Arabs and Lambri by Polo) in which I began to lose sight of the north star, as the earth intercepted it. And in that country the heat is so excessive that all folk there, both men and women, go naked, not clothing themselves in any wise."

The natives of this State are described as " an evil and pestilent generation" who had no formal marriage, all women being in common. This is an allegation often made against savage and semi-savage communities since Cæsar wrote of Britain, and on closer examination it is usually found to be based upon a misunderstanding of native customs.

Odoric's narrative is interesting because he is the first writer to make mention of a "kingdom by name

Sumoltra," doubtless the same as Polo's Samara, which he places to the south of Lamori, a State which later gave its name to the island upon the coast of which it was situated.   It is doubtful whether the fact of the insularity of their native lands was realised at all generally by the inhabitants of Sumatra, of Java or of Borneo, and I greatly question whether the average Malay of these parts, even now, has any true appreciation of these geographical facts.

Odoric also mentions still further to the south " another realm called Resengo," though he tells us naught concerning it.   The name, however, would lead us to infer that the country of the Rejang is indicated, the State in which the British East India Company's station of Bengcoolen was subsequently established.   Its inhabitants, of whom by the way Polo makes no mention, were among the most civilised of the Sumatrans, possessing not only a peculiar language, but also an original written character.

From Sumatra Odoric passed to Java, which he states was ruled by a king who had seven other monarchs tributary to him.   It is, he quaintly says, " the second best of islands that exist," and he was greatly struck by its riches and by the magnificence of the palace in which its sovereign had his dwelling.   He adds that the Great Kaan " many times engaged in war with this king; but this king always vanquished and got the better of him," a statement which is historically true, Kublai Kaan having launched two unsuccessful expeditions against Java during the time which had elapsed between Marco Polo's passage through the Straits of Malacca and Odoric's visit to the island.

Near Java—a somewhat vague term—Odoric places a country called " Panten, but others call it Thalamasyn, the king whereof hath many islands under him." It produced sago, honey, toddy and a deadly vegetable poison, which was used to smear the blow-pipe darts of the natives who were " nearly all rovers," or pirates. All this points with some certainty to Borneo, and Banjarmasin, which was a flourishing kingdom as early as the eleventh century, may have been Odoric's Thalamasyn, or Panten may have stood for Kalamantan, a name by which a portion of Borneo was known in ancient times.

" By the coast of this country towards the south," Odoric continues, " is the sea called the Dead Sea, the water whereof runneth ever towards the south, and if any falleth into that water he is never found more."

At a later period de Barros relates a superstition of the natives to the effect that the currents beyond the Straits of Bâli acted in a similar manner, and it is possible that in this legend is to be found the germ of the tale concerning the current which wrecked Sindbad, and cast him up, more fortunate than his fellows, upon the bone-strewn island whence he escaped by means of the subterranean passage. To Odoric we also owe one of the earliest descriptions of the bamboo " canes or reeds like great trees," and of the rattan, while he further speaks of stones found in these " canes " which were regarded as charms that conferred the advantage of invulnerability upon their wearers. It is curious to note that these siliceous deposits are still treasured by the Malays for similar reasons in the present day.

Champa, or Zampa as he spells it, is the last country in this part of the world of which Odoric leaves us any record, and here he echoes Polo's astonishment at the number of the king's offspring which he places at " a good two hundred."

It will be seen from the above summary that the Blessed Odoric does not add materially to the sum of our knowledge concerning the lands through which he wandered, and his narrative is chiefly noteworthy because it demonstrates that at the beginning of the fourteenth century it was possible for a solitary Italian friar to roam up and down the east without let or hindrance, mainly, it must be supposed, at the charges of those whom he encountered on his journey. The achievement is all the more remarkable because, unlike Ibn Batuta, his religion gave him no claim upon the piety of the ubiquitous Muhammadan communities.

The Arab traveller, who was born in Tangier on February 24th, 1304, set out upon his wanderings in his twenty-first year. He did not return until 1347. In all he covered more than 75,000 English miles, a respectable record even in these days of easy and swift journeying; wandering over a large part of Asia before he finally made his way back to Fez, in which place his book was dictated by the order of the Sultan. It is a marvellous record, and the manner in which it is told is inimitably naive and amusing, but to us its chief interest lies in the fact that it illustrates in a

striking manner the opportunities for travelling which in
the early fourteenth century were open to any adventurous Muslim. Ibn Batuta, professional holy man, regarded
his coreligionists as created for his comfort and convenience. Wherever he went he preyed upon them shame-
lessly, and deemed them sufficiently honoured by being
suffered to minister to his needs, travelling in this fashion to
the very ends of the then known earth. He managed
things on a scale of unexampled magnificence, and it is our
good fortune that he lived to tell his tale for our delight,
but it is probable that he was only a preeminent member
of a class, and that at this period there were numerous
Muhammadans, with a curious taste in wives and a rapa-
cious appetite for " rich presents," who wandered up and
down the world and drew much profit from the ubiquity
of the great religious fraternity established throughout
the East by the Persian and Arabian merchants.

Ibn Batuta traversed the well-worn route to China, and
has little enough to tell us concerning the lands of southeastern Asia. He was duly impressed with the number
of the king of Champa's children, and noted the multitude
of tame elephants used in that country. He touched
at some point in the Malay Peninsula, which he calls
Mul-Java, or the mainland of Java, and he spent a
season awaiting the change of the monsoon on the
island of Sumatra. Here he was present at the marriage
of the daughter of his host—the " king of Sumatra," as
he calls him, though this potentate only ruled over a
small portion of the island—and the account which he
gives of the ceremony might have been written by an

observer of a modern Malay wedding, a striking proof, were proof needed, of the extraordinary conservatism of this people. For the rest he has nothing new to tell us concerning these regions, though he shows us incidentally that ships still adhered as of old to the few well-known ports of call and rarely strayed far beyond the beaten track which had been in use for centuries.

Friar John de' Marignolli, a Franciscan like Odoric, was born in Florence between 1280 and 1290. In December, 1338, he was sent from Avignon on a mission to the Great Kaan, and travelled overland to China, returning to India *via* Zayton and the Malay Archipelago in 1346 or 1347. Beyond the bare fact that he left Zayton and eventually arrived at Columbum (Quilon) he tells us absolutely nothing, but after some travels in India he paid a visit to an island which he names Saba, and clearly imagines it to be the same as the Saba of the Scriptures. The island, we learn, was so far to the south that the polar star was no longer visible; it was ruled by women; its queen possessed a fine palace, the walls of which were decked with historical pictures; there was a huge mountain on the island, and there were beasts in its forests nearly resembling human beings; elephants were in use, especially among the women; a few Christians lived there, and when he quitted its shores he was storm driven into a port of Ceylon. These are all the data which we have concerning Friar John's Saba, and it has been identified with Java by Meinert, and with the Maldives by Professor Kunstmann. Colonel Yule has shown that this latter theory is untenable, and declines to accept Java as the true identification because it is impossible to show that female government ever prevailed upon that island. He has, however, no alternative suggestion to make, and ends by giving the puzzle up as hopeless. To me, however, it seems that the best case can be made out for north Borneo, the native name of which is Sabah. The name alone would be of no sort of importance; but its position satisfies the friar's astronomical requirements; it is dominated by the magnificent mountain of Kinabalu, round which still cluster many of the superstitions of the natives, superstitions which the pious monk might very easily identify, as in truth he does, with traditions of Elias and the Magi; the jungles in which the *mâyas*, or ourang-outang, abound may well be said to contain "monsters" with faces like men; while tame elephants were plentiful in Brûnei when Magellan's ships visited the place in the sixteenth century, and the forests of northern Borneo are the only part of the island in which these animals now run wild. More important than all, however, is the fact that among the Dûsun tribes, which compose the larger proportion of the natives of northern Borneo, women occupy a peculiar position and influence. This is mainly due to a belief that the world —which the Dûsuns rightly regard as a very imperfect piece of work—was created by the goddess Sinemundu during the temporary absence of her husband, Kinhoringan, who had designed a flawless universe, and a woman having thus brought the earth into being, it is felt to be right that women should manage the spiritual affairs of the creatrix's world. Priesthood, therefore, and

not infrequently, the chieftainship of a tribe, are vested
among these people in the women, and this may well be
a relic of female sovereignty such as is described by Friar
John. The palace, if such a building ever existed in
northern Borneo, has utterly disappeared, together with
its paintings, but there is evidence to show that this part
of the island has sensibly degenerated in its arts and in
the standard of its civilisation, while its population has
dwindled and become debased, ever since its rediscovery
by the Spaniards less than four hundred years ago.
Nor need we experience much surprise that all tradition
concerning the existence of a kingdom of such magnitude
and importance as that described by Friar John should
have vanished so speedily from the memories of the
Borneans, for historical facts of a far more recent date,
which are preserved for us in the writings of the European
travellers of the sixteenth century, have also passed into
oblivion, leaving among the natives of the island not so
much as a whisper of story. In the semi-uncivilised
lands of Asia dynasties have risen, have flourished, have
come to proud maturity, have dwindled, pined and disappeared with a wonderful rapidity, and when the waves
of time have closed over them they are forgotten with a
completeness which finds few parallels in Europe. It is
possible that the dense forests of northern Borneo may
even yet yield up to us some traces of the wonderful
palace which filled the Franciscan monk with awe and
admiration. The difficulty of the return voyage which
saw the monk's ship storm driven into a port of Ceylon
need not greatly trouble us. A traveller, who fared from

China to Malabar without saying a single word concerning the places at which he touched upon the way, may be supposed capable of passing through the Straits of Malacca, or even through those of Sunda, on his way from Saba to India, without making any particular mention of the fact.

With Friar John and his mysterious island we take leave of the portion of our enquiry in which from the outset we have found ourselves groping through a fog of doubt and of conjecture. We have noted the frequency with which the sea-route to China was used by men of numerous races from very early times, and the comparatively exact information concerning the Far East which from time to time was brought home by wanderers returning to the West. It is, therefore, a matter of considerable surprise to find that when these regions were rediscovered by the Portuguese and Spaniards in the sixteenth century they were regarded by the whole of Europe as worlds undreamed of. The scant knowledge possessed by the ancients of India *extra Gangem* and of the *Chersonesus Aurea* had been practically forgotten; the more accurate and detailed information supplied by Marco Polo and his successors had been dismissed as incredible, or had been scorned as the purest inventions born of unruly or disordered imaginations; the immense force of Islâm had reared a wall between Europe and Asia which for a long period the former was powerless to scale. Even the Book of Messer Marco himself had come to be regarded as a piece of mere fiction, and accordingly by the time the first Portuguese vessels made their way round the Cape of Good Hope, seeking a new highroad to India, the minds of even the learned of Europe presented something like a *tabula rasa* upon which was inscribed none of the facts concerning southeastern Asia that had been collected by the geographers and mariners of antiquity, which had been added to by many Arabian writers, and which had received detailed confirmation from the European wanderers of the Middle Ages. It is in the coming of the Portuguese, therefore, that the exploration of Malaya and of Indo-China by the peoples of the west may properly be said to have had its beginning.

CHAPTER III

IT was in November, 1497, that Vasco da Gama, after those two desperate beatings to seaward and tacks to the south which have made him famous, during which he faced and overcame, not only the fury of the elements, but the fears and the mutinous murmurings of his comrades, came at last to land on the eastern shores of southern Africa. The story of the last great tack is told to us by Gaspar Correa in a fashion which leaves a wonderful picture upon our memories, and his words may fittingly be quoted here.

" As he (da Gama) was a very choleric man, at times with angry words he made them silent, although he well saw how much reason they had at every moment to despair of their lives : and they had been going for about two months on that tack, and the masters and pilots cried out to him to take another tack ; but the captain major did not choose, though the ships were now letting in much water, by which their labours were doubled, because the days were short and the nights long, which caused them increased fear of death ; and at this time they met with such cold rains that the men could not move. All cried out to God for mercy upon their souls, for now they no longer took heed of their lives. It now seemed to Vasco da Gama that the time was come for making another tack, and he comported himself very angrily, swearing that if they did not double the Cape, he would stand out to sea again as many times until the Cape was doubled, or there should happen whatever should please God. For which reason, from fear of this, the masters took much more trouble to advance as far as they could; and they took more heart on nearing the land, and escaping from the tempest of the sea: and all called upon God for mercy, and to give them guidance, when they saw themselves out of such great dangers. Thus approaching the land, they found their labour less, and the seas calmer, so they went on running for a long time, steering so as to make the land and ease the ships, which they were better able to do at night when the captain slept, which the other ships did also, as they followed the lantern which Vasco da Gama carried: at night the ships showed lights to one another so as not to part company. Seeing how much they had run, and did not find the land, they sailed larger so as to make it; and as they did not find it, and the sea and wind were moderate, they knew that they had doubled the Cape; on which great joy fell upon them, and they gave great praise to the Lord on seeing themselves delivered from death. The pilots continued to sail more free, spreading all the sails; and running in this manner, one morning they sighted some mountain peaks which seemed to touch the clouds; at which their pleasure was so great that they all wept with joy, and all devoutly on their knees said the Salve."

It is true that Vasco da Gama was not the first of the

Portuguese mariners to double the Cape of Good Hope, the feat having already been performed by John Infante and Bartholomew Dias, and that da Gama had with him pilots who had sailed with these captains. It is true also that da Gama, unlike Magellan and Columbus, was not the originator of the design which it fell to his lot to carry into effect, and that he owes his fame, less to his own adventuresome spirit and to his individual enterprise and initiative, than to the happy accident of his selection by the King of Portugal for the post of captain-major of the pioneering fleet. All this must be admitted, but nothing can weaken the impression which we receive from Correa's narrative of the dogged strength, the grim resolution, the unshakable courage, moral and physical of the man. The ships held upon that cruel two-months' tack, through angry seas, through cold and tempest, with seams gaping under the long strain, with crews half-famished by the bitter weather, mad afraid, and worn to death with weary toiling at the sails and pumps, and never once did they swerve from the appointed course, because " *the captain-major did not choose!* " When every soul in all that fleet was calling upon God in his extremity, and was beseiging the captain with entreaties to abandon the desperate enterprise, he alone was determined, fearless, and answered their prayers with fierce threats of yet other tacks which he would take if this one failed to accomplish the purpose upon which his will was set. Here in a few words we have the man revealed to us, and if even in this the hour of his greatest achievement we see traces of the ruthlessness, the absence of all care or sympathy for others, which later led him into the commission of crimes more cruel than those of Cortez or Pizarro, we see also in him the embodiment, as it were, of the strenuous spirit of Portugal at the beginning of the sixteenth century—the spirit which made possible the miracles of conquest which then were wrought in Asia, the spirit which awoke that bitter, impotent hatred of the white men which still lingers in the East in the traditions of a people little apt to forgive or to forget.

After Vasco da Gama had opened up the new highway of trade to the East which, diverting the wealth of Asia from its old markets on the shores of the Adriatic, ruined many an Italian city while it brought a hitherto undreamed of prosperity to the towns of Portugal, it became the custom for a large and well-equipped fleet to sail from Lisbon in the spring of each year. These fleets bore with them reinforcements for the white adventurers in Asia wherewith to carry on the ruthless war which then was raging between the newcomers and the ancient kingdoms of the East. They bore too large numbers of men fired by a desire to win for themselves a share of the plunder concerning which such dazzling accounts had reached Europe—men who, like Alexander, lusted after new worlds to conquer, and regarded the recently discovered lands as mere stepping-stones to wealth. It was in a spirit of frank brigandage that the Portuguese, from the highest to the lowest, swarmed into Asia. They were utterly without any sense of responsibility in so far as the lands and the men who were their appointed victims were concerned, for the belief in the mission of the white races to order the destinies of the East for the greater good of the Orientals is a comfortable doctrine of quite modern growth. Instead they occupied in their own sight something of the position of the Children of Israel, and never doubted but that the spoiling of the Egyptian must be pleasing to the God of justice and love. Moreover, since the Portuguese were a people of the Peninsula, with whom the hatred of the Moors was an inherited superstition, their religious faith tended to stimulate them to ill-doing, and was in no sense a restraining influence. Many of the early adventurers were animated by a sincere zeal for their religion, and by a keen desire to force its acceptance upon all and sundry whom they might encounter, and to these the invasion of the East undoubtedly presented itself in the light of a new Crusade. The religious motive is found cropping up in the most unlikely people, and in the most grotesquely improbable circumstances, throughout the history of the doings of the early filibusters, and the cruelty and ruthlessness which avarice and ambition dictated found their constant justification in Christian fanaticism. It is necessary to appreciate the existence of this double incentive to conquest by which the Portuguese were animated in order to understand how it was possible for so much wickedness to be done under the cloak of religion. To the filibuster of the sixteenth century God fought ever on his side, and the stubborn fight in which he was engaged was battle done for the Cross. The enemy, therefore, was of necessity the child of the devil, and to such all rights of person or property were of course denied. The earth and the fulness thereof was God's gift to his people; the Muhammadan or the pagan who chanced to be in possession was logically to be regarded as a usurper of the Christian's inheritance, and force or fraud were weapons which might be freely used in order to deprive him of that to which, in the sight of the Almighty, he had no just claim. It was in this spirit that the Papal Bulls divided the newly discovered earth between the kings of Spain and Portugal; it was in this spirit that the filibusters set to work to give effect to those sweeping decrees; and it was in this spirit that deeds were wrought in Asia which have done more than aught else to rear up between the brown and the white races barriers which few, even in our own day, have the tact, the patience, the sympathy or the energy to surmount.

With the first few fleets which sailed from Portugal during the years that succeeded the rounding of the Cape of Good Hope, we have at present no concern, since their goal was India, and they did not penetrate to the seas or ports of southeastern Asia. In 1508, however, on April 5th, of that year, Diogo Lopez de Siqueira, the Chief *Almotaçel* of the kingdom of Portugal, set sail as captain of four vessels with royal instructions to explore and conquer Malacca, a rumour concerning the wealth and importance of that city having reached the Portuguese in India, and having by them been reported to headquarters. A great deal has been made of the treachery of the Sultan of Malacca, and of his double-dealing with Siqueira, and it is therefore well to note that the latter came to his kingdom, not merely in the guise of a peaceful trader, as others of many nationalities had come before him, but with the deliberate design of " conquering " the land. It was here that the white men differed so materially from the Arabs, the natives of India, and the Chinese, all of whom had during many centuries carried on an extensive commerce in Asia. With none of these people were exploration and conquest synonymous terms. The Hindus, at a very early period, had deeply impressed Java, Lâmbok and Bâli with their influence, and they have left an enduring mark upon the superstitious beliefs and upon the magic practices of the Malayans. None the less, there is no record of anything resembling a Hindu invasion of these islands. Similarly the Muhammadan traders settled in the Archipelago and in the Malay Peninsula had succeeded, by the beginning of the sixteenth century, in converting the bulk of the native populations to the faith of Islâm, but they had not profited by the moral and intellectual ascendency thus gained to wrest the reins of government from the rulers of the land. The Chinese, too, after the period of the great Tartar invasion and the innumerable expeditions of Kublai Kaan, had traded freely with Persia, with India and with Malaya without seeking to annex an inch of foreign territory. The Portuguese, on the other hand, and many of the white nations after them, trusted, not so much to peaceful commerce, but to lawless pillage for their speedy enrichment, and the annual fleets sent out from Lisbon started on nothing more nor less than a succession of filibustering raids. Their objects were to confirm the power of Portugal in the regions already reduced to subjection, to extend the conquest in new directions, and thus to squeeze the kings and the populations of the East dry of all the wealth which they could be made to yield, employing for that purpose every device which cunning could suggest, and which force, courage, and an unscrupulous ruthlessness could translate into action.

When Diogo Lopez de Siqueira reached Cochim he found the affairs of Portugal in a condition which was far from edifying. The viceroy for the time being was Dom Francisco Dalmeida, but the great Alfonso Dalboquerque, fresh from his furious battles in the Persian Gulf, claimed that the government ought to be handed over to him by virtue of certain documents, giving him the reversion of the viceroyalty, which he had received from the King prior to his departure from Portugal. Dalmeida was very loth to resign his authority to any man, least of all to Dalboquerque towards whom he seems to have entertained a lively feeling of dislike, and at the moment of the arrival of Siqueira the position had become extremely critical. Dalmeida, recognising this, thought to find a way out of his difficulties by inviting Siqueira to assume the governorship of the Indies, declaring that if this could be arranged he, Dalmeida, would forthwith set out for Portugal taking Alfonso Dalboquerque with him. The prudent Siqueira, however, would have nothing to do with any such proposal. "*Laissez moi donc planter mes pois,*" he said in effect; for while he did his best to ingratiate himself with both contending factions, he pointed out that he had come to the East for the purpose of exploiting Malacca, and that his only desire was to set forth upon that undertaking so soon as his ships should have undergone certain much needed repairs. Eventually, therefore, taking with him some of the followers of Dalboquerque who had incurred the anger of Dalmeida, he left the quarrelsome atmosphere of Cochim, and sailed across the Indian Ocean to the Straits.

The Malay chronicler tells us in the *Hikâyat Hang Tûah* that from the first moment of their arrival in the port the strangers began to abuse the hospitality extended to them, and that having obtained a grant from the Sultan of as much land as could be enclosed by a buffalo's hide, they adopted the stratagem of the Pious Æneas, and cutting it into thin strips made it the boundary line for a goodly plot of ground. Upon this, so the chronicler tells us, they proceeded to build a formidable citadel whose position menaced the town and the royal precincts, whereupon trouble ensued. The version which comes to us from Portuguese sources is somewhat different. Here we learn that Siqueira received a warning from a Javanese girl, who was the mistress of one of his men, that treachery was meditated. This girl swam off to the Portuguese ships under the cover of darkness, and brought word that the Sultan intended to massacre the white men at a great banquet to which he would presently invite them, and that when this piece of business

had been despatched, he would seize upon their ships.
This intelligence, which may quite possibly have been
true, does not appear to have been in any way tested by
Siqueira, who seems to have accepted it unreservedly,
and to have acted at once with more, perhaps, of promp-
titude than of wisdom. He sent a native man and
woman ashore " with an arrow passed through their
skulls" to the Sultan, " who was thus informed," de
Barros tells us, " through his subjects that unless he kept
a good watch the treason which he had perpetrated
would be punished with fire and sword." The Sultan
retaliated by arresting Ruy de Araujo, the factor, " and
twenty other men who were on land with him attending
to the collection of the cargo of the ships," though it is
to be noted that the Muhammadan monarch used them
with no such atrocious barbarity as that which the Christian captain had practised upon his Malay victims.

Siqueira, finding his force thus considerably diminished, burnt two of his vessels, since he had not enough
men to navigate them, and sailed out of Malacca, proceeding himself direct to Portugal, after despatching a
couple of vessels to bear the tidings of his abortive enterprise to Cochim, where the great Alfonso Dalboquerque was now reigning unopposed.

The news of the check which Siqueira had received
caused considerable annoyance to the authorities both in
Portugal and in India, and on March 12th, 1510, Diogo
Mendez de Vasconcellos with a fleet of four ships set out
" to go and conquer Malacca." The situation in India,
however, was at this moment so critical that Alfonso

Alfonso Dalboquerque

From The Commentaries of Dalboquerque, by permission of the Hakluyt Society

Dalboquerque refused to allow Vasconcellos to proceed upon his way, and retained him and his fleet to aid him in a combined attack upon Goa. The hands of the greatest of the Portuguese viceroys were more than usually full at this juncture. The coming of the filibusters had set the whole of the western coast of India in a flame of war; the Portuguese settlements on the island of Socotra and in the neighbourhood of the Persian Gulf were importunate in their prayers to Dalboquerque to come to their assistance; and meanwhile, in distant Malacca, a number of white men, held in captivity by the Malays, were scanning the sky-line to the north hoping to sight the rescuing fleet for which, during so weary a period, they looked in vain.

By February, 1511, however, Goa had been retaken, and the Coromandel coast was for the moment cowed into submission, wherefore Dalboquerque had leisure at last to look to the more remote portions of his dominions. In that month, accordingly, he set out for the Straits of Hormuz to carry succour to those of his countrymen in that direction whose clamour, backed by repeated orders from the King to erect a fort at Aden, had distracted him all the time that he was too deeply engaged in India to be able to spare them a man or a ship. But the winds proved adverse, and finding that he battled with them in vain, Dalboquerque decided to make a virtue of necessity, and to turn his face towards the Straits of Malacca. Diogo Mendez de Vasconcellos who, it will be remembered, had been sent out for the special purpose of chastising the Sultan of their kingdom, had throughout shown great restlessness under the restraint imposed upon him by Dalboquerque, and at last, defying the viceroy, he actually set sail for Malacca on his own account. Dalboquerque, however, succeeded in recalling him, and as a punishment for his insubordination sent him back to Portugal in disgrace. Accordingly the task of subduing the Sultan of Malacca now fell to Dalboquerque's lot without the assistance of the men actually appointed by the King of Portugal for that purpose, and the viceroy set about its accomplishment in his own thorough fashion.

The lawlessness which characterised the proceedings of the Portuguese at this period is well exemplified by the first incident recorded by the author of the *Commentaries* as having occurred during the voyage to Malacca. " When they had got as far as Ceilao (Ceylon)," he tells us, " they caught sight of a ship. Alfonso Dalboquerque gave orders to chase her, and they took her, and he was very glad to find that it belonged to the Guzerates, as he felt his voyage would now be carried out safely, for the Guzerates understand the navigation of those parts much more thoroughly than any other nations, on account of the great commerce they carry on in those places." Here we have given to us an instance of the acts of unprovoked piracy which the Portuguese, from the moment of their arrival in the East, were accustomed to commit as a matter of course; and if some excuse be found in the fact that pilots were needed, no similar justification can be alleged for the capture of four other Guzerati vessels which Dalboquerque chased and took

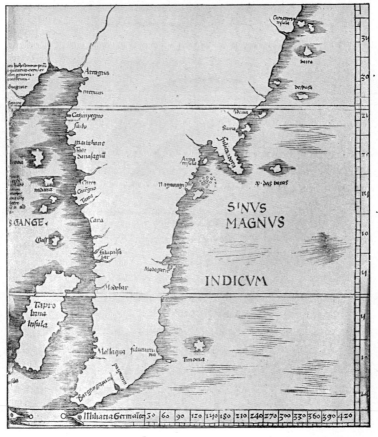

Malay Peninsula, by Waldsiemuller. Strassburg
Ptolemy 1513

(Copied from the Canerio map 1502)

between Ceylon and Sumatra. The man who was acting in this fashion, too, was no irresponsible free-booter, but the Portuguese viceroy of the Indies, and his piracies afford us a just index to the spirit and con-duct of his countrymen in Asia. It is true that sea-brigandage in the East has been suppressed finally by the nations of Europe, but it is well to remember that at an earlier period the white men themselves were the most ruthless and daring of all the rovers who infested Asiatic waters.

The first port touched at by Dalboquerque was that of Pědir in Sumatra, where he found one Joao Viegas and " eight Christians of the company of Ruy de Araujo, who had arrived thus far in their flight from the city of Malacca, and Joao Viegas recounted to him how the king of Malacca had endeavoured to force them to become Moors, and had ordered some of them to be tied hand and foot and circumcised; and they had suffered many torments because they would not deny the faith of Jesus Christ." All of which was probably true, and was, of course, excessively improper, though the Sultan of Malacca's conduct still compares favourably with that of Siqueira in the matter of the arrow passed through the skulls of a man and a woman. Viegas also told Dalboquerque that " a principal Moor of Malacca," named Naodabegea, [Nakhôda Bêgak] who had instigated the Sultan to cut off Siqueira, and had subsequently joined with the Běndǎhâra of Malacca in a plot against the throne, was even then in hiding in the neighbouring Sumatran kingdom of Pâseh. To Pâseh, therefore, Dalboquerque forthwith sailed, and

demanded that the "Moor" in question should be delivered up to him, but the King of Pâseh, as became a
Malayan *râja*, made all manner of specious excuses, and
professed his utter inability to lay hands on the con-
spirator. Dalboquerque, conceiving that the hour had
not yet come for the declaration of hostilities with the
King of Pâseh, concealed his chagrin as best he might,
and proceeded on his way to Malacca. Chance, however, favoured him, for he presently caught sight of a
large native vessel, which his people captured after a hard
fight. On board this ship they found Naodabegea himself, "half dead, without any blood flowing from the
numerous wounds which he had received. Aires Pereira
commanded the mariners to throw him into the sea just
as he was; but when they perceived that he was richly
clothed, they sought first of all to strip him, and then
they found on his left arm a bracelet of bone, set in gold,
and when they took this off his blood flowed away
and he expired." The survivors of the crew informed
Dalboquerque that "the bracelet was formed of the bones
of certain animals which were called *cabals*, that are bred
in the mountain ranges of the kingdom of Siam, and the
person who carries these bones so that they touch his
flesh can never lose his blood, however many wounds he
may receive, so long as they are kept on him."

The term used by the natives was unquestionable
kĕbal (often pronounced *kâbal* by the Malays of Sumatra)
which means *invulnerable*, and all they intended to convey was, we may surmise, that the bracelet was a charm
which conferred this advantage upon its possessor, and

that it had been brought to the Peninsula from Siam. Such charms are worn to this day by many a warrior in Malayan lands.

After taking this vessel, Dalboquerque, for some unexplained reason, retraced his steps towards Pâseh, and fell in with two native ships, one from the Coramandel coast, which struck at once, and another from Java, which was only captured after a very spirited resistance, in the course of which the Javanese set fire to their own craft. On board this vessel Dalboquerque found the unfortunate King of Pâsch, " and when he saw him," the *Commentarios* tell us " he begged his pardon very earnestly for this unfortunate affair "—in truth an euphemistic way of describing such an unprovoked act of piracy—" which should not have happened if he had known of his Royal Highness being on board, and he showed him those ceremonies and that good treatment which is due to a personage of such dignity." Dalboquerque also promised to aid the king in subduing certain of his rebellious subjects,—an engagement which cost him nothing since he never intended to keep it—and he then continued his voyage to Malacca, capturing a " very rich junk " upon the way.

He had already pillaged five Guzerati ships between Ceylon and the port of Pêdir; between Pâseh and Malacca he had taken three, one belonging to the Coramandel coast, one manned by men from Java, and a third whose ownership and nationality are unknown. This was sufficient to spread the evil reputation of the strangers far and wide throughout the seas of southeastern Asia, and to set all the countries bordering them on the defensive, while he now meditated a more decisive stroke—the conquest of Malacca, which then was the head and front of all the Malayan kingdoms—having for his object the establishment of the power of Portugal in the very centre of the commerce of all the eastern Archipelago.

Such then was the first coming of the European filibusters, with which began the real exploration of the lands of southeastern Asia,—lands which were destined, with hardly an exception, to fall under the dominion of the white peoples, lands in which, after a weary period of suffering and of strife, the men of the brown and yellow races were to watch their birthrights pass into the keeping of the strangers.

It was in dramatic fashion that Dalboquerque made his entry into the harbour of Malacca—the entry of the white men into the inviolate lands which destiny had marked for their possession. It was about the hour of sundown, the author of the Chronicles tells us, and to one who knows the Malay Peninsula that phrase conjures up at once a vivid picture. The merciless heat of the tropic day was passed ; a grateful coolness, which yet carries with it a suggestion of melancholy, of spent energies, of exhaustion, had succeeded. The sun lay upon the horizon out yonder in the direction of Sumatra, with great banks of resplendent cloud grouped about it ; enormous fan-shaped rays of light stretched upward from it till they attained the very summit of the heavens,

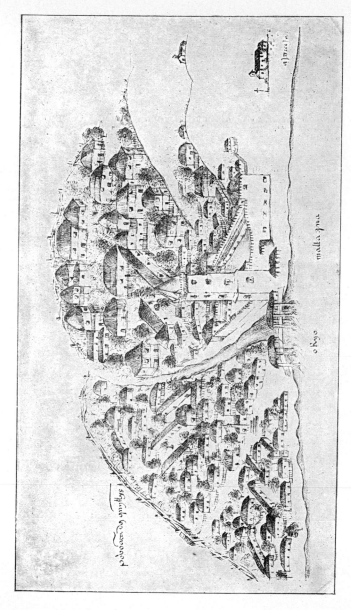

Malacca in the XVIth century

From The Commentaries of Dalboquerque, Vol. III. By
permission of the Hakluyt Society

which stained with every tint of scarlet and purple and gold, showed here and there little inlets of an ethereal azure. Beneath that glory in the skies, the sea, steel-blue under the gathering darkness, heaved gently, monotonously, as a weary sleeper draws his breath, a ruddy sheen marking the furrows between wave and wave. To the landward the native town clung to the beach, swarmed up the sides of small conical hills, and fell away into the heavy forest inshore. Near its centre rose a rude stone building surrounded by a wall draped in crowding creepers, but for the rest the place was a huddle of thatched roofs, rising at all angles, sloping unevenly, set in all directions without order or arrangement, with a blue haze of smoke hanging above them in the motionless air. In the harbour itself junks from China, sharp-nosed *prâhus* from Java or the Archipelago, and fishing-smacks innumerable lay at anchor, and on the yellow stretch of sand before the town, crowds of men and women strolled listlessly, chaffering with the fisherfolk, and enjoying the peace and the coolness after the burden of the day and the heats.

That scene had been enacted daily, repeated in this unchanging climate each succeeding evening for years. It may be witnessed to-day down to its last least detail in the capital of Trĕnggânu which, like ancient Malacca, lies upon the seashore, and as I have sat watching it in this former place, whither as yet the tide of the white man's invasion has not yet attained, it has seemed to me that I have looked back through the centuries upon the

Malayan lands which as yet were free from the aggression of the filibusters of Portugal.

But this evening the beach was thronged more densely than was common, and there was withal a subtle restlessness, a tenseness of expectancy in the air. Word had reached Malacca of the approach of the mysterious strangers from afar, the men with the bearded faces and the corpse-like complexions, the rumour of whose evil doings on the Coramandel coast had carried into the remotest corners of the East. The besetting peril was at hand, even at the gates of the city, but how it might be averted, stayed or met were problems surpassing the wisdom of the wisest.

And then, before the last of the daylight died, as the mobs of gaily clad natives stood upon the shores, oppressed by fear, restless with suspense, their dark faces darker in the gathering gloom, suddenly the West was upon them ere they well knew it. The fleet of Dalboquerque, " all decked with flags, and the men sounding their trumpets," swept into sight from behind the sheltering islands to the north, the great bellying squares of strangely rigged canvas catching the faint breeze. On and on it came, inevitable as Fate, the Power of the West sailing into the heart of Malaya unresisted and irresistible, and with panic in its heart the East stood in impotence watching it from the shore. One by one the vessels came to anchor, and then from all there roared a salvo of artillery, the salute of the white men to their victims, an explosion that broke upon the peace of the quiet scene and sounded the knell of the brown man's free enjoyment of the lands which God had given to him.

We of this latter age know how much, in the fulness of time, the rule of the white man had served to ease the burden of the peoples of the Malay Peninsula at least; but none the less there is something infinitely pathetic in the contemplation of this rude breaking in of the strangers from the West, the hard and restless workers, upon the indolent peace of these ease-loving peoples; the thought of the storm-torn ships from distant Portugal sailing insolently into this quiet haven while the dusky men of the East stood gazing at them fearfully from the shore, seeing in their coming a sure presage of what the future held for them and for their children.

Upon the arrival of Dalboquerque there followed negotiations of the usual wolf-and-lamb character. The Sultan of Malacca made haste to send a messenger to the Portuguese viceroy, asking why he had come with so great an armament, declaring that he had, poor soul, no keener desire than to live on terms of amity with the King of Portugal, "and giving him to know that the Bendará (Běndǎhâra) had been put to death on account of his complicity in the rising which had taken place against the Portuguese captain (Diogo Lopez de Siqueira) who had come to that port, and had resulted in the murder of the Christians who were there in the land, but this was no fault of his." The author of the *Commentaries* characterises this pathetic attempt to delay the inevitable as an "artful apology," and tells us that the great Alfonso

" dissembled with " the Sultan in the hope that he might by that means get Ruy de Araujo and the other Christians—who, by the same token, do not appear to have been murdered—into his hands, and so into safety, before he delivered his contemplated assault upon the town. The unfortunate Sultan, however, who saw in the possession of hostages the only lever by the aid of which he could hope to bring pressure to bear upon the intruders, replied that he could not regard the surrender of the prisoners as a condition precedent to peace. He was fully prepared to hand them over to Dalboquerque, but pleaded that an agreement of friendship should in the first instance be ratified between himself and the representatives of the King of Portugal. In the circumstances this can only be regarded as a stipulation dictated by common prudence, the more so when the reputation which the Portuguese had earned for themselves in Asia be remembered, but this attempt to " curb the spirit of Alfonso Dalboquerque," as his chronicler calls it, served only to precipitate the doom of Malacca.

The author of the *Commentaries* pretends that Dalboquerque at this time was really averse from war, and would have been well contented if a peaceful settlement could have been arrived at. But viewing the matter impartially, we are forced to accept the conclusion that war was intended from the first, and that the only object of the preliminary parleys was the removal of the captives from the power of the enemy before matters were pushed to an extremity. The pious Alfonso, we are told, seeing that the Sultan remained firm and that he was preparing

himself as best he might to repel an attack, arrived at the
comfortable conclusion that " this was a judgment that
had come upon the king, and that Our Lord desired to
make an end of him for good and all, and to cast the
Moors and the very name of Mafamede, out of the land,
and to have his Gospel preached in these regions, and
their mosques transformed into houses of God's praise by
means of the King D. Manuel and by the labours of his
subjects, so he gave orders for an attack with armed
boats and two large barges with heavy bombards, with
the object of viewing the men who rallied at the alarm,
and seeing where they had stationed their artillery, and
how they managed their defence."   For your Portuguese
filibuster of the sixteenth century, while he recognised
the awful finger of God guiding him in even his most
unjustifiable actions, took care that it should lose nothing
of its force through any neglect on his part to " keep his
powder dry."

All being now ready, and the mind of the great Alfonso determined upon war, councils were held, plans
laid, the scheme of attack explained, and two hours before daybreak on the feast of St. James, July 25th, 1511,
a trumpet on board the viceroy's ship called the men of
Portugal to arms.   The force which consisted, according
to the chroniclers, of only 800 Portuguese and 200 natives of Malabar armed with swords and shields, was divided into three bodies which delivered a simultaneous
assault upon the northern and southern quarters of the
city, and upon the bridge by which they were connected.
Sounding their trumpets, and shouting their war-cry of

Sanctiago! (St. James!) the Portuguese rushed to the attack, " and on this," says de Barros, " the air was rent with a confusion of noises, so that the trumpets, the cannon, and the shouts could not be distinguished from one another, the whole forming a doomsday of fear and terror."

The Malays and the Muhammadan traders who fought with them resisted stoutly, though the mosque and many of the stockades were won from them, and the white men began to entrench themselves upon the ground gained. All day long the battle waged, and the Portuguese toiled at the construction of their defences under the merciless Malayan sun, but gloss it over though they will, the chroniclers are forced to admit that in the end the assault failed, and that by nightfall all the Europeans had been obliged to withdraw to their ships, bearing many dead and wounded with them.

One cannot but marvel at the stubborn courage of these filibusters, battling here under a tropical sun at a distance of thousands of miles from their base; bearding the mightiest of the kings of Malaya in his very stronghold; and daring to oppose their puny numbers to the fighting strength of a town whose population was estimated at 100,000 souls.   It was a stupendous enterprise, almost insolent in its scorn of opposing odds, and no parallels to it are found in history save in the story of the European conquests of the earth.   The supreme self-confidence which alone could inspire such audacity as this, the reckless courage, and the pride which held the power of the enemy so cheap, no less than the wonderful energy which made success a possibility, would seem to be qualities which are developed to the full only in the European character, which can be communicated to the Oriental only when he is upheld by the leadership of white men in whom he trusts. If the traditional reward of the meek has fallen to the lot of the white nations, it is not through meekness that they have inherited the earth.

After the first abortive assault upon Malacca there followed a period of nine days during which Dalboquerque instituted a rigorous blockade of the place with a view to starving it into submission. Once more the slender band of Portuguese adventurers flung itself at the teeming native city, and this time the bridge, which was throughout the key to the entire position, was wrested from the Malays, and they and their allies were routed. On each occasion the Sultan of Malacca had himself taken an active part in the fighting, and in the *mêlée* the elephant upon which he was mounted was badly hurt, whereupon, says de Barros, " feeling the pain of its wound, it seized the negro that guided it with its trunk, and dashed him to the ground, on which the king, wounded in the hand, dismounted, and not being recognised, effected his escape." And thus Malacca fell, and passed for ever out of the keeping of the Malays, though it was destined to be reft from Portugal by Holland, from Holland by Great Britain, to be surrendered once more to the Dutch for a little space, and to come finally into the hands of England.

" In this second time of taking the city," says the

author of the *Commentaries*, " many of our men were
wounded, and some of those who were wounded with
poison died, but all the others were cured, because
Alfonso Dalboquerque took very good care to give
orders for their cure, and of the Moors, women and
children, there died by the sword an infinite number, for
no quarter was given to any of them."

The city having now fallen into his hands, and being,
as Dalboquerque rightly foresaw, the beginning of yet
another empire in the East, he next set himself, with all
his accustomed energy, ruthlessness, shrewdness and
wisdom, to the task of consolidating the power of
Portugal in the newly won possession.

Order was also taken for the organisation of the government of Malacca ; a coinage was instituted ; a governor was appointed; and the Javanese headman,
Utemutaraja, a man of ninety years of age, and his
sons, being suspected of a conspiracy against the
conquerors, were publicly executed by way of a salutary
example to all malcontents.   It was their sheer ruthlessness, and their complete freedom from the trammels of a
too exacting sense of justice that alone enabled the
Portuguese to hold what they had gotten, and to rule
teeming native populations, bound to them by no con-
sciousness of benefits received, who were simply cowed
into submission.   But it is to these qualities and to the
methods whose adoption followed from them that the
eventual loss by Portugal of the bulk of her colonial
empire is to be traced.   She made no friends in Asiatic
lands, and when in the fulness of time her European

enemies fell upon her, the men of the brown races, her power over whom she had abused, watched her defeat with jubilant satisfaction, and raised none save reluctant hands in her defence.

But in another direction Dalboquerque showed a sounder and more far-seeing policy. Before the second assault had been delivered, he had allowed the Chinese junks, of which mention has already been made, to start for Canton, only exacting from them a promise that they would put in on their way at the port of Siam. With these traders he despatched one Duarte Fernandez, who had escaped from the captivity which he had shared with Ruy de Araujo and his fellows in Malacca, to act as his ambassador at the Siamese Court. This man was the first European of whom we have any record to visit the ancient capital of Ayutha, some miles further up the Menam River than the modern city of Bangkok, and thus from the fall of Malacca begins also the earliest exploration of Siam by men of the white races.

The rumour of the daring deeds wrought by the Portuguese in Asia had already spread far and wide, travelling with that marvellous speed which is one of the stock wonders of the East, and the King of Siam, between whose subjects and the Malays no love was ever yet lost, hastened to send a return embassy to Dalboquerque, to wish him all success in his adventures in Malacca, and to cement a friendship between the white men and the Court of Ayutha. Dalboquerque in reply despatched a second mission to Siam under one Antonio

de Miranda, who seems to have sailed round the Malay
Peninsula as far as Trĕnggânu (Taranque) on the east
coast, whence he made his way to Ayutha overland
" with horses and draft oxen." Beyond the bare fact
that this journey was undertaken no record of it has
been preserved to us, but even in our own time it would
be long and arduous, and the traveller would have to
make his way, mainly by means of the seashore which
here is for the most part sandy, through Kĕlantan,
Lĕgeh, Pĕtâni, and Sĕnggôra into Lower Siam, and so
along the Isthmus of Kra to the Valley of the Menam.
It is difficult to believe that such a journey was really
performed by a white man as early as the year 1511 or
1512, the more so since sailing craft of many types and
various sizes abound on this coast, and afford far
superior means of transport to any which in the same
regions are found ashore.   There is one fact, however,
which lends *vraisemblance* to the account given to us by
the author of the *Commentaries* concerning the route
followed by Antonio de Miranda. The mission to
Ayutha would seem to have started from Malacca
shortly before Dalboquerque himself set out on his
return to India, that is to say in the autumn of 1511,
and by that season the northeast monsoon would have
begun to make itself felt.   Miranda sailed with the
Chinese junks as far as Trĕnggânu, and it is almost
certain that by the time he reached that port the strong
headwinds would have made further navigation to the
northward impossible to native vessels.   He would then
have to make his choice between wintering in Trĕnggânu

and undertaking the arduous march to Ayutha overland, and as the men of his race and age were little apt to be daunted by obstacles, we may perhaps conclude that he decided upon the latter alternative. If this be so, we must hail Antonio de Miranda, who to us is nothing but a name, as the first if the least articulate of the European explorers of Lower Siam and a portion of the Malay Peninsula.

The noise which the invasion of Malacca had occasioned had not been without its effect upon other kingdoms of Malaya, and before ever Dalboquerque sailed for India, embassies reached him from the Sultan of Kampar, whose kingdom was situated on the western shores of Sumatra, who, though he was a son-in-law of the ill-fated Sultan Muhammad Shah, was moved by his fear of " the fury of the Portuguese " to make terms for himself with the conquerors. From Java too came overtures of friendship, dictated by the wholesome dread which the prowess of the Portuguese had inspired, and the Sultan of the Sumatran kingdom of Měnangkâbau hastened to follow the example set by his neighbours. Thus Dalboquerque's design to build up Malacca as the centre of trade in southeastern Asia, preserving under the flag of Portugal the position which it had occupied under the rule of its own kings,—a design which he had kept steadily in view from the first—was accomplished with little difficulty, and the conquest of this single port served to establish the power of the aliens upon a firm basis in this region, and through the prestige it brought to them secured immediately a political and commercial superiority such as had never before been enjoyed by any single kingdom of Malaya.

One other thing was done by the great Alfonso ere he turned back to India and to the warfare which awaited him at Goa.   He despatched a fleet of three ships, under the command of Antonio Dabreu, who had received wounds and earned distinction in the assault upon the bridge at Malacca, upon a voyage of discovery in the Malayan Archipelago.   "And the instructions which Alfonso Dalboquerque gave to Antonio Dabreu, were, on no account whatever on that voyage to take any prizes, and to go on board of no vessel whatever, nor to consent to any of his men going on shore, but in all the harbours and in all the islands at which he might touch to give presents and gifts to the kings and lords of the country, and for this purpose he ordered there should be given out many pieces of scarlet and velvets of Méca, and many other kinds of merchandise ; and, further, he gave orders that the captains should not interfere with a single ship of Malacca or of the other ports (whether they belonged to the Moors or to the Hindoos) which he might meet with in these Clove islands (*i. e.*, the Moluccas) or Apple islands taking in cargo, but rather show them favour and give them as much assistance as he possibly could ; and in the same way that such ships as these negotiated for their cargo, so also in like manner was he to act for his cargo, observing all the customs of the respective countries."   From which it will be seen that the great Alfonso added the wisdom of a statesman to the reckless daring of a filibuster, and that on occasion even his religious zeal could yield to considerations of policy.

We possess, unfortunately, no details concerning Dabreu's voyage, though there seems to be some reason to believe that he penetrated sufficiently far to the southeast to lay up his ships for refitting at the island of Amboyna, which lies to the south of the western extremity of the island of Ceram. This would lead us to the inference that the southern coast of Borneo was skirted by Dabreu's fleet, and that the islands of the Celebes and Molucca groups were visited and explored in so far, at any rate, as their principal ports were concerned. Moreover, if Dalboquerque's instructions were obeyed, this voyage of exploration was conducted with a policy and in a spirit which were little common among the adventurers of the early sixteenth century, its object being to attract trade to Malacca instead of the commission of acts of piracy and pillage, wherefore the Portuguese, who had earned a great reputation as warriors, must have been free from molestation, and since they were in no aggressive mood must have sailed whither they would without let or hindrance. This voyage, then, although we possess such scant details concerning it, is an event of importance in the history of exploration in southeastern Asia, and to its pacific character is largely to be attributed the rapidity with which during the succeeding fifty years the Portuguese traders spread themselves through the ports of Malaya, a matter which we shall have to examine more particularly in the following chapter.

CHAPTER IV

THE circumstances which led to the establishment of the Portuguese Power in Malacca have been examined in the preceding chapter with a minuteness which is only warranted by the fact that this event marks, as has been already observed, the beginning of a new epoch in the exploration of southeastern Asia. Over the explorations which followed upon the settlement of Malacca we shall now have to pass with much less of detail and particularity, partly because considerations of space forbid more elaborate treatment of this single portion of our subject, and partly because the records of many wanderings are lost to us, while those which exist are too often of a very fragmentary character.

From the despatch by Dalboquerque of embassies to Siam, to Java and to several Sumatran kingdoms, and from the launching by him of the exploring fleet to the Moluccas, dates the gradual founding of commercial posts by white adventurers throughout southeastern Asia and the Malayan Archipelago. Malacca stood to each of these as a base of operations; the prestige of Malacca served to protect isolated outposts and individual traders; and the rumour of the wealth which was to be won in these regions speedily caused a host of hungry folk to quit Portugal in a continuous stream which poured unchecked into the distant East. Riches, rather than power, were the lure which tempted these men away from their fatherland, and in the pursuit of their object no difficulties or hardships sufficed to daunt them, no humanitarian considerations placed restraint upon their actions, and no regard for the rights of person or property vested in their Oriental victims served to shackle their lawlessness or their licence. They kept faith with no man, not even with their native allies; no sense of honour or love of fair-dealing actuated them in their intercourse with the Asiatics, whether questions of policy or of trade were in point; the cruelties which, on occasion, they committed, can only be recalled with horror; their avarice and cupidity were at once shameless and insatiable; and with very few exceptions they abused their power and their positions, seeking none save ignoble, selfish ends. Therefore it is an ugly chapter in the history of the relations of Europe with the East that holds the record of their doings—doings which have bequeathed a legacy of hatred the force of which is not yet wholly spent. But, through all and in spite of all, it is impossible to withhold from these men the tribute that is due to a dauntless courage and a tremendous self-reliance, or to divest them, squalid though many of their actions were, of the cloak of romance which must ever cling about the memories of those who adventured greatly.

Even in the heyday of their extraordinary success the Portuguese in Asia never had at their back the advantage of numbers. They were always a tiny band of aliens battering upon the face of the ancient East, severed by countless miles from their base in Europe, often, in individual cases, cut off entirely from the support of their countrymen. The unshaken conviction in the innate superiority of the white man over the bulk of mankind, which gives to our people to-day so immense a moral force, was at that time a thing of very recent growth, a belief founded upon a barely proved experience, a theory that was still in the testing. Yet in the face of all disadvantages, numerical, physical, moral, the Portuguese by the end of the year 1515—the date which saw the passing away of the strenuous soul of the great Alfonso Dalboquerque—had made good their footing in Asia, not only as a new, but in some sense as a dominant power.

"At the time of the death of Alfonso Dalboquerque," writes the author of the *Commentaries*, " peace was universal from Ormuz to Ceylon; and all the kingdoms of Cambay, Chaul, Dabul, Goa, Onor, Baticalá to Mount de Deli, Cananor, Ciacoulao and the Cape of Comorin—all the kings and lords and marine merchants—and the interior lands he left so quiet and well-ordered that there was never a nation left so completely conquered and subdued by force of arms as this was. And the land had by this time become so pacified that the Portuguese used to carry on their merchant business in every place, without being robbed of anything or being taken captive; and they used to navigate the whole of the Indian Sea in their ships, vessels, small or large *zambucos*, and used to cross the sea in safety from one part to the other; and the natives, on

their part, used to visit Goa with their wares without molestation being offered to them.   And from the Cape of
Comorin eastward Alfonso Dalboquerque left the kings
of those countries in perfect peace and friendship with
the King of Portugal, sending to them ambassadors bear
ing presents in his name, and they sent similarly to him.
Among these I may name the King of Pegu, the King of
Siam, the King of Pasé, and the fortress of Malacca, in
repose.   He remained also in the closest terms of peace
with the King of China, and the King of Java, the King
of Maluco, with the Gores, and all the other neighbouring princes were kept by him in a state of submission and
tranquillity."

This account, which is substantially accurate, shows the
spread of the Portuguese power during the first fifteen
years of the sixteenth century.   It must be remembered,
however, that trade, rather than territorial possessions,
was the lure which tempted the Portuguese adventurers
to the East, and that Dalboquerque, more far-seeing than
the majority of his contemporaries, did not desire an extensive empire so much as the command of the sea and
the acquisition of convenient ports which might be used
as business-centres and suitable bases for Portuguese commerce with the eastern world.   In Malaya, for example,
he was content with the conquest of Malacca, which disposed once for all of a formidable rival; and that accomplished, he did his best to establish friendly relations with
the neighbouring kings and countries.   Command of the
sea and of the trade-routes once secured, the Portuguese
had no great hankering after inland possessions, and ac-

cordingly their explorations were practically confined to
the islands and ports and the coast regions of the East.

The Moluccas or Spice Islands, the home of the clove
and the nutmeg, had from the first been the principal
goal which the Portuguese adventurers were bent upon
reaching, and Dalboquerque, as we have seen, lost no
time in despatching an expedition to explore this archipelago as soon as Malacca had fallen. Antonio Dabreu,
who was in command, was not the first European, however, to visit the group. Prior to the date of Dalboquerque's victory in the Malay Peninsula, the Moluccas
had been visited by the Italian wanderer, Ludovico di
Varthema, and by Barbosa, the former being, so far as
our information goes, the first white man to land upon
their shores. Dabreu returned to Malacca in 1514 with
all his party, except the crew of one vessel who, with
their captain, Francisco Surão, had lost their ship at Ternate and had remained behind on that island. Pigafetta,
the chronicler of Magellan's voyage, who was at Tidor
during the latter months of 1521, mentions that this man,
whom he calls Francisco Serrano, had become the " cap-
tain-general of the King of Tarenate when he was making war upon the King of Tidore," and by his prowess
had so earned the hatred of the latter that means had
been contrived to poison him. Pedro Alfonso de Loroso,
another Portuguese who was living at Ternate at the time
of Pigafetta's visit, came to see the Spaniards and told
them,

" That he had come to India sixteen years ago, and of
these years he had passed ten in Moluco ; and it was just

ten years since these islands had been discovered by the
Portuguese, who kept the discovery secret from us. He
then related to us that a year, less fifteen days, had lapsed
since a large ship had come hither proceeding from Malacca, had gone away laden with cloves."

From this it is evident that direct trade between the
Portuguese of Malacca and the Molucca islands began with
the expedition sent to the group by Dalboquerque, and
was carried on with more or less regularity from that time
forward. It was not, however, until after the coming of
the Spaniards had threatened the Portuguese monopoly of
trade with the Moluccas that any portion of the group
was annexed by Portugal. This was formerly done after
the appointment of Lopo Vas de Sampayo to the post of
Portuguese Governor of the Indies in 1526.

The enormous importance which was attached to the
establishment of trade with this little archipelago by the
nations of Europe is proved by the fact that, while the
Portuguese kept the discovery of the Moluccas a close
secret, the great voyage of Magellan had for its real and
principal object, not the circumnavigation of the globe,
but the opening up of a new sea-route to these precious
islands. Pigafetta tells us that Francisco Serrano was a
personal friend of Magellan, and that he had been instrumental in instigating him to attempt a voyage to the
Moluccas *via* the western route. It was because Magellan was himself a Portuguese who, having served in the
East, was in the possession of what we should call " trade
secrets,"—among the most prized of which was a knowledge of the exact locality of the Moluccas—that his tak-

ing service with the King of Spain was regarded by his
countrymen as an act hardly to be distinguished from
treason. On the arrival of Magellan's fleet at Tidor the
Spaniards felt that the real end of their journey had been
attained, although they were still far from having completed the circuit of the earth.

" The pilot who had remained with us," says Pigafetta,
" told us that there were the Moluco Islands, for which
we gave thanks to God, and to comfort ourselves we dis-
charged all our artillery. It need not cause wonder that
we were so much rejoiced, since we had passed twenty-
seven months, less two days, always in search of Moluco.
. . . But I must say that near all these islands the
least depth that we found was 100 fathoms, for which
reason attention is not to be given to all that the Portuguese have spread, according to whom the islands of
Moluco are situated in seas which cannot be navigated on
account of the shoals, and the dark and foggy atmosphere."

From which it will be gathered that a meticulous regard for truth did not fetter the Portuguese in their efforts
to keep their rivals off what they regarded as their own
preserves!

The Bull promulgated by Pope Alexander VI at the
end of the fifteenth century, decreeing the discoveries of
the West to Spain and those of the East to Portugal, was
the reason which made it appear necessary to the King
of Spain to discover a new sea-route to the Moluccas.
The nations of Europe not only acquiesced in the Pope's
arrangement to a surprising extent, but seem to have re-

garded the newly discovered sea-route round the Cape of Good Hope as in some sort the exclusive possession of the Portuguese. They did not recognise that the trade of Asia was also Portugal's peculiar property, but they seem to have held that if it were to be tapped by them some new means of getting at it must be devised. For a period, therefore, while all the maritime European peoples were fired to emulate the golden successes reaped by Spain and Portugal, the former tried to enlarge her field of operations by beating out a road to the East round Cape Horn and across the Pacific, while the British and the Dutch struggled again and again to discover a North-west Passage, urged thereto by the common hunger for the riches of the Indies.

" The doctrine that the ocean is the common property of the human race," writes Mr. Albert Gray, " was asserted first by Elizabeth and her bold seamen, and afterwards defended on legal principles by Grotius in his *Mare Liberum.* Owing to the disputes with the Dutch as to the North Sea fisheries, the doctrines of Elizabeth were abandoned by James, whose legal champion, Selden, replied to Grotius by his treatise, *Mare Clausum.* It is hardly necessary to add that time has been on the side of Grotius."

The defeat of the great Armada in 1588, however, was the real death-blow dealt to the pretensions, so long advanced by Spain and Portugal, which claimed that the sea was the exclusive property of certain nations, and immediately after that event the invasion of the East by the white races began in earnest.

During practically the whole of the sixteenth century, however, in spite of the incursion of Magellan's fleet, and the ascendency gained by the Spaniards after the accession of Philip to the throne of Spain and Portugal, the Portuguese had the virgin field of Asia very much to themselves, and they took advantage of this to spread their outposts broad-cast throughout the East, establishing trading settlements even in China. It will be convenient, therefore, in this place to sketch in rapid outline the history of European intercourse with Burma, with Siam, and with Indo-China, from its beginning up to the time which saw the arrival upon the scene of the great East India Companies.

A reference to Burma, called by him Mien, occurs in the Book of Marco Polo, though the pagodas, described as having " on the top, round about the balls, little gold and silver bells," are the only distinctively Burmese objects mentioned. There is no reason to believe that Polo himself ever visited Burma, and the honour of being the first white man to land in Pegu is generally attributed to the Venetian, Nicolo di Conti, who returned to his native city in 1444, after spending some five and twenty years wandering through Asia. He went to Racha, which is probably to be identified with Arakan, and thence " after seventeen days passing desert hills came into a champaign country." He must, therefore, have crossed the Arakan Yoma range, possibly by the Aeng pass, and so have reached the banks of the Irawadi. He speaks of Ava by name, and says, mistakenly, that its river is greater than the Ganges. The country he calls Machin

—obviously a corruption of Maha Chin, Great China, a term applied by the natives of Hindustan at that time more or less indiscriminately to all countries lying to the eastward of the Gangetic valley. He also mentions the practice of tattooing, though he ascribes its use to women as well as men, which is no longer the case except among a few hill-tribes, and he is the first traveller to speak of the famous white elephant, the dust-coloured beast with pink eyes and unsightly skewbald patches which is in reality such a disappointing object when seen in the flesh. In 1496 Hieronymo da Santa Stephano, a native of Genoa, landed in Pegu, which he is the first European to call by that name, but he was prevented from visiting Ava by one of the many wars between the two great Burmese kingdoms which was at that time raging. Ludovico di Varthema, whom we have already named in connection with the Moluccas, visited Pegu about the same time, and speaks of bamboos—" great canes as large as a barrel "—and of rubies. He too mentions that war was in progress between Pegu and Ava at the time of his visit.

After the fall of Malacca, Ruy Nunez d'Acunha was sent to Pegu on a friendly embassy by Dalboquerque, and in 1545 the redoubtable Mendez Pinto, of whose voyage along the coasts of Indo-China we shall have more to say presently, was there as a military adventurer. He repeats the myth which had long been current of a great inland lake whence flowed all the rivers of the Indo-Chinese peninsula—a tradition which may possibly have had its origin in the Lake of Tonle Sap—and he adds,

characteristically enough, that he had himself seen it!
At this period there would appear to have been a considerable number of Portuguese traders and adventurers
settled in Lower Burma, men who did their best to keep
the trade of the country in their own hands, sought
service under the native kings as mercenary soldiers, and
unlike the first of the Portuguese invaders discouraged
the missionary endeavours of their priests as calculated
to attract white men to the place and so to interfere with
the monopolies they enjoyed.   In spite of this, however,
the Dominican Gaspar de Cruz visited Burma, which he
calls " Bramer," some time between 1550 and 1560, and
another Dominican, Bomferrus came to India from Pegu
in 1557 after an abortive attempt to convert some of the
inhabitants to Christianity.   In 1569 a Venetian named
Cæsar Frederick was in Pegu and gave a detailed and
interesting account of the country, and fourteen years
later he was followed by another Venetian, Gasparo
Balbi, a jeweller, who went to Pegu with a stock of
emeralds.   Entering the river this man anchored at
Bassein, then called Cosmi or Cosmin, whence he made
his way to Dagon, the modern Rangoon, _viâ_ Dalla.
Robert Fitch, the merchant of London, to whom belongs the distinction of being the first Englishman to
visit Burma, followed the same route as Balbi when he
came to Pegu in 1586.

The accounts which all these travellers, and more
especially Frederick and Fitch, give of the kingdom of
Pegu, even when every deduction has been made for
glamour and its consequent exaggeration, prove that this

empire, established on the delta of the Irawadi, was in the sixteenth century possessed of a might, a wealth, a splendour and an importance which have never since been approached in these regions. Even at that time, however, constant wars were in progress between Pegu and Siam, Tungu, Ava, and Arakan, in many of which Portuguese adventurers took an active part. During the campaign against Siam in 1548, a hundred and eighty Portuguese under James Suarez de Melo fought on the side of Pegu, while James Pereyra led a party of his countrymen under the flag of Siam. During the concluding years of the sixteenth century, however, the Kings of Arakan and Tungu overran Pegu and destroyed its power forever, and in 1600, Boves, a Jesuit priest, thus describes the destruction that had been wrought in the once prosperous kingdom.

"It is a lamentable spectacle to see the banks of the rivers, set with infinite fruit-bearing trees, now overwhelmed with ruins of gilded temples and noble edifices; the ways and fields full of skulls and bones of wretched Peguans, killed or famished and cast into the river in such numbers that the multitude of carcases prohibiteth the way and passage of any ships; to omit the burnings and massacres committed by this, the cruellest tyrant that ever breathed."

The King of Arakan is the tyrant here referred to, and once again Portuguese mercenaries took their share of the fighting. Their leader, Philip de Brito, received from the King of Arakan the port of Sirian as a reward for his services immediately after the fall of Pegu, and for some years he held the position of a kind of rival prince, keeping the son of his benefactor as a hostage for whose release he demanded a ransom of 50,000 crowns! " He also domineereth and careth for nobodie," says a contemporary chronicler, and so secure to all seeing was the eminence to which he had attained that his son married a daughter of the King of Martaban who had established a separate principality upon the ruins of Pegu. In 1613, however, de Brito was besieged in Sirian by the King of Ava, and after a manful resistance was betrayed into the hands of his enemy. The unhappy wretch was impaled by the King of Ava, and actually lived two whole days enduring the most hideous torments.

From this time dates the beginning of the domination of Ava over the whole of Burma. Tavoi was conquered, Tenasserim besieged, although a Portuguese outlaw of Cochin, Christopher Rebello, with forty of his compatriots and a handful of slaves, utterly routed the fleet of Ava which numbered some five hundred sail. Shortly afterwards an alliance against Arakan was sought by the Court of Ava with the Portuguese, and an envoy was sent from Goa to conduct the negotiations. He was treated with the studied insults which always characterised the dealings of the arrogant Burmese Court with foreign embassies, and nothing came of the mission. None the less, step by step, all the country between Assam on the north and Siam on the south, between the Bay of Bengal and the frontiers of China was absorbed by Ava, and though this rule was often inefficient, the hilly region inhabited by the sturdy tribesmen called the

Red Karîns was the only part of Burma which escaped
its domination. The Portuguese, it will be noted, had
never during all this time acquired any territory in
Burma, adventurers like the miserable de Brito having
fought, not for their king and country, but for their own
hands. The opening of factories in Burmese territory
was the work of the British and Dutch East India Companies, and with that we shall have to deal in a later
chapter.

The establishment of the Portuguese in Malaya has
already been recorded, and we can now glance rapidly at
the history of their relations with Siam. The embassy
sent to that country by Dalboquerque after the fall of
Malacca has already been mentioned, and in 1516 Manoel
Falcao established a factory in Pĕtâni, a Malayan kingdom on the eastern coast of the Peninsula which was
subject to Siamese influence, as indeed at that time were
most of the Malay States. This trading-station quickly
assumed considerable proportions, and when it was visited
by Fernandez Pinto about 1540 there were, he states,
some three hundred Portuguese living in the place, and
Antonio de Faria was able to recruit a sufficiently numerous band of adventurers from among them when he set
out, as will presently be related, to harry the coasts of
Indo-China. In Siam itself the Portuguese, though they
neither sought nor obtained any territorial possessions,
settled in considerable numbers, and fought as mercenaries against the Peguan invaders in 1548. Pinto also
speaks of Siam as a place in which Portuguese traders
were in the habit of seeking refuge and passing the

"winter," *viz.*, the period during which the prevalence of the northeast monsoon rendered the China Sea difficult and dangerous to navigation. This commercial and unofficial intercourse seems to have continued unchecked until 1633, and in 1620 the King of Siam actually sent to Goa and invited the Portuguese Government to take possession of a port upon his coast. At that time, however, the position of Portugal in the East was becoming critical, and she was too busy defending what she had already won to be able to devote her energies to the acquisition of new responsibilities. Nothing, therefore, resulted from this mission, and ten years later the Siamese quarrelled with the Portuguese colony, though the difference was patched up in 1633, and in 1636 the King of Siam sent an embassy to the Governor of the Philippines. Intercourse between Siam and the Dutch East India Company, however, had begun as early as 1604, and from that time the influence of the Portuguese in Siam began to wane, just as it waned in India and in Malaya when other white nations appeared upon the scene whose past held no such record of wrong as that which embittered the relations between the peoples of the East and the earliest of the western invaders.

The first exploration of the coasts to Indo-China by the Portuguese would appear to have been undertaken, in somewhat peculiar circumstances in 1540–41. Its story is related by Ferdinand Mendez Pinto, and from him we learn, what is to be derived also from numerous other sources, that the seas of southeastern Asia were by this time teeming with Portuguese merchants and adventurers. In India and at Malacca Portugal was established in force; in Pegu and Tenasserim, in Pĕtâni and Siam she had important trading colonies; and in writing of the port of Liampoo in China Pinto says of his countrymen:

"They had there built above a thousand houses, that were governed by Sheriffs, Auditors, Consuls, Judges, and six or seven other kind of Officers, where the Notaries underneath the publick Acts, which they made, wrote thus, *I, such publick Notary of this Town of Liampoo for the King our Sovereign Lord.* And this they do with as much confidence and assurance, as if the place had been situated between Santarem and Lisbon, so that there were houses there which cost three of four thousand Ducates the building, but both they and all the rest were afterwards demolished for our sins by the Chineses."

The practice of sailing direct to China from the Straits of Malacca, only touching where necessary to take in water, which, as we have seen in earlier chapters, was that usually adopted by mariners bound for the Far East, caused a settlement so important as the one here described to have been established in the southern provinces of the Celestial Empire within thirty years of the fall of Malacca, while even the coasts of Indo-China continued to be practically unknown. It fell to the lot of Mendez Pinto to give us an account of the first detailed exploration of these coast-lines, and though much of the matter contained in his narrative, such as the long-winded orations attributed to various Orientals, obviously owe more than a little to this author's imagination, the general outline of the events which he records bears every mark of sub-

stantial accuracy. His itinerary, with its number of extraordinary proper names, is quite impossible to follow in
detail, but his story owes its value to the fact that it is the
earliest extant account of the exploration of the shores
of Indo-China by men of European race, and because it
is illustrative to a remarkable degree of the spirit which
animated the Portuguese at this period, of their methods,
and of the attitude by them assumed towards the East
and its peoples. After reading Pinto's artless book one
is at no loss to understand why the Portuguese speedily
became an object of such intense detestation to the natives of Asia.

In the spring of 1540, Pinto tells us, he was sent to
Pahang (Pan) on the east coast of the Malay Peninsula to
fetch a cargo which had been purchased by a native agent
on behalf of Pedro de Faria, the Governor of the citadel
of Malacca. During a disturbance which occurred while
he was still in Pahang, Pinto was robbed of all the property in his charge, and he escaped with just his life and
his ship, and sailed forthwith for Pĕtâni. Here he learned
that three junks belonging to some Pahang merchants
were lying at anchor inside the mouth of the Kĕlantan
River, and though it was not suggested that they were
the property of the ruffians who had robbed him, the fact
that they hailed from Pahang was, in these lawless days,
sufficient grounds for making them the objects of repris-
als. Accordingly, the permission of the Râja of Pĕtâni
having been obtained, the Portuguese fitted out a small
fleet, raided the Kĕlantan River, captured the Pahang
junks after a hard fight, and carried their prizes back to

Pĕtâni with all haste, "because," as Pinto naively remarks, "the whole Country thereabouts was in an uproar." This, it may be noted in passing, was a condition into which the visits of the Portuguese adventurers were apt to throw the native States which these gentry honoured with their attentions.

At Pĕtâni there presently arrived Antonio de Faria, who was probably a relative of Pedro de Faria, the Governor of Malacca. He had been sent to ratify a treaty of friendship already existing between the Portuguese and the Râja, but he had brought with him a large con signment of private merchandise, and since he could not sell it at a satisfactory profit in Pĕtâni, he sent Pinto with it to Lîgor, a little State further to the north on the eastern shores of the Malay Peninsula. Here Pinto, while lying outside the bar, was set upon by native pirates, robbed of his ship and her cargo, and only saved himself by swimming ashore with such of his European companions as had survived the fight. After terrible hardships he made his way back to Pĕtâni, and reported what had befallen him to Antonio de Faria, adding the information, which avowedly rested upon the merest guess-work, that the pirate who had used him so evilly was one Coio Acem,—probably Dâto' Kâya Akhim, or some similar name and title. Upon hearing this Antonio de Faria at once determined to put to sea in search of this marauder, whose act of piracy (if indeed he had committed the deed) had ruined the ambassador, since the captured cargo had been bought with money borrowed in Malacca, and de Faria had now no means of discharging his liabilities.

To us the spectacle presented by one who had been entrusted by Government with a special embassy transforming himself with such suddenness into a sea-rover, appears incongruous enough, but such was evidently not the view taken by the Portuguese traders in Pĕtâni. For, says Pinto,

" All the Assistants very much commended his valorous resolution, and for the execution thereof there were many young Soldiers among them that offered to accompany him in that voyage; some likewise presented him with Mony, and others furnished him with divers necessaries."

Accordingly, on Saturday, May 9th, in the year of Grace 1540, Antonio de Faria sailed from Pĕtâni, " and steered North Northwest, towards the Kingdom of Champaa, with an intent to discover the Ports and Havens thereof, and also by means of some good booty to furnish himself with such things as he wanted," a proper spirit, truly, for one who regarded it as his special mission to punish piracy! He first touched at Pûlau Kondor, as Marco Polo and many another traveller had done before him, crossed thence to the shores of Champa and skirted the coast in a northerly direction until a river was reached which formed the boundary between that kingdom and Kambodia. This river Pinto calls " Pulo Cambim," though *pûlau* signifies an island, and he tells us on the authority of the natives that it had its source in a lake named Pinator in the neighbourhood of which there were gold mines, while there was a " diamond quarry" on its shores at a place called Buarquirim. It is

impossible to make anything of these names, but the
river was probably one of the principal mouths of the
Mekong, a branch of which river connects with the great
lake of Tonle Sap, but in any case the mineral wealth of
the interior was greatly exaggerated.   Seventeen leagues
north of Pulo Cambim Pinto places a port called Saleyza-
can, which also defies identification, beyond which was
the river of "Toobasoy."   At this place de Faria was
attacked by pirates, whom he repulsed and captured, his
"bag" including "a Capher slave, one Turk, two
Achens, and the captain of the junk, named Similau, a
notorious Pyrat, and our mortal Enemy."   The variety
of nationalities represented is curious, and it serves to il-
lustrate how much more general was the intercourse subsisting between the natives of different parts of Asia in
the sixteenth century than it has since become.   It is
horrible to add that these prisoners were tortured to death
with quite diabolical cruelty by Antonio de Faria, and it
is typical of the times that this barbarous act was performed just before the feast of Corpus Christi, which religious festival was observed with due form by the Christian souls on board de Faria's piratical fleet !

Sailing on Wednesday from Toobasoy, which was
probably one of the mouths of the Mekong, and continuing to coast in a northerly direction, de Faria arrived on
the following Friday at the mouth of yet another river
which, Pinto states, was called Tinacoreu by the natives,
but Varella by the Portuguese.   The fact that the white
men had given a name of their own to the place would
lead us to infer that it had been visited by the Portuguese

prior to the arrival of de Faria, but Pinto expressly adds
that he and his fellows were the first Europeans whom
the natives had ever seen. Near the mouth of the river
there was a village called Taquilleu, and at some distance
in the interior, the Portuguese learned, there was a town
called Pilaucacem, where the king of the country had his
residence. I conceive that the wanderers were still
among the mouths of the Mekong, and it seems probable
that Pilaucacem was Pnom Penh, as it is described as being the centre of an extensive trade with the " Lauhos,
Pasuaas, and Gueos—very rich people," namely the natives of Laos and the wild tribes, so called, of the interior.
The river of Tinacoreu, Pinto further tells us, " extends to
Moncalor, a mountain distant from thence some four
score leagues," and that further up it was far broader, but
not so deep. The Portuguese also learned of the existence " in the midst of the continent " of a great lake
called " Cunebetea " by its nearest neighbours, and
Chiammay by others in which the river took its source.
This belief in a great central lake in which all the large
rivers of the Indo-Chinese peninsula took their rise was
very persistent, and in writing of Burma, it will be recalled, Pinto declares that he had himself seen it—which
is manifestly untrue. The great lake of Kambodia may
have been the origin of this tradition, a lake at the head
of the main branch of the Mekong being inferred by
analogy with the more accessible branch which joins the
parent stream near Pnom Penh, but it is obvious that the
coast natives did not know that the river ran through a
portion of China, and that it was never regarded by them

as a possible highway for communication with the Celestial Empire.

Antonio de Faria next visited an island situated "in the entrance to the Bay of Cauchenchina forty degrees and a third to the northward," which was probably the island of Cham Collao. Thence he crossed over to Hainan (Ainan), and later returned to the mainland, arriving at the kingdom of Tanququir, which was, of course, Tongking. Coasting thence forty leagues towards the east, he reached a port called Mutipinan (Turon?), whence, Pinto tells us, a great overland trade was carried on with the Laos and other peoples of the *Hinterland*. If this statement is correct the routes over the mountains from the valley of the Mekong into that of the Song Koi, which the French explorer de Lagrée ascertained had formerly been in frequent use, but in his day had been completely abandoned, must have been in existence at a very early period. From Mutipinan de Faria returned to Hainan, and later spent some months cruising about the coasts of Indo-China in a southerly direction with the intention of "wintering" in Siam, but somewhere to the south of Quangiparu, "a fair town of 1,500 fires, as we guessed," in which there were "goodly buildings and Temples," he met with utter shipwreck. The situation of this town cannot be determined, but it would appear to have been on the banks of a river which fell into the sea on the exposed coast of Annam, and it may perhaps be identical with the modern Quang-mai. The spot where de Faria and his fellows were cast ashore was barren and uninhabited, and for some days the survivors

of the wreck—fifty-three souls, of whom twenty-three
were Portuguese, out of a company some five hundred
and thirty strong—wandered about in a condition of great
distress. A Chinese vessel, however, soon put in there
to water, and while her crew were ashore, de Faria succeeded in surprising her, and sailed away in triumph
leaving the dispossessed owners marooned upon an in-
hospitable coast.

They next captured some unfortunate fisherfolk on a
little island called Quintoo, to serve as pilots, and from
them they learned that eighteen leagues distant there was a
" good river and good Rode" called Xingrau. For this
haven de Faria sailed, and thence, after touching at several islands and ports, and committing various acts of piracy, they made their way northward eventually reaching
the Chinese port of Chinchu. How thereafter de Faria
fell in with the pirate of whom he had so long been in
search; how he defeated and killed him; of the rich spoil
which he took, and of the splendid reception accorded to
him by his enthusiastic countrymen at the port of Liampoo, I cannot here tell in detail. De Faria, the sea-rover,
it should however be remarked, was conducted in state to
the church where public thanks were offered to the Almighty for the victorious crusade against the infidel, in
the course of which this Christian hero had broken not a
few of the Ten Commandments, had murdered and robbed
and tortured and pillaged without scruple, and had made
victims of the inoffensive natives of countries who never
before had so much as seen a white man. It was a curious age in which men could see virtue in the perpetrator

of such enormities : it is less curious that before the end
of the sixteenth century the name of the white man had
been made to stink in the nostrils of Asiatics.

The verdict passed by Pinto upon Indo-China is worth
repeating.   After describing its wealth from information
derived from native sources, he says,

" Whereby it may be gathered that if the Country could
be taken, it would without so much labour or loss of
blood, be of greater profit and less charge than the Indies,"
an opinion which its present possessors, the countrymen
of Dupleix would, I conceive, be little likely to echo,
however much they might desire to be able to give it their
endorsement.

After Pinto's day the Portuguese appear to have settled in Kambodia, much as they settled in Burma, at their
own risk and without receiving much active support from
their Government.   The Dominican Gaspar de Cruz
visited the country in 1590, as also did Christoval de
Jaques between 1592 and 1598.   According to the latter
the Lake of Tonle Sap and the Khmer ruins at Angkor
had been discovered by the Portuguese in 1570, and this
would seem to indicate that the intercourse between the
rulers of Kambodia, whose capital was at or near Pnom
Penh, and the Portuguese traders had increased considerably during the half century immediately following the
famous voyage of Antonio de Faria.   In about the year
1580 a Frenchman named Louvet visited the delta of the
Mekong, and was thus the first of his race to set foot in
the region which was destined to become at a later date
the great Asiatic colony of France.   Five years later an-

other Frenchman, Père George La Mothe of the Order
of St. Dominic, went to Cochin-China in the company
of a Portuguese missionary named Fonseca. The two
priests were attacked by the natives, Fonseca was murdered, and La Mothe, sorely wounded, made his escape
on board a Spanish ship, but died of the injuries he had
received before he could reach Malacca. Jan Huygen
van Linschoten, whose book published in 1596 wrought,
as we shall presently see, so much injury to the prestige
of Portugal, had collected much information concerning
all the lands with which the Portuguese held commerce,
and he is one of the first to speak of the great river of
Kambodia by name.

"Through this kingdom (Champa)," he writes, "runneth the river Mecom into the sea, which the Indians
name Captain of all the Rivers, for it hath so much water
in the Summer that it covereth and watereth all the country as the river Nilus does Ægypt." . . . "Upwards
in the land behind Cambaia (Kambodia)," he adds, "are
many nations, as Laos, which are a great and mightie
people, others named Auas (Avas, *i. e.*, Burmese of Upper
Burma) and Bramas (Lower Burmese) which dwel in the
hilles ; others dwel upon the hils called Gueos, which live
like wild men, and eat men's flesh and marke their bodies
with hot irons which they estéeme a fréedome."

The knowledge in his possession, it will be seen, was
not precisely accurate, the Burmese being by no means
hill tribes, anthropophagy being a practice unknown in
Indo-China, and tattooing, which is only in use among
the Burmese and the Shans and hill tribes of the north,

being effected by pigment rather than by "hot irons," which would seem to imply a process of branding. Linschoten, however had had opportunities of ascertaining from the best Portuguese authorities all the facts within their knowledge, and his book probably represented the best information concerning the peoples of the *Hinterland* of Indo-China that was then at the disposal of Europeans in the East.

Late in the sixteenth, or early in the seventeenth century, the Portuguese established regular trading-posts in Cochin-China and Kambodia, the most advanced of these being at Pnom Penh. Beyond this and the district of Siamreap at the north of the Lake of Tonle Sap, they do not appear to have penetrated, and the first organised attempt to explore the interior of Indo-China by the Mekong route was made, not by them, but by the Dutch East India Company. With this we shall have to deal in a later chapter, but the explorations of the Portuguese in southeastern Asia, which began with the fall of Malacca in 1511, may be said to have ended early in the following century. When the other nations of Europe began to flock eastward the Portuguese found the task of defending their own position sufficiently arduous, and thereafter they ceased to push their discoveries into new lands. During the hour of their prosperity they scattered themselves broadcast with a quite extraordinary rapidity, but they were content for the most part with the exploitation of the coasts and easily accessible places at no great distance from the sea, and the heavier work of discovery fell to the lot of other white nations. Yet the traces of the

Portuguese traders have not even now completely vanished, and in almost every town of any size in southeastern Asia men are to be found bearing historic names of
Portugal, speaking a bastard dialect of the Peninsula, and
albeit they are generally more swarthy than the natives
of the land, cherishing in the ignominy of the present a
passionate disdain for the full-blooded Oriental. This
latter sentiment is almost the last relic of the pride of the
once powerful race who for a space ruled the seas and
coast of Asia, and passing bequeathed to the East this
sorry legacy of half-breeds.

CHAPTER V

THERE is a certain characteristic irony in the fact that the nation whose king enjoyed the title of " The Eldest Son of the Church " should have been the first of all the peoples of Europe to set at defiance the Bull of Alexander VI. In 1528 the brothers Jean and Raoul Parmentier of Dieppe sailed from France, rounded the Cape of Good Hope, and penetrated as far south and east as Sumatra, where Jean, the leader and the inspiring genius of the adventure, died in the following year. His friend, the poet Pierre Crignon, who sailed with him, says of his dead captain :

" *C'est le premier François qui a découvert les Indies jusques à l'isle de Taprobane, et si mort ne l'eust pas prévenu je crois qu'il eust été jusques au Moluques.*"

This, however, was not to be, and though the French broke through the ring-fence of Portugal before any other nation of Europe had ventured to do so, their efforts were isolated and of no importance. The first organised challenge to the monopoly enjoyed by the Portuguese in Asia emanated from the city of London, England once again playing the part which has earned for her so much hatred among the nations of the Continent—that of chief thwarter of individual ambitions.

During the concluding twenty years of the sixteenth

century history in Europe made itself apace. The
United Provinces had achieved their independence;
Spain and Portugal had come under the sceptre of Philip
II, who thus united in his single person the sovereignty
of the discoveries in the Eastern and the Western world,
which had been made by the two great nations of the
Peninsula; the globe had been circumnavigated by
Drake and by Cavendish; and most important of all, in
so far as the fate of the East was concerned, the pride and
strength of the greatest maritime peoples of Europe had
been humbled to the dust by the defeat of the Invincible
Armada.   During the sixteenth century the trade of Asia
poured into Lisbon, carried thither in Portuguese bot-
toms, and its distribution throughout the countries of
Europe was mainly conducted by the traders of Holland.
Philip's decree forbidding Dutch merchants to reside in
or to hold commerce with Lisbon was a blow directed
against the material prosperity of the Netherlands; but
though for a time the measure caused considerable distress, it served in the end as a stimulant to the Hollanders
inciting them to find their way to Asia on their own
account, and thus to break up the monopoly so long
enjoyed by Portugal and partially shared by Spain.

The first expedition, which had for its object the establishment of direct commercial relations between English
merchants and the East, sailed in 1591, three years after
the defeat of the Armada.   It consisted of a fleet of three
vessels under the command of Raymond and Lancaster,
and the enterprise was conducted upon lines as frankly
piratical as the heart of an Elizabethan could desire.   On

the way to the Cape of Good Hope a " Portugal carawel laden by merchants of Lisbon for Brasile" was snapped up, containing " divers necessaries fit for our voyage: which wine, oyle, olives and capers were better to us than gold," as Edmund Barker, Lieutenant, appreciatively records. In June, 1592, Lancaster, after cruising off the north of Sumatra, reached " Pulo Pinaon" (Penang), where he decided to await the change of the monsoon. Here many men died of sickness, and when Lancaster put to sea his company numbered only thirty-three men and one boy, " of which not twenty-two were found for labour and helpe, and of them not a third part sailors." None the less the adventurers did not hesitate to give chase to " three ships, being all of burthen sixty or seventy tunnes, one of which we made to strike with our very boat," though her consorts were spared because the goods they contained belonged to natives of Pegu, and not, like those which she contained, to the hated " Portugals." In September Lancaster sailed southward into the Straits of Malacca as far as Pûlau Sămbîlan, a little group of islands situated near the mouth of the Pêrak River, where he lay in wait for shipping passing to and from Malacca. He succeeded in effecting the capture of two important Portuguese vessels, which made only a poor resistance, and then, " douting the forces of Malacca," as well he might, he made his way northward to Junk Ceylon, back to Sumatra, and thence to the Nicobars. After short stays at the first and last of these places, he proceeded to Ceylon, where it had been his intention to await a fitting opportunity to fall upon the

Portuguese ships sailing from India, but his crews had had their fill of wanderings and adventures, and as their leader was stricken down by sickness at this juncture, they insisted upon sailing for the Cape. Lancaster's voyage could hardly be accounted much of a success, but it was memorable because it was the first attempt made by the English to strike right into the heart of the Portuguese empire in the East. Drake and Cavendish had both passed through the Malayan Archipelago, and each had done his best to cause trouble to the Spaniards before ever Lancaster sailed from Plymouth; but Cavendish, at any rate, had had some not unfriendly intercourse with the Portuguese merchants in Java, and both he and Drake had come by the Cape Horn route, and had sailed for the Cape of Good Hope without attempting to penetrate into the Straits of Malacca. Lancaster, on the contrary, though in effect he accomplished little, sailed round Africa by the great Portuguese highway; harried Portuguese shipping from the Atlantic to the mouth of the Pêrak River; and captured vessels almost within sight of the great Portuguese stronghold of Malacca. This was a considerable achievement, for he had given practical demonstration of the fact that the position of the Portuguese in the East was by no means unassailable, and he brought back with him some valuable information, not only regarding routes and trade, but also on the subject of the political situation in Asia.

During the last decade of the sixteenth century, indeed, the secrecy which the Portuguese had been at such pains to maintain concerning their eastern conquests and dis-

J. Huygen Van Linschoten

From his "Voyages to the East Indies," by permission of the
Hakluyt Society

coveries began to be penetrated by the other nations of Europe. A period was set to the time during which all detailed information concerning the geography, the trade, the politics and the peoples of the East was, in a sense, the exclusive and jealously guarded property of Portugal. The capture of the carrack, the *Madre de Dios*, by the English in 1592, on board which was a copy of the "Notable Register and Matricole of the whole Government and Trade of the Portuguese in the East Indies," furnished the merchants of London with much precious information which hitherto had been withheld from all the world, and this document became in fact the prosspectus of the first British East India Company. Dr. Thorne, an Englishman who had long resided in Seville, also supplied his countrymen with a valuable report on the political and commercial relations of Spain and Portugal with the East. A similar service was rendered to the merchants of Holland by Jan Huygen van Linschoten, who had resided many years at Goa under the patronage of the Archbishop, Vincente de Fonseca, and had collected a great store of information relating to all the eastern lands with which the Portuguese held commerce. Linschoten returned to Holland in September, 1592, and two years later the States General granted him a license to publish his work. Its appearance, however, was delayed until 1596, as its author, who shared the then popular belief in the possibility of opening a trade-route to the Indies *via* the north of Europe and Asia, wasted this period upon a fruitless voyage undertaken with that object. Although his book was not given to the public until 1596, it seems probable that the manuscript was examined by many who were interested in the future of Holland's trade with Asia, and its subsequent publication, and translation into many tongues, dealt a tremendous blow to Portugal, for it contained a merciless exposure of the futility of her system and of the rottenness which was eating into the heart of her administration in the East.

On April 2, 1595, a fleet of four vessels, equipped by the newly established Dutch East India Company, sailed from the Texel, under the command of Cornelius Houtman. The Cape route was followed, and in June, 1596, the fleet reached Sumatra. Coasting towards the south, Houtman passed through the Straits of Sunda, and made a considerable stay at Bantam, the town at the northwestern extremity of Java, where a Portuguese factory was already in existence, and where the Dutchmen speedily obtained permission to establish a trading-post of their own. Their coming was, of course, viewed with great dissatisfaction by the Portuguese, and though the latter concealed their hostility, they set to work to intrigue against their rivals, and succeeded so well that serious misunderstandings arose between Houtman and the natives. After leaving Bantam, the Dutch adventurers passed to Jaccatra, the town upon the ruins of which Batavia, the modern capital of the Dutch East Indies, has been reared, and thence, coasting along the northern shores of Java, visited Bâli and Lômbok. At the latter place he found that his crews had been so much reduced that their number no longer sufficed to work all the ships, and the *Amsterdam*, a vessel of 200 tons, was abandoned

Linschoten's map, 1599

From Nordenskiold "Periplus"

and burned. Houtman then set sail across the Indian Ocean, doubled the Cape, and reached the Texel in August, 1597, having with him only eighty-nine men out of the company, 249 strong, which had shipped with him little more than two years earlier.

His voyage is chiefly interesting because it illustrates the different policy adopted from the beginning by the Dutch, as compared with that of the Portuguese. The methods of the latter we have already examined: the qualities which characterised the Dutch system may be summed up in a few words. To begin with the Hollanders had in view a single object—trade. They evinced no desire to proselytise, or to insult the religious or social prejudices of the natives. They made no attempt at filibustering; behaved with considerable self-restraint in very trying circumstances at Bantam; and their generally peaceful and orderly behaviour made a deep impression on the Orientals who had become used to the license of the Portuguese. This favourable view of the newcomers was confirmed at a later period by better acquaintance with the Dutchmen, and Pyrard de Laval, for instance, tells us that at Bantam "the king had an affection towards them and the people loved them." Their claim upon the good will of the natives rested also to no small extent upon their open hostility to the Portuguese, and though they were guilty of many acts of piracy, they tried to make a distinction between the property of their European enemies and that of Asiatic traders. Speaking generally, both the Dutch and the English were well received in the East, principally because they were not

Portuguese, and because their coming was known to be viewed with intense disfavour by those white men who had earned and deserved the hatred of the native populations. Houtman, therefore, was able to bring back with him a very encouraging report of the prospects presented by the newly opened trade between Holland and the Indies, and so quick were the merchants of the Netherlands to seize the advantages thus offered to them that by the summer of 1601—only six and a half years after the sailing of the first expedition—no less than forty-nine Dutch vessels had been sent out bound for Malaya *via* the Cape of Good Hope.

Meanwhile, on December 31st, 1599, the Charter of Incorporation of the first British East India Company had been granted, " Being a privilege for fifteen years to certain adventurers for the discovery of the trade of the East Indies, namely, George Clifford, Earl of Cumberland and 215 knights, aldermen, and merchants." A capital of £72,000 was subscribed, and on February 16th, 1600, Lancaster sailed from England in command of the first fleet of the East India Company. Taking the Cape route, he reached Achem (Acheh) on June 5th, 1602, delivered a letter addressed by Queen Elizabeth to the king of that state, established good relations with him and his people, and opened a factory in his capital. A Portuguese ambassador from Malacca tried vainly to induce the King to have no dealings with the Englishmen, but the Achehnese had from the first constituted themselves the especial defenders of the brown man's birthright against the aggression of the Portuguese, and they

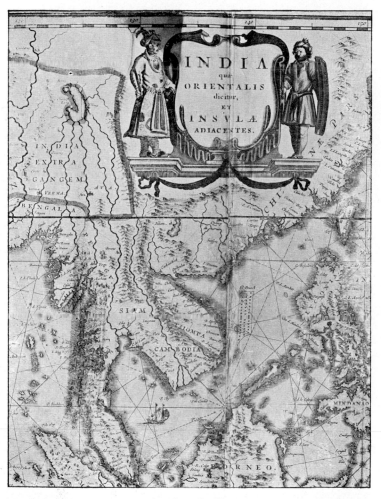

Further India

From Blaew's Atlas, 1663

were accordingly prepared to give a warm welcome to
any Europeans who were enemies of the hated race.
Lancaster not only carried on his trade in Acheh without molestation under the protection of its king, but
actually used the place as his base of operations for a
piratical raid which he presently made upon the Portuguese in the Straits of Malacca—an expedition which
resulted in the capture of one very rich prize. On his return to Acheh a treaty of friendship was made with the
King, and Lancaster coasted along Sumatra, passed
through the Straits of Sunda, and opened a factory at
Bantam. Thence he sailed for England, leaving behind
him eight men and two factors, the chief of whom was
Master William Starkey, whose purely mercantile charge
must be regarded as the germ out of which there grew
in the course of time Great Britain's enormous empire
in the East.

Bantam itself had been first visited by the Portuguese
in 1511, when, immediately after the fall of Malacca,
Henrique Lemé, one of Dalboquerque's captains, touched
at the port. Houtman, as we have seen, established a
trading-post there in 1596, at which time a Portuguese
factory was already in existence, and the station now
founded by Lancaster became later the principal Presi-
dency of the British East Indies to which the agencies of
Madras, Bengal and Surat were alike subordinate. The
importance of Bantam for both the English and the
Dutch lay in the fact that it furnished a convenient centre
from which to trade with Sumatra for pepper, and
especially with the Moluccas for spices, the latter being

the most precious produce in the East. No sooner had the Dutch power in the Malayan Archipelago attained to sufficient proportions than a descent was made upon Amboyna, which was captured by Van Nek in 1599, although the Portuguese had a fort on Tidor. Two years later the Portuguese sent a fleet under André Furtado " to expel the rebel Hollanders," and for the moment Amboyna was retaken. Aided by the Spaniards, who were now strongly established in the Philippines, the Portuguese tried in 1603 to annex Ternate, but the attempt failed, and in 1605 the Dutch made another swoop upon the Moluccas, their leader, Van der Hagen, driving the Portuguese not only out of Amboyna but also out of Tidor. Two years later Pedro de Acuña, the Spanish Governor of the Philippines, attacked the Dutch and deprived them of all their possessions in the Moluccas, except Amboyna.

Meanwhile, in 1606, the Dutch under Matelief laid seige to Malacca itself, thus striking at the very heart of the Portuguese power in Southeastern Asia, and it is to be noted that the Sultan of Johor took part in the campaign against the successors of Dalboquerque. It was in these latter years that the Portuguese began to reap the crop of hatred which they had sown among the natives of the East during the preceding century. The Portuguese Viceroy, Martin Affonso de Castro, sailed from Goa to the relief of Malacca with the greatest armada which had ever quitted that port. In the first instance he attacked Acheh, whose king had, as usual, befriended the enemies of Portugal, and was heavily repulsed. He then passed into the Straits of Malacca, forcing Matelief to raise the siege, but was immediately after trounced most soundly by that redoubtable Dutchman in a great sea fight. For the moment, however, Malacca itself was saved, but a death-blow to the prestige of Portugal in Malaya had been dealt, and from that moment the fate of the first conquerors of Malacca was sealed. Matelief, flushed with victory, sailed to the Moluccas, where in the following year he succeeded in driving the Spaniards out of Tidor. Till 1611 this island was held by the Dutch, but in that year it was retaken by the Spaniards together with the island of Banda, though soon after the Dutch reestablished themselves in Ternate. In 1641, however, Malacca fell before the joint attack of the Hollanders and the Achehnese, and passed into the keeping of the former, as also in the course of time did the Moluccas and most of the islands of the Malayan Archipelago.

After the final defeat of the Portuguese and the conquest of Malacca the power of Holland in Malaya grew rapidly. By means of superior energy and enterprise the Dutch contrived to engross the greater part of the spice-trade, leaving to the English traders only an insignificant residue. In 1682, by fomenting an insurrection headed by the son of the King of Bantam, they succeeded in driving the British out of Java, which they then annexed little by little, till they had made themselves masters of the whole. The English fell back upon Sumatra, where they held factories in Acheh, at Priaman, Fort Marlborough, and at Bengkulen, stations which became of less and less importance as England gradually began to win a new empire in India. On the mainland the Dutch established trading-posts in Pêrak and Sêlângor, but through these were presently withdrawn. Malacca was held until 1795, when it was attacked and taken by the British; it was restored to Holland in 1818 under the Treaty of Vienna, but six years later was exchanged for Beukulen, and this time passed finally into the keeping of Great Britain. The East India Company had meanwhile founded a settlement on the island of Penang, which was leased by them from the Râja of Kĕdah in 1786, and in 1798 the territory on the mainland, now known as Province Wellesley, was purchased for $2,000. Sir Stanford Raffles, whose statesman's eye saw the strategic and commercial value of the position, obtained the cession of the island of Singapore from the Sultan of Johor in 1819, but the territory immediately behind the town of Malacca was not brought under British jurisdiction until 1833. An English expedition invaded and took possession of Java in 1811, but in 1818 the island was restored to Holland. The remaining British settlements on the island of Sumatra were ceded to the Dutch by a treaty concluded in 1871, under the provisions of which Holland abandoned all claims in the Malay Peninsula, and with the extension of British influence throughout the Native States of the mainland, which began in 1874, the real exploration of this Malayan region had its beginning. Up to this time the Malay Peninsula, in all save its coast-line and its ports, at some of which small Dutch factories had from time to time been established, was

a complete *terra incognita* to Europeans. The story of
its subsequent exploration will be told in a later chapter.

To return now to the doings of the East India Companies in the other lands of southeastern Asia, it was not
until 1618 that trade began to be conducted by the British with the valley of the Irawadi, the exploitation of which
by Portuguese adventurers has already been noted. Curiously enough the first of the Company's factors to visit
Burma came, not from India, but overland from Siam.
In 1618 the factor at the Siamese capital, Lucas Anthonison by name, sent a sub-factor, one Thomas Samuel, up
the Menam to Zengomay (Chieng Mai), to investigate
the prospects of trade in that place, which shortly before
had passed into the hands of Siam. The forces of the
King of Ava retook Chieng Mai while Samuel was still
there, and the unfortunate merchant was carried to Pegu
with all his property, and soon afterwards died there. He
was not the first white man to accomplish the journey
from Ayuthia to Pegu, since the Portuguese contingent
which aided the Peguan army in its invasion of Siam in
1548 must have traversed approximately the same line of
country ; but his arrival led indirectly to the opening up of
commerce with that country by the agents of the British
Company. Anthonison, who had meanwhile been transferred to Masulipatam, no sooner heard what had befallen
Samuel than he despatched two sub-factors to Burma,
ostensibly to enquire for the dead merchant's effects, but
really with a view to establishing trade. He was badly
served by his agents, who tried to keep the commerce of
Burma in their own hands and to discourage its exten-

sion, but none the less British intercourse with the country shortly afterwards became freer than it ever was again until after the annexation of Pegu in 1852. The East India Company had settlements at Prome, Ava and Sirian, and a trading-post somewhere on the confines of China, at a place which in all probability was Bhamo, on the Irawadi, over 300 miles above Mandalay. The Dutch Company also had a considerable trade with Burma, possessing factories in the upper districts, and, it is said, occupying the island of Negrais. From 1631 to 1677 they had a factory at Sirian, once the capital of the ill-fated de Brito, and Valentyn attributes their abandonment of trade with Burma to the constant wars which in this region made peaceful commerce impossible. The British trade also languished, but between 1680 and 1684 the Company reestablished its factories in Burma, and in 1686–7 the island of Negrais was surveyed and taken nominal possession of by the English. In 1695 Nathaniel Higginson, the Governor of Fort St. George, sent Edward Fleetwood and Capt. James Lesley to Ava with presents to the King, out of which the sender, who instructed his agents to haggle manfully, hoped to make a profit in the form of return-gifts. A grant for a new factory at Sirian was obtained, and a Resident was appointed there to supervise the trade, but almost immediately afterwards a general expulsion of foreigners took place, and thenceforth the East India Company had no direct financial stake in Burmese commerce. Sirian, however, continued to be the residence of British and other foreign merchants, and when the Siamese and the Peguans, leagued together

Further India

From Danville's Map of Asia, 1755

against Ava, took the place in 1740, these strangers were
not molested. Three years later Sirian was retaken by
Ava, and subsequently was burned by the Peguans, when
the British, whose Resident, Mr. Smart, had acted, as be-
fitted his name, with duplicity in his dealings with both
parties, were obliged to retire. Negrais was settled from
Madras in 1753, while war was once more raging between Ava and Pegu, and two years later the British
factory at Bassein was destroyed by the former. A mission under Captain Baker was sent to Ava to ask for
redress and to offer the support of the Company, which
had been prudently withheld until the defeat of the Peguans had become a manifest certainty. Baker was badly
received, and when he spoke of "assistance" the King
bared his thighs, smote them with his palms, laughed in-
sultingly in the envoy's face and asked him what he
thought such a king as *he* had to do with aid from any
man! In 1757 another envoy, Ensign Lister, was sent
up the Irawadi to Ava, and as the result of a most humiliating interview, a new factory was opened at Bassein.
In 1759 Negrais was practically abandoned, only a small
staff remaining there in charge of the buildings, and the
entire population of the island, including ten Europeans,
was treacherously murdered very soon afterwards by the
Burmese. The weakness which characterised the dealings of the Company with Burma was never better exemplified than by the action taken on this occasion, for
the envoy sent to plead for redress was received with contempt and insult, and there the matter ended. Bassein was
now abandoned, but some trade was carried on with Ran-

goon until 1794, the merchants doing little business, while
the Company's agents possessed no political influence, and
occupied for the most part positions of great humiliation.

Over Chittagong and Assam, however, the Company
had established its hold, and when in 1794 the Burmese
sent 5,000 armed men into the former province " to arrest robbers dead or alive," the British at last showed
fight, and the Burmese yielded without forcing the issue.
The following year Capt. Michael Symes was sent upon
his famous embassy to Ava, a mission of which he subsequently wrote an elaborate account. He was accompanied by Lieutenant Woods, who made the first reliable
survey of the Irawadi from Rangoon to Ava, and by Dr.
Buchanan, who collected a great deal of information
bearing upon the districts traversed. This was the only
really important achievement of the mission, for Symes
was treated with the utmost insolence, was presented to
the King, in circumstances of intense humiliation, upon
a *kodau*, or " beg-pardon day," and effected nothing of
any importance. He moreover carried away with him a
wholly exaggerated idea of the might of Ava, and though
Cox, the next envoy, corrected his predecessor's erroneous
impressions, Symes was regarded at the time as the more
reliable authority, and his book was probably not without its effect in leading the Government of India into
continuing the weak-kneed policy which had too long
been followed towards the arrogant Burmese Court. Between the time of Cox's visit and 1810 three other missions were sent to Ava, each in turn to be subjected to
insults which it is humiliating to recall, and on each

occasion the King declined to take the slightest notice of the letters sent by the Governor-General, deeming it below him to have any dealings with one who was not a crowned head. All these missions followed the river route to Amarapura, the then residence of the King, and no material addition was made to the information which had been collected by the officers attached to Symes's mission. Ava during the whole of this time continued to treat foreigners with the utmost contumely, and in 1805, for instance, all the British subjects in Rangoon were imprisoned, owing to some misunderstanding which arose over the seizure by the Company of a ship in whose cargo the Burmese authorities were in some way interested. The Company, however, was long-suffering, and it was not until Chittagong had been repeatedly raided that war was at last declared. Sir Archibald Campbell ascended the Irawadi and reached Prome on April 4th, 1825, where he went into cantonments until the end of the rainy season. The land column under Cotton, operating in conjunction with him, had been heavily repulsed by the Burmese at Donabyu, but otherwise the resistance offered had been poor. In September the King sent down from Ava to know on what terms the British army would retire. The reply was that Arakan and Tenasserim must be ceded to the Company. The King declined, and hostilities were renewed, the Burmese being badly beaten a little north of Prome. As the British army continued to advance, the King decided to sue for peace, and on February 24th, 1826, the peace of Yandabu was signed, whereby Tavoi, Mergui, and

Tenasserim—together constituting the long strip of country lying between the Bay of Bengal and the frontiers of Siam—were ceded to the British, and with Arakan became the foundation of our Burmese empire.

The same year John Crawfurd was sent to negotiate the commercial treaty which had been provided for in the terms of peace, but the Court of Ava had not yet learned its lesson, for though his reception compared favourably with those accorded to his predecessors, he met with both impertinence and bad faith. On December 31st, 1829, Major Burney was appointed British Resident at Ava, a position which he held with distinction for eight years, only retiring to Rangoon and sailing for England after the usurpation of the crown by the savage and arrogant King Tharawadi had robbed him of all influence. With the appointment of Burney to this post at Ava a new chapter opens in the story of the exploration of Burma, but its details will have to be examined by us later on.

Turning next to Siam, we find that intercourse between this country and the Dutch East India Company began as early as 1604, before a decade had elapsed since the sailing of the first vessels from the Texel; and in 1608 a Siamese mission was sent to the Dutch factory at Bantam. It was not, however, until 1634 that a Dutch post was established in Siam, and in 1663 the Company withdrew its agent, averring that its agreement with Siam had been violated by the latter. That Siam saw the removal of the factors with regret is proved by the fact that in the following year an embassy was sent to Batavia, by means of which friendly relations were once more established. These continued unabated for some years, the Dutch agent in 1685 being the first foreigner ever admitted to the presence of the King. In 1706, however, a differ- ence arose once more, and this time the Dutch were obliged to ask for such terms as the Siamese were dis- posed to grant to them. Subsequently the trade between the Hollanders and Siam languished and almost ceased. In 1740 an effort was made to restore the former state of things, the King of Siam making friendly overtures to the Dutch, but the negotiations led to nothing, and so completely did the intercourse between the Dutch and the Siamese cease that when Bowring visited Bangkok in 1857, he found no trace remaining there to show that the connection, which had lasted for more than a century, had ever existed.

A remarkable figure in the history of Siamese relations with the West is that of Constantine Phaulkon, or Fal- con, a Greek of Cephalonia, who ran away to England in about 1640, when he was a mere child, and afterwards sailed for the Indies in one of Old John Company's ships. Later, having acquired a vessel of his own, he was wrecked near the mouth of the Menam, passed some years in Siam, and learned the language of the country. Sailing from Siam, he had the misfortune to be again wrecked on the coast of Malabar, his whole ship's com- pany perishing, while he alone escaped, carrying with him a sum of 2,000 crowns. Naked and in a sorry plight, he was roaming the shores upon which he had been cast, when he lighted upon another shipwrecked mariner, even more destitute than himself, who was also the only survivor of his crew, and the moment this man opened his mouth to speak Constantine discovered that he was a native of Siam. Enquiry led Constantine to ascertain the fact that this waif was a high official who had been despatched by his King on an embassy to Persia, of all places, —yet another proof, were any such needed, of the extent of the inter-Asiatic intercourse which existed prior to the domination of the East by white men—and the wily Greek, whose charity, we must suspect, was not untainted by self-seeking, invested his all in a ship, in which he conveyed his new-found friend back to Siam. The man whom he had thus so handsomely befriended recommended him to the officials in Siam, and Constantine presently won for himself great renown by his skilful manipulation of the accounts of some Muhammadans, whereby he proved that far from the King being in their debt, they owed the monarch a substantial sum of money! At an Oriental Court tact and wisdom such as this were sure of recognition, and Constantine rose in the public service until he at last occupied the proud position of Prime Minister. He attained this eminence in 1665, and at Lopburi in the Menam valley there are still extant the ruins of the works which were built under his direction. During his youth in England he had abandoned Catholicism, and had become an Anglican, but the Jesuits, who long ere this had established missions in China and in other parts of the Far East, found him out and won him back to the faith of his fathers. Thereafter Constantine appears to have cherished a desire to convert the King of Siam to Christianity, and it was largely through his agency that the missions of which Père Tachard and Père Choisi were the chroniclers were despatched to the Court of Siam by Louis XIV in 1685 and 1687. These embassies, the second of which was under the leadership of the Chevalier de Chaumont, were mainly composed of Jesuits, and their sole object was the conversion of the King. They were well received, and the Chevalier de Chaumont was careful to submit himself to none of the humiliating observances which, until a much later period, were exacted from British envoys to the Court of Ava; but the King, albeit he was a most liberal-minded monarch, far in advance of his age and race, had no intention of adopting an alien faith. De Chaumont, therefore, presently returned to France; but the Jesuits remained behind, and for a period occupied positions of importance in the Siamese service. They were instrumental in helping to suppress a rebellion headed by a Muhammadan, in which some refugees from Macassar took part, but they gradually became hateful to the nobles and the people of Siam, and were eventually massacred to a man, Constantine himself being ignominiously executed.

During the eighteenth century intercourse between Europeans and Siam was confined to the visits of a few traders and missionaries, and Hamilton's *Account of the East Indies*, published in Edinburgh in 1727, is probably the best work on the lands of southeastern Asia which that period produced. It shows, however, an intimate knowledge of nothing save the ports and coast-lines, all information relating to the interior being derived from native sources of no great accuracy. Hamilton may be regarded as typical of his class and age, and a study of his work shows us how slow was the progress of knowledge of these regions after the great discoveries of the sixteenth and the first half of the seventeenth centuries. The missionaries, as ever, were ubiquitous and scornful of risk, but they were for the most part inarticulate for us, and when in 1821 John Crawfurd was sent to Bangkok and Hue on a special embassy, George Finlayson, in his account of the mission, writes of these countries as though they were in some sort being rediscovered. Hitherto, he declares, they had been " almost unknown to us." Crawfurd and his party were coldly received in Siam, and after a short stay at the capital they coasted as far as Pûlau Kondor, touching at several islands on the way. They visited Saigon, where they met a M. Diard, " a lively, well-educated Frenchman," and passed thence to Hue by water after calling in at Turon. At the Court of Cochin-China they found that French influence was predominant, but permission to trade was granted by the King to the East India Company, and the mission then returned overland to Turon. Five years later Burney, afterwards Resident at Ava, was sent to Bangkok to enlist the co-operation of the Siamese against Burma, with which the British were then at war, but he was not too well received, and the peace of Yandabu was concluded before any active steps had been taken. We have now traced the history of European intercourse with Siam up to the time of the first Burmese war, and as the detailed exploration of the country is a work that belongs to the last seventy years of the nineteenth century, it will be more convenient to continue the narrative in a later chapter.

Turning finally to Indo-China—namely, Cochin-China, Kambodia, Annam, Tongking, and the Laos country in the valley of the Mekong,—we find that after the first settlements had been formed by the Portuguese during the sixteenth century, as has already been related, the British and Dutch East India Companies both established factories in this region. The English had their factory on Pûlau Kondor, now the penal settlement of Saigon, establishing it there in 1616, but a mutiny of the Company's Macassar troops, who had been kept on after the expiration of the terms of their agreement, led to its abandonment. This, and the English factory at Pětâni, from the possession of which we were ousted by the Dutch, were practically the only ventures of the Company on the shores of the China Sea. The East India Company of Holland founded a factory in Cochin-China in 1635, in competition with the Portuguese, who had been established there some fifty years earlier, and the Dutchmen had also a trading-post at Pnom Penh, the capital of Kambodia. To them, moreover, belongs the distinction of having been the first to explore the interior by the Mekong route. In 1641 some Laos traders having come from Pnom Penh to Batavia in one of the Company's vessels, Van Dieman, the Governor, decided to attempt the establishment of commercial intercourse with their country. To this end he deputed a sub-factor named Gerard Van Wusthof to visit Laos, then more or less united under the King of Vien Chan. The story of this

remarkable expedition will be examined in more detail in
a later chapter in connection with the French mission of
1866, but it may be mentioned here that the party ascended the Mekong as far as Vien Chan and resided
there some months.   This journey, however, was not
repeated, and did not lead to the opening up of Laos, as
in 1642 the Portuguese contrived to cause the Dutch
factor, Jeremias de Wal, to be murdered while on a
journey to Pnom Penh, and after that the Dutch factories
in Cochin-China and Kambodia were abandoned.   The
Portuguese themselves never penetrated far into the interior, though an Italian missionary priest, named Leria,
reached Vien Chan in 1642, and later travelled overland
into Tongking.   His example, however, found no imita-
tors, and from his time until late in the last century Laos
was not visited by missionaries.

For a space after the departure of the Dutch the
Portuguese who remained in possession exercised considerable influence at the Court of Kambodia and in the
delta of the Mekong, but towards the end of the seventeenth century the native officials, instigated it is said by
China, organised a general massacre of the white men,
dealing a blow to the power of the Portuguese in this
region from which it never again recovered.

From that time onward, the intercourse of Europeans
with the lands of Indo-China was confined to the missionaries and to a few visits from traders.   Most of the missionaries were Frenchmen, though a proportion came from
Spain, and the latter half of the seventeenth century saw
the growth of French influence in these regions.   The

French Bishop, Pigneau de Béhaine, is the commanding figure in the drama. He was born in 1741, came out to Cochin-China, built a church at Saigon, and so won the confidence of the King Ngueyen Anh, afterwards better known as Gia Long, that he was actually entrusted with the custody of his son, whom he took to Paris in 1787 and presented at the Court of Louis XVI. France was at the moment over-busy with her internal affairs, being as she was on the eve of the great Revolution, and beyond a gift of arms and a treaty of alliance, the main provisions of which were never fulfilled, nothing tangible resulted at the time from Béhaine's mission. Subsequently, however, the existence of this treaty was recalled to mind, and the fact was made a foundation upon which to base France's right to interfere in the affairs of Indo-China.

Béhaine's visit, however, attracted the attention of Frenchmen to this distant corner of the world, and a number of adventurers of that nationality visited Annam. By their aid and that of Béhaine, King Gia Long succeeded in conquering the whole of the ancient kingdom of Annam, from the Gulf of Siam to the frontiers of China, thus uniting under a single sceptre Cochin-China, Annam and Tongking. His gratitude to the white men who had assisted him in this work led him to show an unwonted measure of tolerance to the preachers of the Christian religion. When Béhaine died in Saigon in 1789 he was accorded a state funeral, and the monument erected by his patron over his grave still ranks as one of the most interesting historical relics of the place. By 1802 Gia Long had made himself master of his whole kingdom, and for eighteen years more he ruled it with an iron hand and extended open tolerance to the Christians. In 1820, however, he died, and his successor, Minh Meng, expelled the French and persecuted the native Christians before he had been four years upon the throne. A second massacre of missionaries—for the Roman Catholic priests of the Société des Missions Etrangères returned again and again to the charge, as also did the Spanish missionaries,—occurred in 1851, and a war vessel was sent to destroy the forts at Turon. In 1857 Bishop Diaz, a Spaniard, having been brutally murdered by the authorities, France and Spain took joint-action with the result that Cochin-China was invaded by a Franco-Spanish expedition. It was not, however, until the hand of France had been freed by the signing of the Treaty of Peking in 1860, which put an end to the war with China, that really effective action was taken, and Cochin-China was ceded to France.

Kambodia meanwhile had been invaded during the latter half of the eighteenth century by Siam and Annam, and had gradually become subservient to both. In 1857 her King, Ang Duong, appealed for aid to France, and a French protectorate over the kingdom was proclaimed by France shortly after the accession of his successor Norodon in 1859. Siamese influence continued to be predominant at the Court of Kambodia until 1863, when Siam was bought out by France, the provinces of Siam-reap and Batambang being ceded to her without the knowledge or consent of the unhappy Norodon, whose protests, however, were unavailing. These provinces had, as a matter of fact, been occupied by Siam for many years, and from the French point of view it was all-important that Siam's demands should be satisfied, and that a clear field should be left in which the influence of France might operate unchecked. Captain Doudart de Lagrée, of whom much more hereafter, occupied for some time the post of Resident at the Court of Kambodia, and it was on the eve of his departure on the great journey of exploration which cost him his life, that the rebellion of Pu Kombo broke out in that State. Norodon was aided by French troops who rescued him from a precarious position in the beleaguered town of Pnom Penh, and this led to the increase of French ascendency, so that to-day though Kambodia is nominally only a protectorate of France, its finances and administration are entirely in the hands of Frenchmen.

In Tongking a Dutch factory had been established in 1637, but it was abandoned in 1700, and after that time no permanent European colony appears to have been formed in this kingdom. Tongking was conquered and annexed by Annam in 1802, after which period it was in frequently visited by Europeans, save only a few missionaries, until the Frenchman Dupuis, of whom something will be said in a later chapter, attempted to make the Song Koi River a highway of communication and trade with China. This led to interference on the part of France, and eventually to the practical annexation of the country after a period of prolonged and harassing warfare.

The glance which we have now taken at the history of

European intercourse with all the lands of the great Indo-Chinese Peninsula, from the coming of the British and Dutch East India Companies to 1826 in the case of Burma and Siam, to the date of the active interference of France in the case of Cochin-China, Kambodia, Annam and Tongking, to the eve of British expansion in the Native States in the case of the Malay Peninsula,—has been necessitated, not because it adds very materially to our information on the subject of the exploration of these countries, but because it is from these periods that the most important part of our story begins. The establishment of European supremacy, or at any rate the wide extension of European influence, were necessary preliminaries to the great task of exploring the *Hinterland* of Indo-China which had been kept jealously closed to white men from the early days of the seventeenth century when the whole of the East not yet learned begun to fear and suspect her invaders. The true exploration of Burma dates from the appointment of a British Resident to Ava after the first Burmese war; that of Siam was a work left for accomplishment to the last quarter of the nineteenth century; the interior of the Malay Peninsula was almost entirely unknown when Pêrak and Sĕlângor were placed under British protection in the early seventies of the last century; while the valley of the Mekong was first revealed to Europeans with some fulness of detail by the De Lagrée-Garnier expedition of 1866–1868. It is with the last named journey, as being at once the most important and in many respects the most interesting, that we shall now deal.

CHAPTER VI

IN the preceding chapters the knowledge gained by Europeans of the lands of southeastern Asia has been traced from its earliest beginnings, in the imaginary island of Chryse, the Golden, until by the seventeenth century the coast-lines of the whole of the vast Indo-Chinese peninsula had become familiarly known to the geographers and merchants of the West. Similarly we have followed the growth of knowledge of this part of the world, and the events which contributed to it, until in the nineteenth century the spread of European influence in Burma, in Malaya and in Cochin-China and Kambodia opened the gates to enquiry and made the scientific exploration of the *Hinterland* a possibility. The work lay now ready to the hand, and of all the men who took a share in it and succeeded in writing their names large upon the maps of these regions, Francis Garnier, the Frenchman, the naval officer, colonial administrator, explorer, cartographer, man of letters and dreamer of dreams, is perhaps the most arresting figure.

It is no part of my present plan to attempt a biography of Francis Garnier; our concern is with his achievement rather than with his character. Yet in order that a true appreciation of the former may be arrived at, something must be known of the latter. Its keynote is to be found in the strong constructive imagination of the man, in his ability to plan and to organise, in his tireless energy, mental and physical, in a certain largeness of view and quenchless enthusiasm, and withal in an inspiring nobility of spirit. Garnier was born at Saint-Etienne in 1839, but he was brought up at Montpellier within sight of the sea, which early exercised over him a great fascination. He was educated at the naval college at Brest, into which he passed eleventh out of a hundred successful candidates, and from which he in due time entered the regular service after gaining distinction in the examinations. It is immediately prior to his maiden voyage as a naval officer that we get the first, and as I think, the most illuminating glimpse of Francis Garnier the man. It comes to us from certain boyish letters addressed to a friend, and though his opinions are of a nature little flattering to our national self-esteem, they may stand as a picture of a young Frenchman of the best type in early manhood. There are crudities and absurdities in every line. Facts and fictions are accepted at second-hand without enquiry or examination, without test or proof. Passionately patriotic, Garnier is here seen to be the victim of the hate that is ever the fringe of love, and the rank injustice of the verdicts into which it betrays him is too exaggerated to arouse anything save amusement. None the less, Garnier's letters, penned at the age of twenty, are instructive. They show the creed of anglophobia in which, it is to be feared, too many young Frenchmen are educated, and though it so chanced that their author in after life won enough of experience where-

Francis Garnier

with to correct his earlier impressions, it is melancholy to remember that many others, who have imbibed the same opinions in youth, have never had occasion or opportunity to revise and alter them. The inherited and unreasoning dislike of the average English schoolboy for Frenchmen is undeniably strong, but it is of a wholly different brand to the hate which here may be seen to inspire the opinions of Francis Garnier; and the ordinary Englishman of our own time puts such prejudices off when he comes to man's estate together with other things of the child. The fervid virulence of angry hate which finds its expression in the following quotations has no home among ourselves, and the mere fact that we are inclined to laugh at such frenzies unquestionably adds fuel to the flame. It is the Englishman's almost contemptuous indifference to the dislike of which he is the object, and his inability to return the sentiment in kind, which contribute so largely to his unpopularity abroad.

But Garnier's tirade, for all its insensate hatred of England, for all its boyishness, all its folly, gives token of other more estimable qualities. There is here the enthusiasm, the optimism, the tremendous self-confidence, the generous ambition which are bred of youth and inexperience, and above all we see Garnier in the character that made him great, as the dreamer of dreams who is yet a man of action bent upon giving concrete form to his imaginings. His aim was nothing less than the total destruction of England, and he hoped to that end to form a confraternity which should bring about a consummation so devoutly to be wished.

" I tell you," he writes to M. Joseph Perre, his lifelong friend, " that if there be manufacturers with enough heart and intelligence to apply themselves to the impoverishment of Protestant England,—men who understand sufficiently well the interests of civilisation and of France to desire to diminish England's commerce and influence,—there are also young men of sufficient courage, energy, and will to work for an even more difficult end. Ideal, do you call it? But not impossible for them ; and this end is to overthrow her utterly and to strike her name from the ranks of the nations.

" What young and ardent soul is there that is not, during its hours of aspiration after the beautiful and the great, smitten with some noble idea, some immense and magnificent aim? What young man is there who, in the solitude of his soul, has not dreamed of the means whereby he may attain the pure and radiant crown of glory which encircles the brows of those philanthropists who have passed obscure lives in the most toilsome labours in order to ameliorate the lot of their kind? But soon the vortex of the world and the selfish interests which govern it efface the vividness of these impressions, tarnish them, cause them to be forgotten, and so, becoming sensible, as it is called, one loses the illusions and the dreams of youth.

" For those of whom I speak to you it has not been thus. The idea which appealed to them was that of civilisation in general and of the regeneration of mankind in certain countries in particular.

" Behold France, the arbiter of Europe, making use of

Further India, 1840

From Lizar's Edinburgh Map

her influence only for the happiness and for the moral improvement of the peoples. Behold her spreading everywhere, whither her arms have penetrated, benefits and civilisation, pacifying all confusions, appeasing all quarrels, making the peoples abroad listen always to her solemn voice when it has become necessary to make others respect the rights of misunderstood men.

"Now look at England astonishing the nineteenth century by her influence and her expansion. Go to India, visit this country ruined and impoverished by the plunderings of the English Company. See the lands lying waste, the canals dried up, the natives brutalised by a degrading yoke, deprived of almost all the rights of the native and the citizen, and ask yourself if this is the country which of old was the centre of Asiatic civilisation, which was renowned for her wealth, her fertility and for the might of her inhabitants. Is this the part which a civilised nation ought to play towards a vanquished people? Has England fulfilled the duty which her very conquest imposed upon her? Go everywhere else throughout the English Colonies, and you will find only misery, despair and forced labour designed to satisfy an insatiable metropolis. Examine modern history. Who was not disgusted when the Parliament of London declared war on China because her Emperor forbade to his subjects the use of the opium that was killing them, action which was taken because the edict diminished a trade of which England had the monopoly and the profit. What honest heart was there that was not made indignant when, profiting in cowardly fashion by the superiority of her arms, England forced the Chinese Emperor to revoke his edict, and so to sanction the poisoning of three hundred millions of men? But what did this matter to London? She had a few millions more. I say nothing to you of the rôle which the British Cabinet has played and is playing in Italy, nor of the insults which Lord Palmerston lavished upon a white-haired old man! All the iniquities of English policy have for the rest been eloquently denounced by M. de Montalembert in France and by Mr. Brownson of the United States, and to them I refer you.

"And this is the conclusion at which the young men of whom I spoke to you just now have arrived after an examination of a situation which I have been unable even to sketch for you: it is that such a country, such a disgusting picture of disorder and of immorality, such a spectacle of all the miseries, the theatre of all the crimes which afflict and degrade humanity, a country which breathes corruption upon the world, a country whose Machiavellian Government has lies and cowardice for its policy, that England, in a word, the infamous melting-pot in which the lives of men are exploited for the profit of the few, in which, for the enrichment of the two millions of individuals who compose the English aristocracy and Government, one hundred and fifty millions of men waste now and always their sweat and their blood, having only misery, despair, and corruption for their bed, living and dying like brutes—that this country, I say, which presents to the very nineteenth century human degradation on so vast a scale, ought to be put under the ban of

the nations so that such a monstrous abuse of force be
made to cease.

" These young men have told themselves that Europe
will never be peaceful or happy while such a monster
stirs in her breast and sheds upon it its venom, and they
have devoted themselves to a task, slow, patient, but
active, the task of overthrowing her! In making an appeal to unknown races and to the indignation of mankind, to those who have no definite end in view, to those
whose energy stands in need of a stimulant, they have
hoped to succeed. Only a sailor "—a delightfully youthful
and naive touch this !—" can thoroughly understand all the
chances of success of the plan which they are already beginning to put into execution.

" We shall fail perhaps; but we will die in the endeavour, and that which a nation dares not try to accomplish we, at least, shall have the glory of having attempted. *Mon Dieu!* I know that at first sight the enterprise seems foolish. England, you will say, is a Co-
lossus. Granted, but her feet are rotten. Shake her and
she will fall. England is universally execrated, and in
our day public opinion makes and unmakes empires.
When Tell and his two comrades swore in the darkness
to give back her liberty to their country, was not the enterprise a folly? We, we desire to restore liberty to the
world, and the world will be on our side, for it groans
and laments under the painful restraint, the constant
encroachments, which this nest of pirates and robbers,
having become powerful, imposes upon it and makes on
every occasion."

It is impossible to imagine a letter such as this coming from the pen of an English youngster, and our insular self-complacency tempts us to the inference that something resembling a subconscious sense of inferiority is responsible for this and for other similar tirades.   There is an almost hysterical note in this young Cato's reiterated *Delenda est Carthago*, but behind the rodomontade is to be detected the man of ideas and enthusiasms, the man who can conceive great schemes, who is not to be daunted by difficulties, or even by impossibilities, and who, not content with dreaming, is bent upon immediate, energetic and decisive action.   This is the Francis Garnier who, in his riper maturity, when the vainglorious follies of youth had been set aside, and his powers and views had been tested by experience did such magnificent work for France and for science in the *Hinterlands* of Indo-China.   It is satisfactory, too, and creditable to Garnier's impartiality, powers of observation and good sense, that when at a later date he visited the India, of which in his boyhood so deplorable an account had reached him, he puts aside his preconceived prejudices and writes as follows of the British administration of Hindustan.

" Thanks to the genius of Dupleix, the French were able to dream for a season of gaining supremacy over all this vast and rich peninsula.   But a more persevering and more fortunate nation has reaped what they sowed. England has at last succeeded in founding from Cape Comorin to the Himalayas a flourishing empire of two hundred millions of men.   Taught by the hard lessons of a costly experience, she has seriously undertaken to reconcile the elder branch of our race with its younger European branch. Purely mercantile preoccupations have given place to speculations of a more elevated description. To material has succeeded moral conquest which, marching with the torch of science in hand, strives to destroy prejudices, to dissipate misunderstandings, and invites the vanquished to enjoy all the advantages of a generous civilisation. One cannot but admire the magnificent *ensemble* of researches and of deeds which have adorned the efforts of English colonisation. Conquests thus justified are a benefit to those who submit to them and to all mankind. They are the only conquests of the kind which our era has witnessed."

In this passage we have again the enthusiasm, the love of that which is good which always distinguished Francis Garnier, and those of us who know the East must admit that once more his fiery imagination and his inclination to indulge in dreams caused him to do our countrymen something more, as he had formerly done them somewhat less, than justice. If England's main task be that of reconciling the peoples of the East with those of the West it may be questioned whether she has accomplished much more than a magnificent and generous failure. We do not like Francis Garnier any the worse, however, because when he became a convert to admiration of England his impulsive and enthusiastic nature carried him somewhat beyond the prosaic facts and betrayed him into some exaggeration. Nor can we avoid being flattered when at a later date we find this whilom Anglophobe, who by a thousand proofs showed himself a

patriotic, loyal and loving son of France, marrying an
English wife, and once in the bitterness of his soul, echo-
ing unconsciously the sentiment of the great Voltaire,
" What a misfortune it is that I was not born an Englishman! With them I should have been a man at once
powerful and honoured! As bad luck will have it, however, I cannot make up my mind to be no longer a
Frenchman!"

Such was the man the story of whose explorations in
the Indo-Chinese peninsula we shall presently examine,
but before we pass on to this part of our subject we must
trace in as few words as possible the history of his connection with the regions with which his name was destined to be so intimately associated.

On January 9th, 1860, Garnier, having volunteered for
service with the naval expedition then about to sail for
China, left Toulon on board the *Duperré*, and on his outward voyage earned distinction by an exhibition of more
than usual courage. At 11 P. M., on May 30th, when the
vessel was running some five knots an hour, and the night
was very dark, the cry was raised that a man had fallen
overboard. Garnier instantly threw himself into the sea,
seized the life-buoy which was cast after him, swam with
it to the drowning sailor, and succeeded in supporting
him until a boat lowered from the ship had the good luck
to find him and the man whom he had saved. An act of
this kind, which draws its inspiration from no feeling of
personal devotion or affection for the man for whom the
terrible risk is run, which is not born of the intoxication
of battle, which can draw no stimulus from the plaudits

of spectators, argues the possession of a resolution, an un-
selfish and steady bravery, such as is found only in very
exceptional men, and all will agree that Garnier richly
deserved the promotion to the rank of ensign which was
immediately given to him as a reward of his valour.
This was his first opportunity for making his merit
known, and he had seized it in a noble fashion. Vice-
Admiral Charnier at once attached him to his Staff, upon
which he served during the whole of the war with China.

In October, 1860, the treaty of peace was signed in
Peking, and the French Government was able at last to
turn its attention towards Saigon. This place had been
captured by a joint Franco-Spanish expedition in February, 1859, as also had the harbour of Turon, but owing to
the inadequate force at the disposal of the authorities during the war with China, the latter had to be abandoned in
March, 1860, and the retreat at once inspired the natives
of Cochin-China with the hope that they might succeed in
dislodging the French. The Emperor issued a proclamation in which he said :

" Behold they have departed, these noxious and greedy
beings who have no inspiration save evil, no aim save
sordid gain ! They have departed, these pirates who de-
vour human flesh, and who fashion garments from the
skins of those whom they have eaten ! Put to flight by
our valiant soldiers, they have shamefully saved themselves ! "

Thus encouraged, the forces of Cochin-China beset
Saigon, in overwhelming numbers the city was then garri-
soned by only 800 men, of whom a fourth were Spaniards,

aided by two corvets and four despatch-boats. In July two night-attacks were made, but the little force repulsed them with considerable slaughter, and after that, though Saigon was closely invested, no attempt to take it of any determined character was made. The innate inefficiency of the Oriental to which, more than to the prowess of the white races, is due the conquest of the East by the West, resulted, as it had so often resulted, in delay when all depended upon no time being wasted, in aimless manœuvres when the only chance of success lay in striking a decisive blow. In the months during which the little force, completely isolated, and without any immediate prospect of succour, held out inside Saigon, the fate of Cochin-China was sealed. Her people had their opportunity, which circumstances combined to render unwontedly favourable, and failing to take it a similar chance of success never again presented itself.

In February, 1861, Admiral Charnier, upon whose Staff Francis Garnier was still serving, arrived at Saigon with a large force which included 230 Spaniards and a corps of native Christians who had been recruited at Turon. The siege was raised in triumphant fashion, more than a thousand of the enemy being killed in an engagement in which the French lost only twelve men killed and 213 wounded, and in which Garnier had the good fortune to distinguish himself under the eyes of the Admiral. He was present later at the taking of Mytho, and had the satisfaction of seeing the real work of conquest accomplished before he returned to France with Charnier in the following October.

In France he devoted himself to study, chiefly of an historical, geographical and scientific character, and to the dull round of his routine duties. His recent experiences had served only to whet his appetite for adventure; the glamour of the East had cast its spell upon him; the mystery of lands in which no white man had set foot since the beginning of things had fired his imagination; the itch of travel was upon him, goading him to restlessness. The reaction of the enforced inactivity to which he was now condemned irked him, seemed the veriest bathos after the experiences of the strenuous days in which he had delighted. " I am in Lower Brittany," he writes to M. Perre, " occupied in drilling marine riflemen for seven hours a day, a task which develops one's intelligence very little and satisfies one's heart even less! " So depressing was the life which he now was leading that he speaks, in true French fashion, of the final setting of " his star," and seems even to have thought of throwing up the naval service.

The young officer, however, had already made his mark, and when the conquest of Cochin-China was accomplished, and the Treaty of June, 1862, had been signed between France and the Court of Hue, Garnier was remembered, and was presently appointed inspector of Native Affairs in the new colony. By this Treaty the Provinces of Bien-Hoa, Gia-Dinh (Saigon), Dinh-Tuong (Mytho), and the island of Kondor were ceded to France; the free exercise of the Christian religion by all who desired to adopt it was formally permitted; French warships were granted access to the Mekong River, and

French merchants were given the right of trading upon its banks. An indemnity of four million dollars was also paid by the Emperor of Annam.

Garnier reached Saigon in 1863, and though he was still a youth of barely twenty-four years of age, he was appointed to the charge of Cholen, a suburb of Saigon. His post was now what we should call that of District Officer, though he was more under-staffed than is usual with even our short-handed administrations, and appears to have combined in his own person the duties of half-a-dozen offices. He paid special attention to public works, and his rule of the little town was characterised by the energy, the enthusiasm and the imagination which distinguished everything to which he set his hand. He early perceived that the country ceded to France had no natural boundaries, and that an extension of territory was imperatively necessary in the interests of the new colony. This view he expressed repeatedly both in his private and official writings, and though an Annamite embassy to Paris in 1863 all but succeeded in persuading France to relinquish her conquests, Admiral de la Grandière, the Governor of Cochin-China, contrived in 1867 to obtain permission to annex Vinh-Long, Sadec, Chandoc, and Hatien.

It was while he was at Cholen that the idea of exploring in detail the *Hinterland* of Indo-China first presented itself to Francis Garnier as a definite scheme. France had now established her supremacy on the delta of the Mekong—that " Captain of all the Rivers," as Linschoten named it,—and to Garnier, the man of strong imagina-

Doudart de Lagrée

tion, that mighty stream flowing out of the heart of the land, whence no one precisely knew, was the propounder of a tremendous riddle. The fascination of the Unknown, for those whom it has no power to awe and discourage, is a force greater, perhaps, than aught else, and Garnier's was a nature to which it made an appeal more than usually vivid. A dreamer of dreams he saw visions of an empire won for France which might equal, if not transcend, the empire which Clive had wrested from the hold of Dupleix ; a statesman bent upon developing the resources of the colonies which France had already conquered, he thought to find in the upper reaches of the Mekong a trade-route which should divert the commerce of the Chinese Empire from her own coast-ports to those of French Indo-China ; a man of science who loved knowledge for its own sake, he longed to learn the secrets hidden so closely since the beginning by that untrodden wilderness. His official memoranda embodied the earliest proposals for the exploration of the valley of the Mekong, and the matter excited the interests of the authorities in France and on the spot. It was not until June 1st, 1866, that his representations were translated into action, and then he was considered to be too junior in years and service to be entrusted with the chief command of the expedition which owed its inception to his energy and imaginative foresight.

The leadership of the party was vested in M. Doudart de Lagrée, a post-captain in the French navy, who was then holding the important position of what we should call " Political Agent " at the Court of Norodon, King of Kambodia, the protectorate over whose country had been declared by France largely as the result of the influence which her agent had acquired. Garnier occupied the post of second in command, and to him was entrusted the geographical, astronomical and meteorological work of the expedition. He was instructed to determine the precise positions of all points of importance, to make a map of the country traversed, to take soundings and ascertain the navigability of the rivers, to note the means of navigation employed by the various native tribes, and to compare the advantages presented by the river and the neighbouring land-routes. The other members of the expedition were M. Thorel, a naval medical officer, who was the botanist of the party; M. Louis Delaporte, a naval ensign, who was a clever artist; M. Eugène Joubert, another medical officer, a geologist; and M. Louis de Carné, an officer attached to the Ministry of Foreign Affairs, who owed his selection to the fact that he was related to the Governor of Indo-China. De Lagrée took with him also a sergeant of marines named Charbonnier, who spoke Siamese and Annamite, a private of marines, and two sailors. The expedition was moreover accompanied by a number of native interpreters.

On June 5th, 1866, the little band of white men left Saigon on the first organised journey of exploration ever made by Europeans into the more remote portions of the unknown *Hinterland* of Indo-China, from the shores of the China Sea.

From Th[...] of An[...]

CHAPTER VII

A DESPATCH-BOAT had been sent to Bangkok by the Colonial Government for the purpose of obtaining passports and a supply of Siamese money of which the expedition would stand in need when it quitted Kambodian territory and began to make its way through districts under the dominion of Siam. Pending the return of this vessel, the main design of the explorers—the ascent of the Mekong to its source—could not be proceeded with, and De Lagrée decided to utilise the time of forced inactivity by paying a visit to the immense ruins of Angkor, the most remarkable of the many relics of a forgotten civilisation which are to be found scattered throughout Kambodia, in the districts of Siamreap and Batambang (which had been wrested from that kingdom by Siam), and in some parts of the Laos country. De Lagrée, while serving as political officer in Kambodia, had visited Angkor on more than one occasion, and had taken a scientific interest in its monuments and in the problems which they present for solution. Neither he nor any of his companions, however, can claim to be regarded as in any sense the discoverers of these ruins, their existence having first become known to Europeans as early as 1570, as we shall presently see. None the less, the accident of their sojourn at

Angkor affords us a convenient opportunity of taking in
this place a rapid glance at the ruins themselves, at the
few facts concerning them which can now be ascertained,
and at the theories, conjectures, and surmises, to which
they have given birth.

The expedition steamed up the Mekong to Pnom
Penh, the point at which the branch of the great Kambodian lake of Tonli-Sap falls into the river on its right
bank, and thence up the whole length of the lake to its
northern extremity. Here, about a couple of miles inland, standing isolated in the centre of a plain, is a small
hill crowned by two peaks, the higher of which is
covered by a grove. Within this are the ruins of an ancient
temple—the Pagoda of Mount Krôm—overgrown, almost hidden by vegetation, but displaying to the eye of
the astonished traveller its graceful towers, its wealth
of sculpture, its bas-reliefs and its gigantic stone figures, intact or pitifully broken and defaced. It is a
wonderful sensation—as all who have experienced it bear
witness—to come thus suddenly, without the smallest
preparation, after travelling for weeks through a wilderness of forest broken by nothing more imposing than a
cluster of thatched huts, upon this beautiful work of art,
whereof the graceful lines, the slender domes and arches,
the delicate detail of the carving, all attest the high culture
and civilisation of the men who wrought so greatly.

A few miles further on, between Mount Krôm and
Angkor, lies the modern town of Siamreap, an unsightly
collection of hovels dominated by the stone fort occupied
at the time of Garnier's visit by the Siamese Governor of

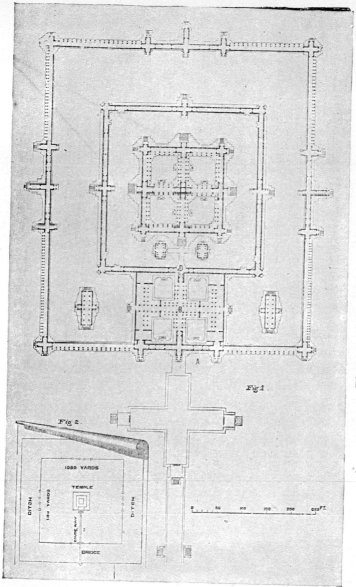

Fig 1.

Fig 2.

1080 YARDS

TEMPLE

DITCH   DITCH

BRIDGE

0   50   100   150   200   250 FT.

Plan of the Temple of Ankor Wat

From Thomson's "Antiquities of Kambodia"

the province and his body-guard. Leaving this place behind him the traveller passes once more into the forest,
and then, again without a moment's warning, comes face
to face with the magnificent temple of Angkor Wat.
The force of the contrast between the apparently primeval forest and this finished work of man is tremendous
and dramatic. Its unexpectedness and the isolation of its
situation give to the ruined temple an impressiveness
such as even its beauty and its immensity could not otherwise claim, yet these are in themselves sufficient to
fire the most languid imagination. " Its endless stair-
cases and galleries," writes Garnier, " its inner courts and
colonnades of an uniform aspect appeared to me, in spite of
their symmetry, or rather because of their very symmetry,
to form an inextricable labyrinth. The enormous proportions of each part of this great entity prevented one
from taking in the whole. . . . It required some
time to appreciate the exact disposition of an edifice
which measures, within ditches, five and a half kilometres
(over three miles) in circumference."

This immense building is constructed of sandstone
brought from quarries distant some twenty-five miles.
Some of the blocks are of great size, weighing more than
eight tons, and though no cement was used, they are
fitted together with so nice an accuracy that a line traced
on a piece of paper laid over the junction between two
stones is as straight as though it had been ruled. What
were the mechanical contrivances by means of which these
huge blocks of stone were cut, were transported to the
site selected for the temple, and were hoisted into their

destined places in the building, is a riddle to which it is
by no means easy to supply an answer, but the amount
of human labour at the disposal of the architects must
have been enormous, and the civilisation which could conceive such designs and could carry them into successful
execution must have attained to a very high standard.

Even more astonishing than the Titanic character of
the ruins is the wealth of beautiful detail which they dis-
play. Almost every individual stone is curiously carved.
Statues of immense proportions, figures of Buddha, of
giants and kings, of lions, dragons, and fabulous monsters
abound. The bas-reliefs show processions of warriors
mounted on birds, on horses, tigers, elephants, and on
legendary animals, combats between the king of the apes
and the king of the angels, boats filled with long-bearded
rowers some of them dressed in the Chinese fashion, cock-
fights, women at play with their little ones, soldiers armed
with bows, with javelins, sabres, and halberts, and innumerable other scenes. The men who wrought these
carvings must have been possessed by a veritable passion
for artistic presentment, by a love of art for its own sake
such as would seem to argue a degree of intellectual re-
finement which has no counterpart among the peoples of
the Indo-Chinese peninsula in our own day.

About two and a half miles north of Angkor Wat is
another ruined temple—the Pagoda of Mount Bakhêng—
standing like that of Mount Krôm on the summit of a hill,
the foot of which is guarded by two magnificent stone
lions, each formed with its pedestal out of a single block
of stone. A broken stairway leads to the cap of the hill,

Sculpture at Ankor Wat, Kambodia

From a photograph by J. Thomson

" whence," writes Henri Mouhot, " is to be enjoyed a view so beautiful and extensive that it is not surprising that these people, who have shown so much taste in their buildings, should have chosen it for a site. On the one side you gaze upon the wooded plain and the pyramidal temple of Ongcor, with its rich colonnades, the mountain of Crome, which is beyond the new city (Siamreap), the view losing itself in the waters of the great lake on the horizon. On the opposite side stretches the long chain of mountains whose quarries, they say, furnished the beautiful stone used for the temples; and amidst thick forests, which extend along the base, is a pretty, small lake, which looks like a blue ribbon on a carpet of verdure. All this region is now as lonely and deserted as formerly it must have been full of life and cheerfulness; and the howling of wild animals and the cries of a few birds, alone disturb the solitude."

The temple of Mount Bakhêng is obviously the most ancient of the Angkor ruins, just as the great temple of Angkor Wat is plainly the most recent; in the former the idols are somewhat rudely fashioned, and would seem to belong to a period when the art of the Khmers was in its infancy and had not yet attained to the delicacy and precision of a later age.

All the buildings hitherto mentioned were designed only as places of worship, and as such bear unmistakeable testimony to the religious enthusiasm which animated the people who fashioned and conceived them. Half a mile beyond Bakhêng, however, ruins of a wholly different character are met with. Here, though temples are not

lacking, most of the edifices were built for the accommodation or the protection of man, for this is Angkor Thôm
—Great Angkor—once the capital of a mighty empire.
" The outer wall," says Mouhot, " is composed of blocks
of ferruginous stone, and extends right and left from the
entrance. It is about twenty-four miles square (*sic*), three
metres eighty centimetres thick, and seven metres high,
and serves as a support to a glacis which rises almost
from the top." An ancient road, in which, though it is
partly obliterated, the ruts ploughed by the heavy traffic
of a bygone age are still descernible, leads to the main
entrance across a wide ditch full of the débris of broken
columns, portions of carved lions and elephants, and fallen
blocks of stone. The portal is an arch some sixty feet in
height surmounted by four immense heads, described by
Mouhot as being " in the Egyptian style," these and the
whole building being constructed of sandstone. At each
of the four corners of the great rectangular city there is
another gate, and there is a sixth on the east side.
Within the vast enclosure formed by the walls the forest
riots wantonly—an inextricable tangle of grey-black
trunks and spreading branches, of striving saplings, dense
underwood, twining creepers and hanging curtains of
parasitic growths, such as only the warm moist earth can
produce in these prolific tropical lands. Hidden under
this splendid pall of verdure, reverently concealed beneath
God's green coverlet, lies the city of the dead. Here are
pagodas, now the lairs of forest creatures, in which men
of a forgotten generation put up their prayer or plaint,
houses in which they were born, in which they lived and

planned and loved and laboured and quarrelled and suffered and died, the great store-treasuries which held the wealth of an empire, the gorgeous palaces within which dwelt kings and the fathers of kings.

> " They say the Lion and the Lizard keep
> The Courts where Jamshyd gloried and drank deep:
> And Bahrám, that great Hunter—the Wild Ass
> Stamps o'er his Head, but cannot break his Sleep."

The romance, the wonder of the lost story of this once great city, of the lives of the men and women who dwelt in it,—of the hopes and the ambitions, the passions and the desires, the joys and the sorrows, of the thousand trivial, but to them all-important, happenings which made up their myriad individual lives, even more than the thought of the great catastrophe which must have brought destruction upon them, grips you here "at the quiet limits of the world," as you look upon the traces they have left behind them—the silent stones, wrought with such love and labour, mouldering under the calm dome of the slumbering forest. With eager curiosity you grope amid the lumber of the centuries, seeking some hint that shall have the power to breathe the spark of life into this buried skeleton of majesty; but when you have learned all that is at present known the enigma remains unsolved, and the conclusions indicated are of a character little calculated to satisfy the judgment of those who know Asia only at second-hand.

The earliest known record of Angkor is found in the work of an anonymous Chinese diplomat, who in 1295 was ordered by the Emperor of China to proceed to the kingdom of Chin-Lá, the name by which Kambodia was then known. His book has been translated by M. Abel-Rémusat, in whose *Nouveaux Mélanges Asiatiques* it occupied a prominent place. The author tells us that he was entrusted with the duty of promulgating certain orders of his Emperor (Kublai Kaan) in Kambodia, over which State China exercised something in the nature of suzerainty; that he left Ming-Cheu in the second month of the year following the reception by him of the imperial instructions—that is to say in 1296—travelled thence to the port of Wen-Chu, whence he put out to sea on the 20th day of the same month. On the 15th day of the third moon—namely twenty-five days later—he arrived off the coast of Cochin-China, but he relates that he then encountered such adverse winds that he did not succeed in reaching his destination until the seventh moon. He returned to China, once more travelling by sea, in 1297. It is worthy of notice, in view of the hopes so persistently entertained by the French administration of Indo-China of tapping the trade of the Celestial Empire by means of the Mekong, the Red River, or some other inland route, that even when Kambodia was a flourishing and highly civilised kingdom, communication between it and China was maintained by sea, and not viâ the Provinces of Yun-nan or Kwang-si.

The Chinese ambassador next gives us a detailed account of the capital of Kambodia, in which mention is made of the rectangular shape of the town, the high wall by which it is encompassed, the two gates on the eastern face, and the great Causeway of Giants which leads to the western entrance, and which, even in ruins, is so remarkable a feature of Angkor. He also mentions particularly a temple without the walls, which even then was accounted very ancient, and which according to the legend current in his day was built by one Lu-pan in the space of a single night. This would appear to be the pagoda of Mount Bakhêng. On the other hand, the Chinese author speaks of two lakes, one on the east of the town about 100 *li* in circumference, and another, the dimensions of which are not given, some five *li* to the north. Only one such lake is now in existence, and this is not easily to be identified with either of those mentioned by the ambassador from China. Angkor Wat, the immense temple which from internal evidence is proved to be the most recent of the Angkor ruins, is not spoken of, and we are therefore driven to conclude either that it had not been built by the year 1296, or that a description of it was omitted by accident, or, as has been suggested, that the Kambodian capital described in the Chinese manuscript is some place other than Angkor. Before entering into a discussion of this point, however, it will be more convenient in the first instance to undertake an examination of the references to the ruins which occur after the invasion of the East by the peoples of Europe.

The discovery of the ruins of Angkor is stated by Christoval de Jaque, who in a book published in 1606 gives an account of travels in Indo-China undertaken by him between 1592 and 1598, to have been made in 1570.

" It is surrounded," he says, " by a strong wall which is
four leagues in circumference, of which the battlements
are carved with great care," and he gives to this place
the name of Anjog, which would seem to be sufficient to
identify it with Angkor even if he did not also furnish
recognisable descriptions of the Causeway of the Giants
and other remarkable features of the ruins. He states
too—a fact which deserves special attention—that even
in 1570 many of the inscriptions at Anjog were written
in a tongue which none of the natives understood or
could interpret.

In his History of the Islands of the Archipelago, published five years before de Jaque's work, Ribadeneyra
also notices these ruins. He says, " There are in Cambodia the ruins of an ancient city, which some say was
constructed by the Romans or by Alexander the Great.
It is a marvellous fact that none of the natives can live in
these ruins, which are the resort of wild beasts. These
Gentiles have a tradition that the ruins will some day be
restored by a foreign nation."

In 1672 there occurs another mention of Angkor in
the work of a French missionary named Père Chevruel.
" There is an ancient and very celebrated temple," he
says, " situated at a distance of eight days from the place
where I live. This temple is called Onco, and it is as
famous among the Gentiles as St. Peter's at Rome;" and
he adds that in his time pilgrimages were made to it from
Siam, Pegu, Laos and Tenasserim.

From these accounts of Angkor it will be seen that
when the place was first discovered by Europeans in 1570

it was as ruined, as deserted, as much given over to the forest and the beasts of the jungle, as completely a monument of a prehistoric past, as it is in our own day. If then we are to accept the work of the anonymous Chinese official as an authentic account of Angkor Thôm at the end of the thirteenth century, we must ask ourselves to believe that this mighty civilisation, whereof its magnificent architecture was the ripened fruit, not only declined and perished, but passed into oblivion all within a space of less than 280 years. Nay, more than this : for if the omission of any description of the temple of Angkor Wat from the account given in the Chinese manuscript is to be taken as evidence that that splendid edifice, which was of a kind little likely to escape attention, had not yet been built at the time of the ambassador's visit, we must believe that the Khmer civilisation reached its point of culmination at some period in the fourteenth century at the earliest, and nevertheless was thereafter obliterated so effectually that in less than 200 years it had left behind it hardly so much as a tradition.

Apart from the more obvious difficulties in the way of accepting any such supposition, the inscriptions found on many of the monuments of Angkor present an additional obstacle to the adoption of this conclusion. These inscriptions are of two kinds, the one written in a character similar to that now in use among the Kambodians, the other in a strange, and as it is thought, an older character which is unintelligible to even the most learned natives of the country. The former can be deciphered with little difficulty by the Buddhist monks, but unfortunately the inscriptions of this class are devoid of historical interest or importance, being chiefly religious formulæ, prayers, invocations, and the like. The remaining inscriptions have of late years been studied by a number of learned Frenchmen, but, so far as can be judged from the published results, they have not yet served to throw much new light upon the lost history of the Khmer empire. It is deserving of attention, however, that both kinds of inscription are found on the walls of Angkor Wat, although that temple is admittedly the most recent of all the buildings at Angkor. At the first glance this would seem to indicate that even the least ancient of the Khmer ruins was built in an age of great antiquity when a language, now forgotten, was in use. This conclusion, however, is open to question, for in the East from time immemorial the various priesthoods of Asia have always favoured the adoption of some ancient tongue as the special language of religion—usually some language which was not generally understood by the people. India alone gives three notable instances of this, while the Kâwi was the religious language of Hindu Java, just as Latin is the language of the Roman Catholic Church and Arabic that of the Muhammadan faith. It is at any rate possible, therefore, that the inscriptions written in the older character were never legible by the commonalty in Kambodia, their interpretation being the exclusive privilege of the priesthood, and if this were so, it would account for the presence of the unknown characters carved upon the stones of even the most recent of the ruins. The presence of both characters, however, is a puzzle, for it would seem to imply the existence of two distinct epochs—the first during which the ancient character was used, and the second when the more modern form of writing was in vogue—and this would relegate even Angkor Wat to a period of very remote antiquity. In these circumstances, the finding of a satisfactory explanation which might account for the failure of the author of the Chinese manuscript to mention the great temple, becomes even more difficult, and many have concluded that the town therein described must have been some other city of Kambodia and not Angkor Thôm at all.

Although M. De Lagrée himself was of this latter opinion, a careful examination of the account of the Chinese ambassador yields evidence which seems to me to be conclusive that Angkor Thôm and no other place was referred to by him. The details concerning the shape of the town, its size, and the number and position of its gates ; the minute description of the Causeway of the Giants leading to it, and of a temple without the walls corresponding to Bakhêng ; the legend which he relates of the nine-headed serpent, the " patron spirit," as it were, of the kings of Kambodia, whose effigy in stone is still in existence ;—these and many other things all apply perfectly to Angkor, and are inapplicable to any other known ruins in Indo-China. The reason why Angkor Wat escaped mention is, and must remain a mystery, but this omission is at the best only negative evidence of its non-existence at that period, and all the indications would seem to prove it clearly to have belonged to a much earlier age than the thirteenth century.

I am inclined, therefore, to conclude that the capital of Chin-Lá described by the Chinese diplomat is indeed no other than Angkor Thôm, but I conceive that the empire to which it belonged, though still flourishing, was even then in its *décadance*. The Chinese author does not speak of any great works having been in course of construction at the time of his visit, and the fact that even some of the older buildings show signs of never having been quite finished would seem to indicate that the artistic zeal and skill, which in the past had accomplished so much, had declined before ever Angkor Thôm was deserted by its inhabitants. Furthermore, at a very early period of our era, Kambodia, as we learn from the Chinese Annals, had become subservient to China, and this alone would suffice to show that the Khmer empire was even then a decaying power. Buildings of such a character as those of Angkor must have been the work of dynasties who ruled supreme over a populous kingdom, who could command an almost infinite amount of human labour, and who were so free from menace from without that they could devote all the energy of their subjects to the construction of gigantic public works instead of to fruitless war. No such edifices ever yet were conceived or executed by kings who occupied the position of mere vassals, or who had aught to fear from imminent invasion.

If then by the end of the thirteenth century Angkor was still great, still inhabited, but none the less was tottering to its fall, all we have to suppose is that events occurred which hastened the catastrophe and accelerated the process of decay, and here we seem to find a hint in the Chinese manuscript of what may have been the nature of the calamity which precipitated the abandonment of the royal city. The ambassador, as already stated, makes mention of lakes in the neighbourhood of Angkor which are no longer to be located in the directions indicated by him, while another lake appears to have come into being since his time. A change such as this wrought in the natural configuration of the surrounding country could only be the result of seismic convulsions, and such an explanation would also account for the battered condition of many of the buildings and the very general dilapidation of the roofs. It is noticeable, too, that no human remains are found in large numbers in the houses of Angkor Thôm, as would be the case in all probability if the town had been abandoned on account of plague or pestilence, and it would seem to be more likely that the evacuation was due to sudden panic. When we remember the innately superstitious character of these Oriental races, it is not difficult to conceive of the conviction that might have been bred in them by a succession of slight earthquake-shocks that it was the will of the gods that their ancient home should be deserted, and if once such a belief spread among the populace of an Asiatic city, nothing could save it from abandonment. The faith of the Oriental, which, not content with believing in the languid European fashion, has a wonderful power of realising as an actual fact the thing proposed for its belief, would in such an event prove strong enough to overcome all attachment to home, all love of things ancient and sacred, all personal and private interests, all respect for the value of property. The will of the gods, once plainly indicated, once grasped, would be obeyed no matter what the sacrifice demanded by obedience, and something of this kind, I conceive, must be held to account for the abandonment of the noble edifices of Angkor to the encroaching jungle and to the wild creatures of the forest.

Picture then a population driven suddenly forth into the wilderness, as were the Children of Israel, but unlike them with no Moses for their leader and lawgiver. As I have already indicated, it is probable that before the exodus occurred the numbers of the race had diminished, while its arts had languished or had been lost, as so many wonderful arts have been lost completely in Asiatic lands. The kings would have lacked the men, the means and the resources wherewith to create new cities to rival their deserted capital. Stonework, such as had been fashioned in ancient times by thousands of toiling men, would be altogether beyond their reach, and the limitless jungle spreading around them would yield timber and palm-leaves for roofing at the cost of little labour. It would naturally follow that the exiles would easily content themselves with the more modest accommodation at their immediate disposal, and that the sons of the men who had lived in royal Angkor would speedily resign themselves to the thatched huts of the modern Kambodians. The fact that they were already a rapidly decaying people would make the decline more fatally easy. They would have in them no power of rebound, and the blow which would have been dealt to their national importance and prosperity by the abandonment of their cities would be one from which they had not enough of energy to recover.

For the rest the legend of their former greatness would very soon pass into a mere myth. The Malay hero, Hang Tûah, who as chief of the fleets of Malacca fought against the Portuguese, both at the time of the taking of that city and for many years after it had passed into the keeping of the white men, is to-day, and has been for the past two hundred years, a figure as fabulous in the popular imagination as Hercules or Agamemnon. Around him has been woven a maze of marvellous story and miraculous tradition; it is, as Crawfurd has remarked, much as though our own Sir Walter Raleigh had become by the eighteenth century a solar-myth. Things such as this are constantly happening in the East, where the power of faith is stupendous, where the imagination is strong, where people have a natural leaning towards the marvellous, and where the unlettered populace know nothing of written history. To me it seems in no wise strange that in a matter of something over two centuries the Kambodians should believe that Angkor was fashioned from potters' clay by the god Prea En, or should give credit to any other fabulous legend concerning the origin of buildings which in their present degenerate state these people are unable even to conceive the possibility of designing or executing.

As regards the encroachment of the forest, that, I think, need occasion no surprise. I have myself seen a ploughed field in tropical Asia covered in the space of fifteen months with dense undergrowth twelve feet in height, through which a man could pass only with the greatest difficulty, with the aid of a stout wood-knife. If Angkor after its desertion was protected by the tradition, already quoted above from the work of Ribadeneyra, that the natives could not live in it, two centuries would be ample time for the forest to take back its own, and this tradition would seem to support the explanation of the abandonment of the city which I have here ventured to put forward.

The origin of the Khmers is wrapped in obscurity, but the features of the men represented in the ancient monuments, as may be seen from the statue of the Leprous King, here reproduced from the work of M. Mouhot, are distinctively Hindu. The type is found to this day prevalent among Kambodians of pure descent, and it presents a very marked contrast to the broad-faced, flat-featured Mongolian races of China and Siam. Kambodia in our time, however, is not peopled by a single nation, but rather by a very heterogeneous population. The mountains are inhabited for the most part by aboriginal tribes of a very low standard of civilisation, who from time immemorial have been pillaged and enslaved by their more advanced neighbours. The trading and energetic portion of the community is composed almost exclusively of Chinese—mostly natives of Fok-Kien, for Kambodia still communicates with China by sea, and very rarely by the overland route. Here and there there are colonies of Malays scattered about the country, who came there no one precisely knows how, and the Kambodians themselves have in most cases intermarried with strangers and so have lost their ancient purity of blood. In Batambang and Siamreap the Siamese have also established a few colonies.

Of the heyday of the Khmer empire we have no record whatsoever, but we may safely conclude that it dates from a period prior to the reduction of Kambodia by China. This is said to have taken place under the Chinese Emperor Yao, who was also the first of his race to cause the Yang-tze valley to be colonised by Chinese. The practical dominion of China in Kambodia ended with the Thang Dynasty, which perished during the latter half of the tenth century of our era. One building at Angkor is believed to have been constructed in the second century, an inscription which has been deciphered seeming to warrant this conclusion, and it is possible that some of the edifices may be even older than this. A legend is still extant of a king of Kambodia who not only built Angkor, but who also subjugated many of the islands of the Archipelago and monopolised for a space the trade between China and the West. To him also are attributed the great roads, traces of which are still to be found in parts of the country. No reliance is to be placed upon such traditions as these, but Angkor itself and the numerous other ruins are triumphant evidence of what the might of the Khmer empire must once have been. That it derived its inspiration direct from India cannot be doubted—the character of the carving, the features of the statues, the practice by the Khmers of the cult of Buddha, all indi-

cate this, while the appearance of the Kambodians of our
own time seems to confirm the belief that the ancestors
of these people came originally from the peninsula of
Hindustan. We know that Hindu influence extended in
very early times as far south as Lômbok and Bâli, and it
is highly probable that Kambodia may also have been
peopled from India by sea. The enormous encroachments of the land upon the ocean, caused by the immense
amount of the deposits washed down by the Mekong,
have added largely to the flat coast-lands of the country
during historical, as opposed to geological times, and a
thousand years ago Angkor was certainly much less distant from the sea than it is to-day. None the less, since
other seaward States in its vicinity escaped the Indian invasion, it is at least possible that the Khmers may have
made their way into Indo-China overland, as is contended
by some French writers, though the opinion is one which
it is not easy to accept.

To sum up, all that we can really ascertain at the present time concerning the Khmer civilisation is that it
flourished and came to full fruition before its subjugation
to China ; that the Chinese dominion ended before the
conclusion of the tenth century of our era, though it had
a nominal and more or less formal existence for more
than three centuries later ; that Angkor and the other
towns of Kambodia were occupied by the natives of the
country well into the fourteenth century, although by that
time the civilisation of the Khmers had decayed, their arts
would appear to have declined, and the numbers of their
subjects to have dwindled. It further seems probable that

some time in the fourteenth century the ancient buildings were deserted owing, it may be surmised, to a superstitious belief that it was no longer the will of the gods that they should be occupied—a superstition which exists to the present day, and which may have originated in, or have impressed itself upon, the public mind by reason of one or more earthquake-shocks. We have, it must be confessed, only a slender base upon which to build our theories, but the evidence of the Chinese ambassador, so often quoted in these pages, is something tangible and concrete which cannot easily be thrust aside. For the rest, I trust that I have succeeded in showing that the desertion of Angkor at a period subsequent to his visit is at any rate a possibility, and that the condition of the ruins at the present time, and the maze of myth and legend in which the imagination of the native population has entangled them, need excite little surprise when we remember the Titanic nature of the buildings on the one side, and the appeal which they would inevitably make to a marvel-loving, superstitious, and unlettered people. When all has been said, however, the problem of the Khmer civilisation remains unsolved, for of the story of the great empire which existed before ever China effected conquests in Kambodia we know nothing. Judged by the gigantic remains which they have bequeathed to us,—the expression at once of a tremendous energy and of a passionate love of art—the Khmers must have been a wonderful people, and such a people cannot have failed to have a marvellous and inspiring history. What that story was we know not, and perhaps shall never know; but we must

all subscribe to Francis Garnier's tribute to the men of
this vanished race.

"*Jamais nulle part peut-être une masse plus imposante
de pierres n'a été disposée avec plus d'art et de science.
Si l'on admire les pyrammides comme une œuvre gigan-
tesque de la force et de la patience humaines, à une force
et une patience égales il faut ajouter ici le génie!*"

CHAPTER VIII

IT was only on July 7, 1866, that the de Lagrée-Garnier
expedition at last began its ascent of the Mekong
River from Pnom Penh. A short visit was paid to
the pagoda of Pnom-Brashe, an ancient Khmer ruin situated opposite to the Sutin islands. This is a magnificent
temple, in general appearance not unlike a Gothic
cathedral, and according to an inscription found in it, a
translation of which was furnished to the explorers by a
Buddhist monk, it dates from the second century of our
era. De Lagrée, who found it impossible to get over the
difficulty presented by the omission from the manuscript
of the Chinese ambassador of all mention of Angkor Wat,
thought that the town described in that work was to be
looked for in the neighbourhood of Pnom-Brashe, but
there is little to be advanced in favour of this view, since
the account of the capital of Kambodia as it was in the
thirteenth century corresponds in almost every detail with
Angkor Thôm, and is not applicable in an equal degree
to any other of the great Khmer remains.

On July 9th, Kratieh, on the left bank just below the
Sombor rapids, was reached, and here the two shallow-
draft gunboats, in which the expedition had so far been
conveyed, were abandoned. Up to this time, no steamers

had ascended to a point so far from the coast, and the
difficulties in the way of navigation which had been encountered since leaving Pnom Penh had been great.
The gear and supplies of the explorers were therefore
transferred to native boats—long crafts fashioned from
tree-trunks, warped open by fire, their carrying capacity
being increased by plank sides built up from the solid
keels. Each boat was furnished with a bamboo deck,
supporting a low, thatched cabin amidships, and was
propelled by a number of punters armed with long, iron-
shod poles.

Heavy rains had already begun to fall in the interior,
and the river was some sixteen feet above its normal
level. On July 16th the first formidable rapids of the
Sombor flight were reached, and thus early in his journey
Garnier was forced to resign one of his most cherished
dreams. On each bank of the great river rose marvellous tangles of untouched forest—giant trees with but-
tress-roots, treading on one another's toes, standing knee-
deep in striving underwood, their branches interlocked,
and bound each to each by vine and creeper, shaggy with
ferns and mosses, draped with hanging parasitic growths,
and set here and there with the delicate stars of orchids.
Between these sheer cliffs of vegetation the great river
rolled, sullen and persistent, its brown waters sweeping
downward with irresistible force their freight of wallowing
tree-trunks, rushing with a fierce hissing sound through
the brushwood on either bank, foaming and fighting
around the islands which here bespatter the surface of
the stream, and squabbling noisily with the rough-hewn

sandstone outcrops which form at this point a broken bar at right-angles to the current. Looking at this wild scene, Francis Garnier, the lover of beauty and of savage nature, felt that his eye was filled with seeing,—filled with visions of sheer delight; but Francis Garnier the practical statesman, the utilitarian, the naval officer, took small comfort from the conclusions which were now forced upon his recognition. No highway of trade was to be beaten out of this whirling wilderness of troubled waters. Within ten days from his departure from Pnom Penh the hopes which he had cherished of discovering in the Mekong a practicable route, by means of which the trade of Yun-nan might be diverted to Indo-China, had been brought to nought.

Reluctantly and not without a struggle did he admit this truth. The river ran in flood three and a quarter miles in width, and he could not but hope against hope that in all that great expanse some possible channel for a steamboat might be found. Taking a small canoe with two or three native boatmen, he put out into the stream towards the right bank, but before he was well within sight of the great rapid of Preatapang his crew struck work. They refused flatly to carry him beyond an island in mid-stream, whence he could see nothing to his purpose. He coaxed, cajoled, bribed, entreated and finally had resort to threats, but all in vain. He had come into collision with the stolid, unshakable resolution of the Oriental whose mind is made up, and storming with rage he was obliged to return a defeated man to his jeering companions.

Still hugging the left bank of the river, and travelling for the most part through the submerged forest, where alone the punters could find bottom with their poles, the party crept painfully up-stream, reaching the mouth of the Se-Kong on the 21st, and the town of Stung-Treng, in Siamese territory, on the same day.

From Stung-Treng, Garnier, who felt that he still bore a grudge to the rapids of Sombor, set off down river to explore the right bank of the Mekong. After many risks in the rapids and difficulties with his boatmen, Sombor was reached, and finding there a boat containing belated supplies for the expedition, Garnier got on board her, and after five laborious days spent in punting up-stream, rejoined his comrades at Stung-Treng.

Meanwhile de Lagrée had utilised his leisure in exploring the Se-Kong, which falls into the Mekong on its left bank a little below Stung-Treng. The neighbourhood of the latter place had also been examined, and some curious stone towers, yet other relics of the Khmer civilisation, had been discovered. Concerning these Gerard van Wusthof, the leader of the Dutch expedition to Vien Chan in the seventeenth century, of which more will be said in a later chapter, has the following passage :

"On August 17th, we passed the night at Bætzong (Stung-Treng) near a stone church, ruined through age, where the Louwen (Laos folk) perform ceremonies and sacrifices. Candles were burning in this church on the altars of two idols. About fifty years ago the Kings of Kambodia resided in this place, but forced to retreat before the incessant attacks of the Louwen, they left this church to itself in the solitude of a grove, and descended to the spot where they now reside."

Similarly in van Wusthof's time Kambodians occupied villages in the upper reaches of the Se-Kong, whereas long since the descendants of the once dominant race have retreated to the country lying below the Sombor Falls. Stung-Treng itself, an insignificant place of less than 1,000 inhabitants, is peopled by Laotines, though here as elsewhere in Indo-China, what little trade there is remains almost entirely in the hands of the ubiquitous Chinese.

"*Sans l' intervention de l' élément chinois,*" writes Garnier, "*ces contrées éloignées mourraient bientôt à toute relation extérieure,*" and indeed the same may be said with truth of every portion of Indo-China and Malaya. The Chinaman possesses in a remarkable degree those very qualities of diligence, energy, business capacity, perseverance and thrift which the men of these regions most singularly lack, and any plan which has for its object the placing of the prosperity of the peninsula on a sound economical basis, and the endowing of them with the blessings of material prosperity, must include a scheme for the free immigration of the Chinese, under which they shall be granted full rights of citizenship.

The valley of the Se-Kong is encompassed by mountains, and the country between it and the main range bordering Cochin-China is inhabited by wild tribes. For the rest the population is Laotine, and the standard of civilisation does not compare favourably with that of the Kambodians, all trade, for instance, being still conducted on a system of barter.

De Lagrée explored the Se-Kong on this occasion as far as Sien-Pang, and he later completed the work using Bassak as his *pied-à-terre*. To the latter place he now decided to push on, his object being to establish a base from which to conduct further explorations, and in which he might fix his headquarters during the coming rainy season. His design was somewhat delayed by the severe illness—a malignant form of fever—by which both Garnier and Thorel were prostrated, but though the former was still delirious a start was presently made from Stung-Treng, and by the time the rapids of Khon were reached on August 17th, the second-in-command was sufficiently recovered to be able to take his usual eager interest in all that was going on around him.

Above Stung-Treng the river is so bespattered with islands that it was rarely possible to catch a glimpse of both banks at the same time, but just below the Khon Falls the stream opens out into a great basin, some three and a-half miles across. The northern end of this is occupied by a compact group of islands, divided each from each by narrow channels through which the river tears its way, its waters being precipitated into the basin below. In many of these channels all obstacles have been worn away, and here the waters glide downward in long, unbroken waves, the force of which is terrific. In the channels of Salaphe and Papheng, the two principal falls, however, the stream runs in absolute cascades, the body of water being more than 1,000 yards across, and plunging vertically from a height of fifty feet. From bank to bank the broken line of rapids, rushing through the group

of islets, measures between seven and eight miles in width,
while immediately above, the river is twelve miles across,
though a little further up it narrows down again to its
original breadth of about three and a-half miles.

"Everything in this gigantic country," wrote Garnier,
"breathes an unheard of force and clothes itself in overwhelming proportions." The land is thickly populated
and highly cultivated. The principal villages are Sit
andong and Khong, and with the Governor of the latter place the expedition speedily established very friendly
relations. For the rest the scanty trade consisted in the
exportation of jungle produce obtained from the hill-
tribes and brought to the river by means of a track leading inland from its left bank.

The province of Tuli-Repu, on the right bank of the
Mekong, was formerly a part of Kambodia, but the chief
in charge of it having rebelled and obtained the support
of Siam, it passed, without any formalities of cession, under the dominion of Bangkok, as have so many other
fragments of the ancient Khmer empire. After that
event it became almost a desert, the mountainous parts
being infested by lawless bands who lived chiefly by pillage, and Garnier saw in its annexation by France its only
chance of salvation. This is an opinion which has since
found much favour with French colonial statesmen, but
even under the administration of France this part of the
Mekong valley seems hardly likely to produce a trade of
any remarkable proportions.

Using Khong as his base, de Lagrée ascended and explored the Repu or Se-Lompu River, and on the banks

of the Mekong, to the south of the island, he discovered
a few vestiges of ancient Khmer buildings.   On September 6th Khong was left and a start made for Bassak.   The
river, for the first time since Sombor, was found to flow
in a single channel, its width being between 1,400 and
1,800 yards from bank to bank.   For the first time, too,
high mountains became visible to the north, and at the
end of the fifth day the explorers found themselves beginning to describe a great curve, formed by the Mekong
as it skirts the foot of a high range of hills.   On September 11th Bassak was reached, the whole of the country
traversed from Khong to that place being densely populated.

Bassak is situated on the right bank of the Mekong,
which here measures over a mile and a quarter in width;
it lies opposite to the big island of Don-Deng, and mountains rise up at the rear of the town.   A little to the north
there is a plain on the right bank, and beyond this a chain
of mountains, skirted by the river, runs to the peak called
Phu Molong.   To the west is a peak called Phu Bassak,
and east-northeast are seen the distant volcanic mountains, the most southerly of which was subsequently
named Mount de Lagrée by Francis Garnier when death
had claimed his chief.   The expedition had cause for
congratulation in the selection of Bassak as its headquarters, for the climate was found to be delightful; the
thermometer registered between 57° and 60° F. in the
early mornings of January, the place being, in fact, far
cooler than any district of Kambodia, and even than
many spots higher up the river.

Ravine near the Mekong

From Garnier's "Voyage en Indo-Chine"

The explorers were now well into the Laos country, and they were much struck by the intelligence and gentleness of the natives. Garnier fancied that he discerned in them some traces of that vitality and mental energy which are the germs of progress, and for a period he cheated himself into the belief that they might have a future before them such as is surely denied to the spent peoples of Kambodia. The people of Laos he says, *" peuvent renaître à l'activité et à la richesse, au milieu des contrées admirables qu'ils habitent, sous l'influence civilisatrice de la France,"* an opinion which may or may not be true, but which has certainly not yet been justified in the smallest degree. It is to be feared that Garnier, deluded by his love of Indo-China and by his very natural enthusiasm for the future of countries with which he had become so closely identified, allowed himself to be blinded to some obvious facts. Compared to the Kambodians the Laotines were doubtless less utterly past hope, but the people of southeastern Asia who are most vital, most alive to-day are, without question, the Siamese, whose energy has been sufficient to achieve the reduction of so many of their neighbours; yet no one who has studied modern Siam with any care, and has not had his vision confused by personal predilections and prejudices, can cherish many illusions concerning the future that awaits its people. As for the Laotines, such achievement as was possible to their limitations belongs to the days of Vien Chan's prosperity; compared with that of Siam or Burma, leaving entirely on one side the great empire of the Khmers, it is a paltry thing, and as regards their future,

the very tolerance of alien creeds, which Garnier found so
worthy of praise, sets a seal upon their fate.   This is a
virtue which, in the East, never yet sprang from intellectual energy.   It is in the Oriental a sure sign of the
apathy of decay.   Among the Kambodians, who have a
proud past behind them, fanaticism is the last vestige of
their ancient self-esteem : it is an expression of their
hatred, their resentment of the foreign aggression which
they fear, but are powerless to resist.

From September 11th to Christmas Day Bassak continued to be the headquarters of the expedition.   The camp
was formed in deluges of rain, and for many days the downpour continued unabated, but when fine weather returned a number of interesting explorations were made
from this new base.   Garnier, Delaporte and Thorel began by visiting the plateau situated to the north of
Bassak, but did not succeed in reaching the summit.
Next Garnier was sent by de Lagrée to explore the
lower reaches of the Se-Dom, a river which falls into the
Mekong on its left bank some miles above Bassak.   Up
this stream he proceeded to a point where it bifurcates,
and thence up the western branch to the great falls which
are some fifty feet in height.   Thence he returned down-
stream, and set off with elephants in search of some
silver mines, the existence of which had been rumoured by
Mouhot.   At the end of a laborious day's journey he
found himself in the village of one of the wild tribes, and
was informed by his guides that there were no mines to
be seen, and that they had thought from the first that he
desired to visit the habitations of the " savages."   Neither

he nor his interpreters had any great knowledge of the
Laotine dialect; "varied gestures and ingenious drawings," he tells us, "were called to the aid of our ignorance of words, and it was rarely that by this process we
did not obtain, at the end of half an hour of effort,
seven or eight entirely contradictory answers." In these
circumstances there was room and to spare for misunderstandings, but Garnier believed, and perhaps justly, that
the locality of silver mines was being purposely concealed from him. He was unable to prove the truth of
his suspicions, however, and eventually had to return to
Bassak without having obtained any information concerning the object of his search.

He reached headquarters on October 9th, and found
that the Mekong had fallen more than sixteen feet during
his week of absence. The end of the rainy season had
come; on every hand preparations were being made
for planting the land which had been enriched by the
overflow of the river, and during the last days of the
month, the travellers witnessed the great feast of Hena
Song, which is a kind of public thanksgiving annually
made for the harvest that is to be. Immediately after the
feast Garnier set off down the Mekong, his object being to
get word of the mail-bags of the expedition which were
long overdue. Leaving Bassak on November 4th, Garnier reached Stung-Treng four days later, and there
learned the disquieting news that the insurrection which
had broken out in Kambodia under Pu Kombo had
assumed serious proportions, and that the valley of the
Mekong to the south of Stung-Treng was in the hands of

the rebels. Garnier therefore sent his interpreter, Alexis,
down river with letters for the French authorities,
and himself returned up-stream on November 12th,
reaching Bassak on November 23d, after spending much
time in the detailed exploration and survey of the
Mekong and its banks.

Meanwhile de Lagrée had led an expedition up the Se-
Dom, hauling his boats up the rapids already discovered
by Garnier, and ascending the river until the village of
Smia, on the right bank, was reached. From this point
his party trudged up the left bank of the Se-Dom to the
falls of Keng Noi, and then struck across open grassy
plains, broken by occasional rice-fields and patches of
forest, to Saravan, where the Se-Dom was once more met
with. From this village they continued the ascent of the
stream, walking up its banks and crossing and recrossing
it at frequent intervals, for four days, when they finally
quitted it and struck across the dividing ridges in the direction of the head waters of the Se-Kong.

The Se-Kong, when first encountered, was already
more than 100 yards in width, but the travellers had to
tramp down its banks for two days before the first inhabited villages were met with. At Ban Kumkang boats
were obtained, and in these the foot-weary men were carried to Attopeu, the village which is the chief trade-centre
of the valley and is situated in the heart of a district inhabited thickly by wild tribes. Ethnologically these tribesmen are distinct from the Laotines, their noses being straight
and fine, their foreheads more developed. These tribesmen
are known in Laos by the generic name of Khas, are

The Mekong at Hsin Tu Ku

called Moi in Annam, and Pen-nong in Kambodia, and
though it is probable that they belong to different
branches of a single race, they are known among themselves by more than a dozen distinctive names. They
furnish one of the many riddles propounded by southeastern Asia to the ethnologist. The Negrito, who is
represented by the Sĕmang and Pangan tribes of the
Malay Peninsula, is not found in Indo-China, but on the
other hand the hillmen of a brown race, corresponding
to the Sâkai of Malaya, count many thousands of individuals in Kambodia, Annam, Laos and the Shan States.

In their character these unhappy folk to the south of
Luang Prabang, who from time immemorial have been
the prey of their more civilised and therefore stronger
neighbours, appear to be peaceable, gentle and timorous.
Some of the more remote tribes, who dwell in the fast-
nesses of the mountains and hold communication only spar-
ingly with even the tamer aborigines, are reputed to be
ferocious, but the same legend is current wherever such
tribes exist, and its origin may perhaps be traced to a desire on the part of the slave-traders to enhance the value
of their wares. That the aborigines look upon all other
human beings as their enemies is likely enough, since
time out of mind their children have been abducted and
sold into slavery. That they will fight on occasion to prevent this is also possible, but none of these down-trodden
races have any love of fighting for its own sake, and they
always prefer flight to battle, after the manner of all other
denizens of the jungle. Garnier, in writing of some of these
poor creatures, mentions the horror with which he noted

the miserable eyes of their women following him when he chanced to look admiringly at some of the children. The fear was upon them lest he should seize the little ones, in which case the bereaved parents would have had no choice but to submit, and the women's eyes were eloquent of pitiful memories of the lot to which the wild tribes-folk are born.

Leaving Attopeu, de Lagrée descended the course of the Se-Kong as far as Tapak, whence he journeyed overland to Bassak. Attopeu itself had been visited by van Wusthof in the seventeenth century, but the whole of the Se-Dom and the head waters of the Se-Kong were now explored by Europeans for the first time, as also was the country between Tapak and Bassak. Careful surveys had been made and the course of two large rivers, together with much of the country lying between them, had been added to the map, an important piece of work to have been accomplished in the space of two and thirty days.

The officers left behind at Bassak, and Garnier himself after he had rejoined them, had been busy exploring the ruins of Wat Phu, a pagoda perched upon a hill, which presents most perfect and finished examples of Khmer art. It is noteworthy that parts of this building are incomplete, and that some of the more recent carving is of inferior workmanship and obviously belongs to a period after the decline of the Khmer people had begun.

During their stay at Bassak, the explorers had taken careful note of the rise and fall of the river. Its flow on December 5th, when its waters had subsided to their ordinary level, was estimated by Garnier at 9,000 cubic metres per second, whereas in flood time, on September 20th, the volume was increased to 50,000 cubic metres per second, although both the Se-Kong and the Tonli-Repu fall into the Mekong below this point. The estimate for the river at Pnom Penh, in seasons when the river is full, is between 60,000 and 70,000 cubic metres, while Garnier's estimate for the Mekong at Bassak at dead low water was only from 2,000 to 3,000. On the other hand the Irawadi, at the head of the delta, is estimated at 2,130 cubic metres per second, while the waters of the Ganges at a similar point, and at high water, is estimated at no less than 167,000 cubic metres. With this the Mekong can, of course, make no comparison, yet the rise of the river from low to flood level between Kratieh and Pnom Penh is at least forty feet in the course of the year, a fact which accounts for the constant changes wrought in its bed, and for the immense inundations which serve to enrich and fertilise so large an area of its valley.

As regards the navigability of the river, Garnier arrived at the conclusion that it was feasible for shallow-draught steamers as far as the Sombor rapids, which are at a distance of nearly 400 miles from its mouth; that above this point big poling-boats could be used for its ascent, and large bamboo rafts for its descent; and that below Bassak the Khon rapids presented the only really serious obstacle to navigation. Here, however, even if a safe channel could be found, the force of the current was such that no steamer could possibly, he thought, make headway against it.

While the expedition was still at Bassak, Alexis, the native interpreter, returned, having failed to get through to Pnom Penh, and after much discussion it was determined to send him overland to the capital of Kambodia, *via* Angkor, while the explorers pushed on to Ubon, on the banks of the Se-Mun, a right-bank tributary of the Mekong. Accordingly, on December 25th, the camp at Bassak was broken up, the explorers taking leave of the King and the natives, who had shown them much courtesy and kindness, and proceeding on their journey upstream. The expedition passed through the defile by means of which the Mekong flows round the foot of Phu Molong on December 26th, skirted the big isolated mountain of Phu Fadang, where the stream, imprisoned between smooth, rocky walls, measures barely 200 yards across, and entered the Se-Mun on January 3rd. On the same day the village of Pi-Mun, was reached, and here the gear of the expedition had to be transshipped into boats sent for the purpose from Ubon. Above this point the Se-Mun runs down a succession of long, straight reaches which have the air of having been hewn out by the labour of man, and on each side a great grassy plain spreads away to the horizon.

Ubon was reached on January 7th, " *l'agglomération la plus vivante que nous eussions encore rencontrée,*" as Garnier described it, a very large village on the left bank of the Se-Mun, the centre of the trade of this part of the Mekong valley. From this point all commerce is conducted, not by river with Kambodia and Saigon, but overland with Korat and Bangkok. For all practical

purposes, Bassak may be described as the most distant
trade-centre in the Mekong valley which traffics with the
districts of the delta. It is, and always has been, the
dream of the French colonial authorities to divert the
trade of the *Hinterland* in such a manner that it may be
made to flow through the possessions of France, and
Saigon having come, through fortuitous circumstances
rather than by design, to occupy the position of capital
of Indo-China, it has been thought that commerce should
be forced to pass through that town. The oppressive
custom-dues formerly exacted by Kambodia and the
conquest of Laos by Siam may both have contributed to
the selection of the overland in preference to the river-
route, but apart from political considerations, the question
is in the main one of convenience and cheapness. The
bulk and value of the trade involved are not great, and it
has been found that goods can be conveyed to Korat and
Bangkok with less trouble than to the coast of the China
Sea. The long and tedious return-journey against the
current is a labour that cannot be lightly faced, and it may
be predicted with some degree of certainty that Saigon
will never be the recipient of the bulk of the trade exported from the interior.

At the present time Bangkok and Korat are already
joined by a railroad, and the French are negotiating for
the extension of this work eastward from Korat, whence it
would pass almost due east to Hue, crossing the Mekong
at Kamarat, and eventually finding the sea at Turon.
The country between Kamarat and Hue is mountainous,
and the construction of this section would be excessively

costly.   Were the engineering difficulties to be overcome, however, it is possible that Turon might become the outlet for the bulk of the trade of the upper valley of the Mekong : on the other hand it is equally possible that Bangkok would maintain its old commercial supremacy, in which case the enormous expenditure upon the construction of the line would be a sacrifice made in vain. In any case the trade of this region would have to undergo an immense expansion before the proposed railway could conceivably become a paying concern.   Curiously enough, however, fear of injuring Saigon, rather than any sounder reason, is mainly responsible for the opposition offered by Frenchmen to the scheme; this is to be regretted, because the present capital can never hope to claim the bulk of the inland trade.   Until French administrators can learn to regard their colonial possessions in Indo-China as a whole, and to seek their good as such, without paying too close an attention to purely local interests, the prospects of that empire are none too hopeful.

From Ubon Garnier started on January 10th on a flying visit to Pnom Penh, for the purpose of bringing back the missing mails.   He ascended the Se-Mun for three days, passing through open, grassy plains from which the forest had long before been cleared by burning; then, leaving his boats at Sam-Lan, he proceeded overland to Si-Saket, where for the first time for many months he again encountered Kambodians.   Having procured four rough carts drawn by trotting-bullocks, he crossed some twenty miles of grass country and entered the forest, which

was not too dense to admit of the use of vehicles.
At Kukan, thirty-eight miles to the south of Si-Saket,
he found himself once more in Kambodian country, the
natives being all Khmers who spoke none save their own
language, in spite of the fact that the province had been
annexed by Siam at a period anterior to the conquest of
Batambang and Siamreap.

Still using his carts, and crossing the rivers by means
of good wooden bridges constructed by the Kambodians,
Garnier drove west-southwest to Sankea, a distance of
some twenty-five miles, where the track bifurcates, one
branch leading west to Korat, the other south to Angkor. Taking the former by the advice of the local
authorities, who seem to have misled him through sheer
inability to understand that any one could possibly be in a
hurry, he went out of his way as far as Suren, whence he
again turned towards the south, reaching Su-Krom on
January 22nd. Here he was assured that the road ahead
of him was impassable for vehicles, but declining to be
moved by these representations, he pushed on resolutely.
Despite the desertion in mid-forest of all his guides and
native drivers, he presently found himself, with the little
knot of French sailors and non-commissioned officers
whom he was taking back to Kambodia, on the lip of a
precipitous cliff some 600 feet in height; he had reached
the abrupt ending of the plateau across which he had been
travelling ever since his departure from Ubon. A path
down the face of the cliff was discovered, but it was of a
nature which necessitated the bullocks being unyoked and
the carts being taken to pieces before it could be nego-

tiated. Garnier set doggedly to work to perform this heavy task. A merciless sun beat down upon the toiling white men ; the bullocks, intensely offended by the scent of Europeans, gave an infinity of trouble ; the heat became unendurable, and presently the little party was racked with thirst. One by one the men gave in, and threw themselves gasping upon the ground, but Garnier wandered far and wide over the dry river-courses in search of water, and at last found a deep, tepid pool. The good news was carried to his comrades, and soon they were sufficiently revived to resume their labours. By 10 P. M. the work was at last accomplished ; the carts and bullocks, together with all the gear, had been conveyed to the plain below ; camp-fires had been lighted and a well-earned rest was enjoyed. It was precisely at this moment that the Governor of Su-Krom arrived with a large rescue-party. He was mightily astonished to find that the difficult descent had been effected without his aid, and Garnier was careful to treat the matter lightly in order that the chief might be the more impressed by the energy and resource of the French explorers.

After quitting the Ubon plateau, Garnier traversed a waste of sandy plain, and on January 25th reached Konkan, where he discovered the dried-up bed of an ancient lake,—yet another trace of the seismic convulsions which may, perhaps, have caused the abandonment of the Khmer towns. Near Suren he had already noted the existence of ruins, and now close to Konkan he discovered a magnificent stone bridge standing thirty metres above the level of the stream, three great fragments of which still

span the Stung-Treng river. The central span is 148
metres long and fifteen metres broad; the parapets are supported by carved monkeys and by dragons with nine
heads, similar to those found at Angkor; the arches are
thirty-four in number, and the whole is fashioned from
sandstone.

Beyond this point more ruins were found, and the villages became numerous. The Kambodians of the district, although they were under the rule of Siam, struck
Garnier as being more faithful to the ancient usages of
their race, and more wedded to its traditions, than are
their countrymen to the south. Given the time, he
thought that here, perhaps, might be learned something
concerning the lost story of the great Khmer empire; but
Garnier could not allow himself the leisure even to turn
aside to examine some of the ruins of whose existence
the natives told him, and was obliged to push on to
Siamreap, where he arrived on January 29th.

He here received reliable news concerning Pu Kombo's
rebellion. At one time King Norodon had been besieged
in Pnom Penh, but he had been rescued from this precarious position by French troops. None the less most of
the shores of the Great Lake and of its southern arm
were still in the hands of the insurgents. Garnier thus
found himself separated from his countrymen to the south
by a narrow zone of country held by the enemy. Turning a deaf ear to the protests of the Siamese Governor of
Siamreap, he procured a boat and a crew of Annamites,
and slipping past the rebel post at Kompong Pluk just
before the dawn on February 5th, found a French gun-

boat at Kompong Luong, and the same evening reached Pnom Penh after a dangerous and toilsome journey extending over twenty seven days.

Pnom Penh was occupied by French troops, and the precious mails were found at last. Most of the private letters, and all the scientific instruments destined for the explorers, had been wantonly left behind at Saigon ; but the Chinese passports were forthcoming, and Garnier contrived to procure the loan of a barometer. Judging rightly that safety lay in speed, and in starting upon his return journey before word of his project could reach the rebels, he allowed himself only two days' sojourn at Pnom Penh, and left that post again on February 8th. Once more he successfully ran the gauntlet of the rebel war-parties, and on the sixth day reached Siamreap. From this point he struck out for Ubon, taking as direct a line as possible. Leaving Angkor Wat, he crossed a desert plain, passed over the Pnom Kulen range,—upon one of the highest peaks of which he discovered some new Khmer ruins,—and so entered the Pre Saa, or " Magnificent Forest," through which he had great difficulty in taking his bullock-carts. After traversing thirty miles of uninhabited country, he abandoned his carts at the first village, and thereafter was handed on from place to place by relays of porters. In some villages the men were busy with the harvest, and only girls were procurable for the transport of his baggage. Woman, as a beast of burden, he discovered, left much to be desired, for the damsels treated him and his business as an immense joke. When he entreated them to hasten and not to tarry by the way, they giggled delightedly, but took no sort of notice of his prayers. At each stream they cast aside their scanty garments and bathed themselves elaborately, while he, in outraged modesty, stood protesting on the banks. It was with a sigh of intense relief that he at last saw their burdens transferred to the shoulders of sober-minded respectable men, who were innocent alike of their follies and their feminine caprices.

Travelling in this fashion from hamlet to hamlet, Garnier crossed the Stung-Treng close to its source, and scaled the cliff, in which the Ubon plateau has its abrupt ending, at a point somewhat to the east of that at which he had descended it with so much labour. He discovered, however, that his guides had not taken him sufficiently far in the desired direction, and that he was even now only two days' march from Kukan. For this place he accordingly made, and thence followed his original route to Ubon where he arrived on February 26. The rest of the expedition had left for Kamarat more than a month earlier, so Garnier hastened to overtake them, descending the Se-Mun to its mouth and poling up the Mekong until, on March 10th, thirty days after his departure from Pnom Penh, he saw the French flag flying over a hut at Hutien, and knew that his solitary journey was ended.

Since parting with de Lagrée at Ubon he had traversed over a thousand miles of country, the greater part of which had never previously been visited by a European; he had filled in a blank which had long disfigured this part of the map; he had fixed the position of numerous landmarks, had discovered several Khmer ruins of im-

portance, and had twice run the gauntlet of the Kambodian rebels.   Above all, he had brought back with him
the Chinese passports which were to open the doors of
Yun-nan to the expedition.   It was a goodly list of
achievements, all of which had been effected in the space
of two months, and de Lagrée had indeed ample reason
to congratulate himself upon the possession of such a
lieutenant.

CHAPTER IX

DURING the two months spent by Francis Garnier in making the flying visit to Pnom Penh described in the preceding chapter, the rest of the expedition had continued its explorations around Ubon and to the north. The province of Ubon at this time supported a population estimated at 80,000 souls, and the chief object of interest was the salt-pans which supply the natives of the district with a large part of their livelihood. A patch of country some forty miles in length, on the plateau of Ubon, appears to cover great reservoirs of brine, and each dry season the salt is precipitated on the surface in the form of a white, powdery dust. This is collected by the natives, cleansed in water, and is once more precipitated in a purified condition in large caldrons, which are exposed to the rays of the sun. A single worker wins about fifteen pounds *per diem*, and the industry is in full swing for a period of three months. As soon as the dry season shows signs of breaking, the ground from the surface of which the salt has been gathered is sown with rice; good crops are obtained, and the soil thus yields, as it were, two harvests annually to its owners.

On January 15th, Delaporte left Ubon and descended the Se-Mun, for the purpose of surveying the Mekong

from the mouth of the former river to Kamarat. The
rainy season had not yet begun, and the exposed bed of
the Mekong was seen to be a mass of enormous rocks and
boulders which lay about in wonderful confusion, piled
one upon another like a heap of gigantic pebbles, amid
which the river made its way in numberless shrunken
streams. In places its channel was barely 200 feet
across; in no part did its width exceed 1,000 yards.
At its narrowest and deepest, soundings could not find
bottom at 300 feet. Each narrowing of the fairway produced rapids, the ascent of which was difficult and even
dangerous, while here and there the current ran grandly
between sheer cliffs of water-worn rock. The river, in
fact, was now running through a mountainous zone,
which it enters a little below Chieng Kang, and its course
from that point to the mouth of the Se-Mun is beset with
difficulties. None the less, it is freely used for the big
rafts upon which the Laos people transport their goods
down-stream, and it is also navigable for native craft of
light calibre.

De Lagrée, meanwhile, and the rest of the party, had
left Ubon on January 20th, with fifteen bullock-carts and
fifty Laotine porters, bound upon an overland march to
Kamarat. Four days' tramp over a flat and often sandy
plain, covered with rice-fields and clearings, and traversed
by an unmade cart-track, brought him to Muong Amnat,
thirty-five miles due north of Ubon. Here the cultivation
of silk-worms and of the *coccus lacca* were found to be
the principal industries of the natives, and here too de
Lagrée paid off his carriers and engaged fresh men for

Alexandre Henri Mouhot

the march to Kamarat. The meticulous conduct of the Frenchmen, who insisted upon paying for services rendered to them, occasioned considerable surprise throughout their journey. The chiefs openly lamented the waste of good brass wire upon mere peasants, and thought that if such things were going cheap, they themselves should have been selected as the recipients. The porters could barely comprehend a love of justice which declined to defraud the labourer of his hire, and which at the same time restricted his indubitable rights; for when performing a like service for Siamese officials they had always been permitted to rob the villagers of the whole countryside, and this de Lagrée would by no means allow. On the whole it may be questioned whether the justice of the white man impressed the natives as anything more admirable than an inexplicable eccentricity. The point is interesting because it illustrates in an amusing fashion the divergent views of the East and the West, and the frequency with which the principles of the latter fail to make any appeal to the understanding or admiration of the former.

From Amnat the way led through wild and sparsely peopled country, separated from the Mekong by a belt of forest, to a district broken by gentle undulations, where the previously sandy soil, bespattered with out-crops of iron-stone, is replaced by rice-fields. On January 30th the travellers found Delaporte awaiting them at Kamarat. This place, the point at which the proposed railway will cross the Mekong, is situated on the right bank, as indeed, since the subjugation of Laos by Siam at the beginning of last century, are all the principal villages in the valley above the Khon rapids.

Using Kamarat as his base, de Lagrée undertook a short journey of exploration into the valley of the Se Bang-Hien, a left bank tributary of the Mekong which falls into the latter river opposite to Kamarat. He was absent eight days, and during that period travelled on elephants to Lahanam, where he found the Se Bang-Hien measuring 900 yards across. Thence he proceeded up the valley to Muong San Kon, below the mouth of the Som Phon, and so across marshy country, to Phong; then east and north to Ban Najo and Lomnu; and so south to Kamarat *viâ* Ban Tang Sum and Laha Kok. From Ban Najo the country traversed was populous, and the short trip served to fill in a small blank upon the map. Its interest, however, was mainly ethnological, de Lagrée making the acquaintance of three remarkable tribes, the Sue, the Phu Tai and the Khas Denong. These "savages," and especially the Sue, are comparatively civilised, and the last named, it is worthy of note, practise a form of ancestor worship, while their dialect is apparently a variant of Kambodian.

During this journey de Lagrée also succeeded in establishing the fact that up to 1831 Annam had exercised control over the whole of the country situated on the left bank of the Mekong between the sixteenth and seventeenth parallels of latitude; this region had paid tribute regularly to the Court of Hue. The information was of political importance in view of the position which France has since acquired in the Kingdom of Annam. De Lagrée ascer-

tained that up to the time mentioned trade routes to the
Annamite capital had been in constant use, and that the
prosperity of the district had been considerable. In 1831,
the Siamese, fresh from their reduction of the Laos States
on the right bank of the river, invaded the country on the
left bank, but were defeated by the Annamites. They
returned to the charge, however, and this time they
transported the entire population across the Mekong,
leaving the left bank a desert. In this devastated and
depopulated area the Annamite armies could not operate,
and at a later period the Siamese began quietly to colo-
nise the abandoned territory afresh. The absence of pity,
which distinguishes the Oriental as opposed to the Occi-
dental, stands him in good stead when he is bent upon
conquest. No consideration bred of sympathy with
human suffering,—let those who endure it be never so
innocent and helpless, let the scale upon which it is conceived be never so great,—causes him to stay his hand when
ruthless action will bring about the result at which he
aims. It is appalling to think of the misery which the
removal of the entire population from one bank to the
other must have inflicted upon its victims—agriculturists
who lived from season to season by such harvests as they
could garner; but by no other means, it is probable, could
the Siamese have possessed themselves of the country
which they coveted, and from which they had already
been driven when they attempted to seize it by
force.

Kamarat was left on February 13th, by boat, and the
ascent of the Mekong, the bed of which is here strewn

with great sandstone outcrops and obstructed by numerous flights of rapids, was begun anew. At Keng Kabao
the boats of the expedition had to be unloaded before
they could be hauled up the falls, but a little above this
point, at Ban Thasaku, the river was found running
through an immense plain covered with forest, and as it
widened out the difficulties which it presented to navigation ceased for a space.

On February 15th, Ban Nuk was reached, a big village
below which is the handsome temple of Tong Bao, with
a façade inlaid with porcelain ; and a week later the party
landed at Peu Nom, a pyramidal structure which is one
of the most famous Buddhist shrines in all the Laos
country. The upper portion is obviously modern, but
its base, the work of a Kambodian princess the wife of
a King of Vien Chan, dates from early in the seventeenth
century, and is believed to have been built upon the site
of a far older pyramid.

Leaving Peu Nom on February 24th, the expedition
made its way up-stream to Lakon, opposite to which village some enormous limestone bluffs spring suddenly
from the plain ; from these the natives prepare large
quantities of quicklime, both for building purposes and as
an ingredient of the betel-quid. Here a small Annamite
colony was met with, and the near neighbourhood of
Annam suggested to Garnier the possibility of opening
communications with the sea *viâ* Hue, an idea which has
since been furthered by the labours of other explorers.
Huten was reached on March 6th, and thence de Lagrée
and Joubert ascended the Nam Hin Bun for two days,

and visited some lead mines situated in the valley of the
Ban Haten.

De Lagrée, on his return, found Garnier at Hutien with
the precious passports in his possession, and on the morrow the journey up the Mekong was resumed. At San
laburi, at the mouth of the Sum Kam, the boats of
the expedition were changed, and by March 16th the
explorers found themselves once more passing through
forest country, though four days later Bun Kang, "a
large and beautiful town," was reached, and the surrounding district was found to be richer and more civilised than
lower Laos. The Mekong River, which had been flowing from the west since above Lakon, was now discovered
to be running definitely from that direction, and its wind-
ings so enormously increased the distance from point to
point that cart-tracks were used by the natives in preference to boats, though a few monster rafts continued from
time to time to loaf down-stream. On March 23rd, a more
thickly populated country was entered, and Nong Kun,
opposite to the important tributary, the Se Ngum, was
reached. This river is navigable for six days' journey
from its junction with the Mekong, but time prevented
its exploration by the expedition.

At Pon Pisai, on March 24th, boats were once more
changed, and a day and a half brought the party to
Nong Kai, near which is situated the ruined city of Vien
Chan, once the capital of a united Laos. The river to
this point had frequently been difficult of navigation, but
the rapids of Hang Hong are the only very formidable
obstacles, necessitating a complete cessation of traffic for

some weeks at a time at certain seasons of the year. The rains had not yet come, and the heat was intense, the thermometer registering 92° F., even after sundown.

Nong Kai itself, founded after the destruction of Vien Chan, is a very important place, the largest town which the travellers had seen since their departure from Pnom Penh nine months earlier. The Governor of Nong Kai treated the party with courtesy, and undertook to send one of the interpreters, named Seguin, overland to Bangkok, as de Lagrée had decided to dispense with his services. At a later period this man was able to furnish Garnier with some useful information concerning the country traversed by him between Nong Kai and the Siamese capital.

On April 2nd, the ruins of Vien Chan were visited. Though the town was not destroyed and forcibly abandoned until 1828, it was already completely overgrown with jungle. From an architectural and archæological point of view this place is not more interesting than Bangkok or Ayuthia, and it claims our attention solely on account of its historical associations and the tragedy of its destruction. It was formerly the capital of a Laotine kingdom, which, founded in the thirteenth century, extended from the Khon rapids to the twentieth parallel of latitude, thus including Luang Prabang itself. In 1528 revolutions drove from the throne the last member of the dynasty which had ruled over this great state, and thereafter a subdivision of its territories ensued. The Laos people were further weakened by protracted wars with the Gueos—hill-tribes whose identity is uncertain— and in a weak moment the aid of Siam was invoked.

From that time the influence of Siam increased, and by the middle of the eighteenth century the subjugation of the whole of Laos was an accomplished fact. In 1767 Ayuthia was sacked by the Burmese, and Laos, which had endured the yoke of Siam with little gladness, took the opportunity to revolt. The insurrection failed, and all went on as before until early in the nineteenth century. About 1820 the King of Vien Chan, finding that he and his people were being mercilessly pillaged by the Siamese officer accredited to his Court, and having failed to obtain redress from Bangkok, caused the obnoxious official to be assassinated. A large Siamese army was at once sent against Vien Chan. Its ruler, King Anu, tried to raise the whole of Laos against the common enemy, but Luang Prabang prudently declined to take any hand in the matter. Vien Chan was taken and destroyed; its population was expelled; large numbers of people were burned alive in barns, and all manner of barbarities were practised by the invaders with the object of impressing the wrath of Siam upon the memory of the vanquished. Anu himself sought refuge in Annam, but his rendition having been obtained, he was brought to Bangkok and imprisoned in a cage, in which he presently died a miserable death. His son, having contrived to escape, and having thereafter been recaptured, committed suicide by precipitating himself from the summit of the pagoda in which he was incarcerated. Some of the survivors of this tragedy were used to populate the new town of Nong Kai; others were driven off in herds to more distant places; while others again were distributed as slaves

among the victors.   Hundreds died of hunger, or fell by
the way on that awful march which was to lead them to
a lifelong captivity.   Vien Chan, wrecked and shattered,
was left to the forest and to the wild things of the jungle,
after everything portable had been looted from it.
The dream of an independent Laos was ended for ever.
To this day children are cowed into obedience throughout
the Laos country by the whispered name of the Praya
Mitop, the Siamese General who commanded this bloody
punitive expedition.

The dread of being overtaken by the rains caused de
Lagrée to push on from Vien Chan with as little delay as
possible, and twenty miles up-stream a narrow gorge succeeded by difficult rapids was encountered.   Progress was
slow, and on April 8th the rapid of Keng Kan necessitated the abandonment of the boats, the explorers walking up the left bank to Sanghao, limping bare-shod over
burning rocks and through thorny jungles, and taking five
painful hours to cover a distance of six miles.   New boats
were obtained, and at Ban Kuklao, reached on April 11th,
other craft which had been sent to meet them were
found.   Next day the last of the rapids was passed, and
at Chieng Kang the Mekong once more expanded as the
explorers won free from the mountainous zone through
which for so many miles they had been following it.

For some time the Frenchmen had been greatly per-
turbed by rumours of a party of English explorers, some
forty strong, which was said to have cut in above them
from Burma.   So far the members of de Lagrée's expedition had been passing, for the most part, through

country which, though it had not been examined in detail, had already been visited by Europeans. In only a few places had they been able to look around them with that peculiar pride and triumph which belong to the white man who knows that for him has been reserved from the beginning the tremendous privilege of gazing, the first of all his kind, upon scenes never beheld before by European eyes. That joy of joys to one bitten by the love of wandering was to be theirs when they should win free at last of the places over which their fellows had scored a trail; but if an English expedition of imposing numbers, and presumably far better equipped than themselves, had slipped in ahead of them, this experience was like to be indefinitely postponed. They never dreamed of questioning the accuracy of the report: it was felt to be *vraisemblable*, to be completely in keeping with the ubiquitous character, the unblushing intrusiveness of the Englishman. They could only set their teeth and determine to die rather than to suffer themselves to be outdone, while they said bitter things of England and of Fate, and Garnier's anglophobia revived of a sudden with something of its old passionate force. Intense therefore was their relief when, shortly after leaving Chieng Kang, they met three rafts journeying down-stream, on board one of which was a Dutchman, named Duyshart, a surveyor in the employ of the Siamese Government, who turned out to be the egg from which, through the incubation of the native imagination, this monstrous *canard* had been hatched. This man, the record of whose journey and surveys seems to have been engulfed in the files of one of the Government Departments at Bangkok, had ascended the Menam to Chieng Mai, had thence struck across country to the Mekong, striking it at Chieng Khong, about 130 miles above Luang Prabang, and had rafted down the river from that point. This prolonged the distance which the Frenchmen would have to cover before they could pass into utterly unexplored country, but this fact notwithstanding, the transformation of an English expedition into a single Dutchman raised their spirits and sent them on their way rejoicing.

On April 16th, the boundary of the province of Luang Prabang was crossed, and on the morrow Pak Lai, which had previously been visited by Mouhot who had come thither from Muong Lui, was reached. This was the first point on the Mekong at which Mouhot's route had been cut by that of the expedition, and Garnier found that the former explorer had misplaced it by sixty-four geographical miles, an error which repeated itself with more or less persistency in all his latitudes. The correction which Garnier was now able to make was one of considerable importance, and necessitated a material rectification of the maps compiled from Mouhot's notes. From Pak Lai there is a cart-track along the right bank of the Mekong, now little used but formerly a highway over which annual Chinese caravans passed from Yun-nan to Ken Tao, a province between Muong Lui and Pak Lai. To-day Chieng Mai and Muong Nan communicate with Yun-nan *via* Chieng Tong, the route partially explored by McLeod in 1837.

Some distance above Pak Lai the expedition passed

through uninhabited forest country, where the river is obstructed by rapids every few miles; above this stretch the stream flowed for some distance between magnificent marble cliffs, while limestone bluffs reappeared on its banks. The rapid of Keng Luong necessitated the unloading of the boats, and this operation had to be repeated at Keng Saniok. At Ban Koksai, a Laotine village, the hills in the vicinity were found to be peopled by the wild tribes called Khmus, whose numbers and spirit have enabled them to occupy towards their more civilised neighbours a position vastly superior to that of most of the hill-folk of southeastern Asia. These wild folk are, as it were, the rats of humanity, but while the Khas of lower Laos and the Sâkai of the Malay Peninsula are the timid and defenceless water-rats, the Khmus may be likened to the old, grey, English house-rat, and have like him an excellent notion of how to stick up for themselves.

On April 29th, Luang Prabang was reached, the largest town which the Frenchmen had met with since their departure from Cochin-China. Garnier estimated the population of this place at 8,000 souls; that of the province at not less than 150,000. It owed its prosperity partly to the fall of Vien Chan, when Luang Prabang stood neutral, and partly to the fact that it alone among the States of Laos had fallen less effectually than any of its neighbours under the yoke of Bangkok. Founded in the eighteenth century, it did not come into prominence until after the decline of the power of Vien Chan, and its prudent rulers were content with a much-tempered form of independence, paying tribute to China and Annam as well as to Siam. The result of this policy is that, after all the vicissitudes which have befallen its neighbours, Luang Prabang remained the most important trade-centre of the Mekong Valley above Cochin-China, and this in spite of the fact that it does not possess natural advantages equal to those of lower Laos.

Although, even when continuing their ascent of the Mekong above Luang Prabang, the travellers were not yet traversing country never previously visited by white men, their arrival at this, the last and greatest of the towns of Siamese Laos, presents a convenient opportunity for taking a rapid glance at the explorations which had been effected in the *Hinterland* of Indo-China by Europeans prior to the coming of the French mission.

The earliest of these was undertaken by the Dutch traders led by Gerard van Wusthof[1] in 1641, of which frequent mention has already incidentally been made. The account of it was originally published in Flemish, nor was it rendered into any other tongue until M. P. Vœlkel translated it for Francis Garnier, who printed it with his own notes in the *Bulletin de la Société de Géographie* in 1871. This has caused the narrative which tells of the first visit paid to Laos by white men to be very generally overlooked, nor indeed is the relation itself of any extraordinary interest from a geographical or even from an historical point of view. It appears that in March, 1641, certain Laotine merchants visited Batavia

---

[1] Vide Supra, pp. 93, et seq.

on board one of the Dutch Company's ships, and that
their coming suggested to the Governor, Van Dieman,
the idea of despatching a mission to their country for the
purpose of establishing trade relations with its inhabitants. For this duty Gerard van Wusthof, a sub factor,
was selected, the party under his leadership consisting
of four Dutchmen, a servant, and one Malay. A
start up the Mekong was made on July 20th, 1641; the
party travelled by boat, and Sambor was reached on
August 5. Bœtzong, which may be identified with
Stung-Treng, at the mouth of the Se-Kong, was reached
on August 17th,[1] and when on the 19th the party found
itself among the maze of islands which here divide the
river into many branches, Wusthof believed that he had
left upon his west the mouth of a huge stream which
took its rise in Burma. How this mistake arose it is impossible to understand, but it must be remembered that
long after Wusthof's day the belief prevailed that the Mekong took its rise close to the Bay of Bengal, while even
later the theory was entertained that the Mekong and the
Menam were joined together in the interior by a waterway was widely accepted. Earlier still it was thought that
the Mekong had an out-flow in the Bay of Bengal itself.

On August 25th an island was reached, called by
Wusthof Saxenham, which would appear to be the
island of Sitandong, to this day an important place,
situated above the Khon rapids. On September 25th,
Ocmum—obviously Pak Mun, the mouth of the Mun
River,—was reached, the country above Khong being

[1] Vide Supra, p. 123.

wilder and less thickly populated than Garnier afterwards found it. On October 18th, the party spent the night at Lochan, which is probably to be identified with Lakon. " The Laos-folk," says Wusthof, " regard Lochan as a great town, although it is no bigger than Harderwijk. We walked in the streets by the light of the moon. . . . This town is quite the most dreadfully pagan place there is in the world;" for the worthy Dutchman was horrified at the behaviour of his native companions, though he adds characteristically, " Much gold is found here at a cheap price."

On the night of November 3rd, orders were received from the capital that the mission was to halt at a mile from the town of Vien Chan (Wincian, Wusthof calls it), and on the morning of the 16th, the party was conveyed on elephants to the temple without the city, to which it is joined by an avenue of trees; in this temple the audience with the King of Vien Chan was to be given to them. The King treated them with kindness. Wusthof himself, whose term of service with the Company was near its expiration, obtained permission to depart alone on his return journey, and after some delay he was able to set forth, charged with certain pacific messages from the King of Vien Chan to the Court of Kambodia, which he undertook to deliver.

Here his individual narrative is interrupted by a description of the Kingdom of Laos. From this it may be gathered that Wusthof's notions of the geography of the country were vague and inaccurate, and that his understanding of the teachings of Buddhism was even less exact. It shows us, however, that at this period the Kingdom whose capital was Vien Chan was one of considerable power and importance : that it reckoned itself, and was reckoned by its neighbours, to stand on an equal footing with Siam, with Kambodia and with Tongking ; that it was rich and prosperous ; and that it was distinguished then, as now, by the religious zeal of its people which manifests itself in the number and the beauty of the temples, pagodas and pyramids scattered through the country, and in the immense influence exerted over them by the innumerable bonzes who make it their business to live by the gospel and upon the faithful.

On December 14th, Wusthof's comrades, left behind at Vien Chan, did not receive their permission to depart until August 11th, nearly nine months after their first audience with the King, a characteristically inaccessible Oriental monarch of whom they do not appear to have subsequently seen anything.

The Dutchmen reached Bassak on the 17th, September, at which point their narrative ends.

The Dutch merchants also mention that during their stay at Vien Chan a " Portuguese " priest named Leria visited the capital and tried unsuccessfully to obtain permission to preach Christianity to the pagan population. This man was not in truth a Portuguese, being a native of Piedmont. He was a Jesuit, and his full name was Giovanni Maria Leria. To him belongs the distinction of being, not only the first, but up to the latter half of the nineteenth century, the only Christian priest who had endeavoured to spread his religion through the Laos

country.   He met with tremendous opposition from the
bonzes, but in spite of this continued to reside in Laos
for five years, and did not leave Vien Chan till December, 1647.

The next traveller, with whose journeys in Indo-China
we need concern ourselves, is Henri Mouhot, of whom
mention has already been made in connection with the
Khmer ruins at Angkor.[1]   A native of France, brought
up in that country, he had resided successively in Russia,
in England and at Jersey: by profession a photographer
in the days when photography was a new art, he had
cultivated his taste for natural history, devoting himself
particularly to ornithology and conchology.   In 1858 he
went out to Siam on a mission which received practical
encouragement from the learned societies of England and
France, his object being to explore the little known countries of Indo-China and to examine the problems of their
ethnology, and their flora and fauna.   Making his headquarters at Bangkok, he first ascended the Menam to
Ayuthia, the ancient capital of Saam, and paid a visit to
the famous temple of Prabat Moi, which he describes as
having about it little that is remarkable.   Its chief distinction, however, and the fact which makes it celebrated
and holy throughout Indo-China, is the footprint preserved in its sanctuary which is piously believed by the
faithful to be that of Buddha himself.

After visiting Saraburi and ascending the Menam to

---

[1] Vide supra, pp. 149, 150.

Pak Priau, above which point the navigation of the river
becomes more difficult owing to the number and the size
of the rapids, he walked to Petawi for the purpose of visiting another famous pagoda.

Mouhot subsequently returned down river to Bangkok,
whence he travelled by Chinese junk to Chantabun, exploring the islands lying off the coast and later the country in the vicinity of his new headquarters. He also
made a short journey into the neighbouring province of
Batambang, and on his return travelled down the coast
to Komput, in Kambodian territory. He visited Udong,
the then capital of Kambodia, made a short stay at
Pnom Penh, the present capital, and passing over the
border into Annam spent three months among the wild
tribes called Stiens, who occupy the Brelam country.
After this he returned once more to Udong, ascended the
branch of the Great Lake which joins the Mekong at
Pnom Penh, and explored in detail the immense Khmer
ruins of Angkor, which he was the first European to describe minutely and with some pretence to scientific accuracy. This work accomplished, he passed a period of
four months in the mountainous country of Pechaburi,
thence returning overland to Bangkok, examining by the
way some of the Khmer ruins in the province of Batambang.

During all these wanderings Mouhot had broken little
new ground, for almost everywhere the ubiquitous Roman
Catholic missionaries, Frenchmen of the wonderful
Société des Missions Etrangères, had been before him;
but on his return to Bangkok he set about making prep-

arations for his last and most important journey. It is at this point that Mouhot's travels begin to assume such geographical value as can be claimed for them.

Proceeding up the Menam, he struck across country to Korat, and thence to Chaipun, where he arrived at the end of February, 1861. The governor of this place showed little inclination to assist him, and Mouhot found himself obliged to retrace his steps to Korat, the governor of which was more courteous and more amenable. With the transport here obtained, and armed with letters of introduction from the friendly governor, he set out once more to Chaipun. From this point he pushed on in a northerly direction to Muong Lui, and thence to Pak Lai,[1] the place at which he first struck the upper reaches of the Mekong, a river whose acquaintance he had already made from Pnom Penh to its mouth.

Even after he had reached the banks of the Mekong, Mouhot continued to travel, not by boat, but by bullock-waggon, following the trade-track along the right bank of the river. The arduous and difficult journey which he had accomplished had already tried him sorely, and Mouhot's journals show at this period unmistakable signs of acute mental depression. His instruments, in the rough journey across country, appear to have fared no better than their master, and an examination of the map filled in from his notes, which was the best information on the subject of upper Laos available prior to the de Lagrée–Garnier expedition, shows that he had fallen into gross errors both in distance and in direction. The value of

[1] Vide supra, p. 202.

the work which he had achieved at the cost of so much labour and pain was further depreciated by the fact that Mouhot did not survive to correct and explain the notes which he had made, and it is possible that some of the errors which resulted were due to misinterpretation of his memoranda.

Luang Prabang itself was reached on July 25th, and after some sojourn in the place and an interview with its king, Mouhot started to explore the country on the left bank of the Mekong. On October 15th, his diary shows, he started on his return-journey to Luang Prabang. On the 19th, he notes that he is stricken down by fever, and ten days later comes the last pitiful entry, the voice of one crying in the wilderness, the despairing appeal of the lonely white man, far from aid and home and comfort, dying among aliens in a distant land:

" *Octobre 29me.—Ayez pitié de moi, O mon Dieu!* "

Was ever the outcry of a human soul concentrated more pathetically into a single phrase?

Five years later his countrymen found his grave in mid-forest near the little village of Ban Naphao, on the banks of the Nam Kan, at a short distance from Luang Prabang, and over it they reared a simple monument. The spot where the dead explorer lies is finely described by Francis Garnier, and I quote his words here as in the original. Translation could only mar a passage whose beauty, if it stood alone instead of being but one of many striking pieces of word-painting, would serve to prove that Francis Garnier, the man of action, united to his other great qualities those of the literary artist.

" Le paysage qui encadre le mausolée est gracieux et
triste à la fois : quelques arbres au feuillage sombre
l'abritent, et le bruissement de leur cimes se mêle au
grondement des eaux du Nam Kan qui coule à leur pieds.
En face s'élève un mur de roches noirâtres qui forme
l'autre rive du torrent : nulle habitation, nulle trace hu-
maine aux alentours de la dernière demeure de ce Français aventureux, qui a préféré l'agitation des voyages et
l'étude directe de la nature, au calme du foyer et à la
science des livres. Seule parfois une pirogue légère
passera devant ce lieu de repos, et le batelier laotien
regardera avec respect, peut-être avec effroi, ce souvenir
à la fois triste et touchant du passage d'étrangers dans
son pays.

" Nous nous étions rendus au lieu de la sépulture en
suivant à pied les bords du Nam Kan ; nous revînmes en
barque à la fin du jour, en nous laissant aller au fil du
courant. A chaque détour de la rivière, nous décou-
vrions, sous les aspects les plus divers, le panorama
animé de Luang Prabang, apparaissant et disparaissant
tour à tour derrière le rideau mobile des arbres de la
rive ; de nombreux pêcheurs tendaient leurs filets au
milieu des rochers et jusque dans les rapides que nos
légères pirogues franchissaient comme des flèches ; des
troupes de baigneurs et de baigneuses folâtraient près
des bancs de sable qui parfois élargissaient le lit de la
rivière. Autour de nous, le soleil couchant faisait étin-
celer les eaux de mille reflets de pourpre et d'or. Tout
dans ce paysage, sans cesse renouvelé par la rapidité de
notre locomotion, respirait une tranquillité et un bonheur
apparents qui invitaient à l'oubli du monde bruyant et

agité dont le souvenir bouillonnait encore en nous. Quel
contraste entre ce calme tableau du Laos tropical et cette
Europe, dont le nom même était inconnu à ceux qui nous
entouraient? Devions-nous les plaindre ou les féliciter
de leur ignorance et de leur sauvagerie? Plus encore
que la distance, ces différences entre la civilisation pour
la cause de laquelle nous nous étions exilés, et la civilisation dont nous étions devenus les hôtes, nous semblaient
creuser entre nous et notre patrie un abîme chaque jour
plus grand."

Mention has already been made of the Dutchman
Duyshart,* whose surveying expedition undertaken at
the behest of the Siamese Government had been magni-
fied by native rumour into a wholesale invasion of upper
Laos by the scientists of Great Britain. The fact that
no detailed account of his journey appears to have been
published leaves the nature of his discoveries somewhat
vague. He seems, however, to have ascended the Menam
from Bangkok to the mouth of its western branch, the
Me-ping, and that river to Chieng Mai, whence he
trekked across country, striking the Mekong at Chieng
Kong, a point some 225 miles above Luang Prabang. It
had thus fallen to the lot of this obscure Dutchman to
be, so far as is known, the first white man to traverse
the country lying between Chieng Mai and Chieng Kong,
and without doubt the first to descend and survey the
portion of the Mekong which lies southward of that
point and between it and Luang Prabang. More than
this we do not know concerning Duyshart's work, but

* Vide supra, p. 201.

it is possible that his papers may have been disinterred from the pigeon-holes in Bangkok and have been utilised by Mr. J. M'Carthy in the preparation of the great map of Siam published by the Royal Geographical Society, which is so largely the fruit of his own surveys and explorations extending over a period of more than twenty years.

The last, and in some respects the most important, of the travellers whose work, since it joins that of the de Lagrée-Garnier expedition, calls for notice in this place, is the Scotsman, Captain, afterwards Major General, McLeod. As his starting-point was Maulmain, his journey belongs properly to the story of Burman exploration, with which we shall presently deal in a separate chapter, but the more important part of his achievement having been connected with the Shan States of Chieng Tong and Chieng Hong, and with his visit to the Mekong at the last named place, he is to be regarded in a special manner as the forerunner of the French mission, wherefore it will be more convenient to study his route now than later.

McLeod started from Maulmain on December 13, 1836, in the company of Dr. Richardson, who had already thrice visited Chieng Mai from lower Burma. On the present occasion Richardson was bound for Ava, whither he eventually made his way through the hill country of the Red Karins, while McLeod's immediate objective was Chieng Mai, whence he hoped to make a journey to Yun-nan through the eastern Shan States tributary to Ava. The travellers ascended the Gyne

River in boats, reaching the last village in British territory on the 16th December. From this point they proceeded northward on elephant-back, crossing the Siamese boundary on Christmas Day, and parting company on the 26th, Richardson continuing his journey in a westerly direction to Mein-lung-hi, while McLeod headed for Muong Haut, or Muong Hal, by a route somewhat to the south of that followed by Richardson in his previous journeys to Chieng Mai. McLeod's path led into the valley of the Tsen-tsue, a tributary of the Salwin, and thence through the mountains to Muong Haut on the Me-ping, the river upon the banks of which Chieng Mai stands. On January 9, 1837, he reached Muong Lampun, or Labong as it was always called by the explorers from Burma, and after a sojourn of three days in that place passed on to "Zimmé" (Chieng Mai), where he remained over a fortnight, the local authorities endeavouring to prevent him from proceeding upon his journey. The explorer, however, had satisfied himself that the road leading to Chieng Tong was the only one which was of any importance for merchants bound for Yunnan, and he therefore turned a deaf ear to the persuasions of the rulers of Chieng Mai and determined to travel by that route and by no other. At last on January 29th, accompanied by some Shan officers sent to escort him, he left Chieng Mai with six elephants, and on February 6th reached the village of Puk Bong on the frontier of Chieng Mai territory, whence the road to Chieng Tong branches off. The first village under Chieng Tong jurisdiction was reached on February 13th, and thirteen days later McLeod entered Chieng Tong itself, all the country from Chieng Mai having never previously been traversed by a white man. The traveller had made a survey of his route, and he fixed the latitude of Chieng Tong at 21° 47' 48" N., and the longitude at about 99° 39' E. His latitudes were very fairly exact, as he was able to determine them by astronomical observations, but his longitudes were confessedly only approximately accurate.

At Chieng Tong McLeod was well received by the Shan king of the place. Although incidentally he was doing geographical work of great value, his mission had as its primary object the establishment of trade between Maulmain and the Burmese Shan States. He had from the first been accompanied by a number of merchants who had brought with them British goods for sale in the local markets, and for these there was so great a demand in Chieng Tong that the traders decided that it would be unnecessary for them to go any farther with their leader and protector. McLeod, however, was bent upon penetrating into Yun-nan if that could by any means be done; he therefore bought some ponies for the journey, and at last persuaded the King of Chieng Tong to suffer him to depart. With this potentate the Scotsman succeeded in establishing most friendly relations, and it is pleasant to recall that when de Lagrée and Thorel visited the place thirty years later, they found McLeod's memory still green, and the King ready to aid any white man for the sake of the friend whom he remembered with so much affection.

McLeod left Chieng Tong on March 1st, and passing through Muong La, reached Chieng Hong on March 9th. He here struck the Mekong at a point farther from the coast than any at which it had previously been visited by a white man, and it should be noted that the de Lagrée-Garnier expedition, which had for its primary object the exploration of the course of the great river, never succeeded in attaining to a point above that reached by the Scotsman. McLeod estimated the average width of the river at 100 yards at the season of his visit, and at 220 yards at full water, its rise being at least 50 feet; he judged its velocity to be about 3 miles an hour. He remained at Chieng Hong for more than a fortnight while the authorities in Yun-nan were communicated with, but the answer to his request to be permitted to proceed was unfavourable. He was told that if he desired to enter the Celestial Empire, the front door, so to speak, was at Canton, a portal through which all foreigners were allowed to pass by the authorities at Peking, and that backdoors, such as the road into Yun-nan, were not open to visitors. He was also gravely told that " there was no precedent " for a foreign official coming by this route, and as, unlike the French travellers who later walked in his footsteps, he had not been furnished with letters of authority from Peking, he had no choice but to return to Burma. Accordingly on March 26th he began his ride back to Chieng Tong, arriving there on the 31st; starting again on April 4th, he reached Chieng Mai on April 18th. Here he entered into long discussions with the King, his object being to get the road to Chieng Tong declared open to traffic for merchants from Maulmain, but in spite of the friendly nature of his intercourse with the authorities, he failed altogether in this object.

McLeod fixed the latitude and longitude of Chieng Mai

at 18° 47′ N. and about 99° 20′ E.; he collected from the natives a considerable amount of information concerning the neighbouring States of Muong Nam, Muong Phe and Luang Prabang; and when he left Chieng Mai it was by a new route, the high road to Bangkok. This runs south as far as Pang Nan Dit, then south-west to the Me-ping, which river McLeod crossed at Ban Nat. Up to this point the way had been through flat and grassy plains, but the Me-ping once crossed, more hilly country was entered, though only one really big hill had to be climbed. There were no cart-tracks here, but the difficulties in the way of making one were not great, and McLeod cherished the hope that the trade with Yun-nan might be tapped by this route and the Lakon road. Nothing, however, resulted from this suggestion. McLeod made his way back to Maulmian *viâ* Kokarit and Mikalon.

I have not dealt in detail with this traveller's description of the Shan States through which he was the first to pass, as an account will be found in the chapters recording the journey of the French mission. It should be remembered, however, that McLeod was the first white man to visit and map these regions.

The summary which has now been given of early explorations in the Indo-Chinese *Hinterland* will enable the reader to understand when and to what extent the de Lagrée-Garnier expedition was breaking ground entirely new, and when and to what extent they were stepping in the footprints of others. Even when the Frenchmen were not the first in the field, however, the almost unlimited time at their disposal and their superior scientific equipment rendered it possible for them to achieve valuable geographical results such as had never been within the reach of their predecessors, to many of whom commercial advantage, rather than abstract knowledge, had been the primary object of their journeys.

CHAPTER X

THE SHAN STATES AND YUN-NAN

AT Luang Prabang, in spite of a certain frigidity which at first marked the relations of the authorities with his party, de Lagrée's tact and firmness speedily succeeded in overcoming the prejudices of the natives. He obtained an audience of the King on conditions honourable to himself, and was well treated in the matter of accommodation and provisions. But he found the opposition raised to the continuance of his journey less easy to remove. The Muhammadan rebellion in Yun-nan had been the signal for endless disorders in the Shan States which owed allegiance to China, and Luang Prabang had seized the opportunity thus afforded to omit sending the customary tribute, the contention of its authorities being that the roads to Yun-nan were impassable. It was therefore against their interests that a small party of Europeans should penetrate into China and so demonstrate the thinness of this pretext, and much was made of the difficulties which were declared to lie ahead of the explorers.

Three routes were open to de Lagrée's choice: firstly, that which led up the valley of the Mekong; secondly, that up the Nam Hu, a left influent of the great river; and lastly, the route to Kwang Si, which traverses country inhabited by mixed tribes situated between China and Tongking. The first route was also the longest, and it had further the disadvantage of running through districts which had been devastated while their ownership was in dispute between Burma and Siam; it moreover led through the Shan States tributary to the Court of Ava, from which the explorers had obtained no letters of authority; but on the other hand, from a geographical and political point of view it was by far the most interesting. The Nam Hu route was more direct, and in Yun-nan the Mekong River, which the explorers were loath to abandon, would again be struck; otherwise, however, it presented no special attractions. The Kwang Si route was perhaps the most difficult of all, for the King of Luang Prabang was at that moment fighting in that region, and also with the Annamites on the east, aid being lent to him by Siam.

The large number of merchants from all parts of Indo-China found in the markets of Luang Prabang enabled the explorers to obtain a considerable amount of information concerning the various routes, and de Lagrée long continued to be strongly biassed in favour of that *viâ* the Nam Hu. Garnier, on the other hand, who confesses that he was obsessed by "*la monomanie du Mekong*," pleaded hard that his beloved river should not be prematurely abandoned. In the end he succeeded in persuading his chief to adopt the first of the three routes, and de Lagrée induced the King of Luang Prabang to provide him with letters of authority which should pass the expedition through all the country under his control. This was but another sign of the excellent relations which the Frenchmen had succeeded in establishing with the natives; indeed, their camp had become the fashionable resort of the *élite* of Luang Prabang of both sexes. It was somewhat of a blow to the self-complacency of the explorers when the King's niece, a buxom young damsel whose behaviour had been most *empressé*, volunteered the opinion that the advanced age of the visitors, as proved by their flowing beards, rendered them in the last degree innocuous, and made the bare idea of their exciting jealousy in the breasts of the most suspicious altogether farcical and absurd.

The baggage of the expedition was now lightened as much as possible. Already the first rains had fallen, and the Mekong was coming down in semi-spate; but fighting their way doggedly against the current, the explorers reached Chieng Khong on June 5th. Joubert and de Carné were sent from Ban Tanun to explore some "volcanoes," which were reported to exist in the neighbourhood, but discovered that they were merely fissures in the ground emitting volumes of sulphureous and other gaseous vapours. Garnier took a few soundings in the Nam Hu.

The character of the Laotine natives inhabiting these upper reaches of the Mekong was found to differ materially from that of their neighbours in lower Laos. The "black-bellied" folk, as the northern Laotines are called on account of the tattooing from waist to knee which they practise, are somewhat more vigorous in body and in mind than the "white-bellied" men of the south. They are more independent, more proud, more self-respecting, and Garnier declared them to be at once more frank and more lively than the people of lower Laos, who are losing little by little all that remains to them

of energy, initiative, and resource. Climate has doubtless had something to do with this, the constant and
enervating heat of the tropics sapping in the long course
of centuries the energy of the natives of Kambodia and
lower Laos; but over and above climatic influence, political circumstances must be taken into account. Their
own decay contributed to their subjection to Siam, but
the rule of any Oriental race by another, and especially
the rule of any alien people by the cruel, corrupt and
inefficient officers of Siam, inevitably makes for the destruction of all that is best in the character of the subject
people.

From Chieng Khong the explorers passed up river to
Chieng Hsen, a ruined city which is situated some three
or four miles above the junction of the Nam Kok and
the Mekong. Under Thama Trai Pidok, one of the most
famous of the many kings who ruled over a Laotine
principality, and who in his time extended his conquests
almost to Ayuthia, this place throve and prospered
mightily. The exact period covered by its prosperity
cannot be definitely ascertained. Chien Hsen itself was
finally destroyed by the Siamese in 1774. The story of
the numberless kingdoms of Indo-China has never yet
been fully told. What knowledge we possess of it is in
the nature of fragments, but even these suffice to show
the welter of struggle and strife, invasion, attack and
defence, travail of kingdoms suddenly reared and as
suddenly destroyed, which taken together make up the
recorded past of these unhappy lands. The end of their
sufferings is not yet, but one cannot rise from an examination of their history without a genuine sense of satis-

faction that the influence of France on the one side, and of Great Britain on the other, has done much, and in the future will do more, to establish lasting peace among these troubled and contending nations.

Above Chieng Hsen the Mekong was found once more to flow through a mountainous region, and on June 18th the foot of a rapid called Tang He was reached, an insurmountable barrier past which it was not possible to carry the boats. Messengers were sent forward to Muong Lim, a dependency of Chieng Tong, to obtain transport, and Garnier, loath to quit the river, tramped alone up the left bank, passing through untouched forest in which the beasts had not yet learned to fear man, a little expedition of which he gives an account that is one of the finest passages in his works.

Muong Lim, standing on a plain, was reached by crossing two small ranges of hills, and in these days, when it has become the fashion to decry the ingenuity and the enterprise of our merchants, it is gratifying to note that the admiration of the Frenchmen was excited by the discovery that the cottons here exposed for sale were all of English manufacture, and that they had evidently been woven specially with a view to the Burmese and Shan markets, their colours being those most popular among the natives, and the designs printed upon the stuffs being pagodas and other objects of local veneration. At this place, too, the near neighbourhood of China began to be apparent. Money was weighed, for instance, in the Chinese fashion, and Chinese as well as Burmese weights were in use. The confusion thus caused was worse confounded by the practice, almost universal in the East, of employing two separate sets of scales—the one with very light weight, for selling, the other, preposterously heavy, for buying! The wild tribes encountered at Muong Lim, called Mu Tseu, Colonel Yule believed to be identical with the Miao-Tseu, people of Caucasian origin inhabiting some districts of southern China, who almost alone afford an example of a race which has had sufficient resistant power to escape assimilation with the Mongolian element. As will be seen from the illustration here reproduced from Garnier's book, the Mu Tseu are a Gipsy-looking folk, much given to personal adornment with silver ornaments and tinsel. In appearance and costume they resemble curiously the Kadayan tribes of western Borneo.

On June 28th leave to proceed was received from "the King of Khemarata and of Tungkaburi," as his majesty of Chieng Tong styled himself, but the Frenchmen were warned that fresh authority would be needed before they could visit the capital. On July 1st, therefore, a start was made, the objective of the expedition being Chieng Hong. The health of the party had of late suffered severely owing to the prevailing rains, both Garnier and Thorel being prostrated by fever, while Delaporte had such badly ulcerated feet that he had to be carried in a litter. The resources of the expedition were also becoming perilously slender, and a further reduction of baggage to save cost of transport was decided upon. It is impossible not to admire the pluck, endurance and tenacity displayed at this juncture by the Frenchmen, and it is enormously to their credit that the bare notion of turning back or of abandoning their enterprise does not even seem to have been mooted among them.

Paleo, the place at which the reduction of baggage was made, is distant only two miles from the banks of the Mekong, and although he had just completed a tramp of five hours' duration over wooded hills, Garnier was drawn to his river as by an irresistible magnet. He found the left bank still owing allegiance to Siam, though the northern boundary lies only a few miles higher up. The river was flowing down, magnificent, imposing, beautiful as ever, but as a highway of trade it had ceased to be used, all goods being transported overland by preference.

On July 9th, after tramping over hilly country covered with dense forest, broken only here and there by a few cotton plantations, and after being drenched to the skin continually by heavy showers, the explorers reached Siam-Lao, where a halt was called until July 23rd. Garnier, indefatigable as ever, paid a visit to the Mekong, which he found still quite navigable, and in this district wild tribes called the Khas Khos and the Khas Kuis were met with, the former wearing their hair in pig-tails and shaving their scalps, the latter resembling the Burmans in appearance but wearing the dress of the Shans. On July 16th an invitation to visit Chieng Tong was received from the King of that place, but de Lagrée decided to decline it, and two days later letters came in authorising the party to proceed to Chieng Kheng. A long day's march across country in which the rivers were in spate, the tracks submerged, and the only practicable paths so overgrown through disuse as to present formidable diffi-

culties, brought the explorers to Sop Yong on the banks
of the Mekong, of which river, rolling down in high
flood, glimpses had been obtained from time to time
throughout the tramp. On the way a hot stream, in
which the mercury registered 218.8° F., was discovered,
and the Nam Yong, a large and beautiful river which
joins its waters to those of the Mekong at Sop Yong,
was crossed in boats. Sop Yong itself was a miserable
little village, containing only four houses, and proved
to be quite unequal to the task of supplying a new
relay of bearers or even a sufficiency of provisions.
Accordingly on July 27th Francis Garnier, filled with
joy at finding himself once more afloat on the bosom
of his beloved river, ascended the Mekong in a canoe
for the purpose of enlisting porters. At Nam Kung he
fell in with a Lu headman who, for one of his race and
opportunities, had been a great traveller in his day, having actually journeyed to the sea *via* Tongking. Through
the good offices of this man a number of human beasts
of burden were procured. The expedition next travelled
up the valley of the Nam Yong, reaching Ban Pasang,
a cluster of villages lying in the centre of a rice plain,
on August 1st. The province of Muong Yu had now
been quitted for that of Muong Yong, which is under the
jurisdiction of Chieng Tong, and to Muong Yong itself
the party proceeded on August 7th. This place, situated
in the foot-hills to the west of the Yong valley, was a
powerful city in its day. It is girt about by a moat and
wall, within which the ground slopes up gradually to a
pagoda. The Burmese agent stationed at Muong Yong
professed to be friendly to the visitors, but secretly he

placed many obstacles in their way, and eventually de Lagrée found it necessary to go in person to Chieng Tong, his refusal to accept the invitation sent him by the King of that city having proved prejudicial to the interests of the expedition. Taking Thorel with him, he presently started on this mission, leaving the rest of the party at Muong Yong with fever rampant in their midst. Garnier took the opportunity thus afforded to him to examine some ruins in the neighbourhood, which proved to be interesting and to resemble those of Angkor, albeit they are inferior to the great Khmer remains. The Tat, or sacred monument, of Chom Yong was also visited, and was found to be older than the ruins of Muong Yong, while the tradition of Tevata Nakhon—"The Kingdom of the Angels"—as the ancient Khmer empire is called in Laos, was universally cherished by the learned classes in this Shan State.

De Lagrée and Thorel meanwhile made their way to Chieng Tong *viâ* Muong Khai, traversing country mainly peopled by the tribe called Doe, whose civilisation is equal to that of the Shans, and whom Yule believed to be merely Shans who have escaped the modifying influence of Buddhism. Chieng Tong was reached on August 23rd, and the King of that place was most cordial, his friendship for McLeod, who had left an excellent reputation behind him, predisposing him in favour of Europeans. The Burmese agent, on the other hand, who had taken great umbrage at his omission from the list of those to whom de Lagrée had sent presents, did his best to thwart the visitors, and it was not until September 3rd that the necessary passports were forthcoming.

The country around Chieng Tong and Muong Yong, in common with most of the Shan States, has constantly been in dispute between its more powerful neighbours, and has consequently been a battle-field for all. At the time of the Frenchmen's visit, though Burmese or Siamese agents were stationed in each Shan State, the control exercised over the local authorities was by no means as complete as in the Laos kingdoms below Luang Prabang.

Chieng Tong at this time was built upon a cluster of little hills, and was surrounded by a moat and wall some seven and a half miles in circumference. The palace was a wooden building with a tile roof; there were a score of pagodas in the place, the architecture of which showed unmistakable signs of Chinese influence; and a remarkable Tat, that of Chom Sri, stood without the walls.

Leaving Chieng Tong, de Lagrée and Thorel passed over the hills into the valley of the Nam Lui, striking that river at Muong Uak, a point at which it begins to be navigable, and crossing to the left bank climbed over another range into the province of Muong Sam-Tao. Ban Kien, the capital, a big town built on the highest point of the surrounding plateau, was visited, where an important armoury which was turning out some 3,000 muskets *per annum* was found. The plateau is thickly populated, principally by Does, who number some 10,000 souls. On September 11th de Lagrée reached the junction of the Nam Lui with the Nam Lem, and two days later arrived at Muong Yu on the right bank of the former river, where he rejoined Garnier and the rest of the party who had come direct from Muong Yong. After a halt of five days the expedition once more crossed the Nam Lui, and struck out for Muong Long.

Following a path which zigzagged up the hillside until the summit was reached, the explorers passed down into the valley of the Nam Nga on September 19th, and continued their journey through numerous villages, set in the midst of rice-fields, to Muong Long. This is a place of 1,500 to 1,800 inhabitants, situated on the banks of the Nam Kama, a tributary of the Nam Nga, and is reached from the stone bridge which spans the latter stream by means of a paved road. The bridge, the road, and a number of carved lions which had been broken and cast aside during some period of destructive warfare, were all found to be of distinctly Chinese design, and the near neighbourhood of China—the goal towards which the Frenchmen had been toiling for so many weary months—was further attested by the presence in the gaping crowd which turned out to meet them of two indubitably Chinese women.

" *Les Chinoises en question,*" says Garnier, " *étaient vieilles, sales et décrépites, mais ils avaient les petits pieds —cela suffisait pour affirmer leur nationalité d'une manière incontestable et justifier l'admiration de mes compagnons.*"

Here the explorers were at last on the very frontiers of the Promised Land. What room for wonder if, after all their privations, all their labours, all their struggles, this precious knowledge served to hearten them again, and to nerve them to renewed endeavour?

In other respects, too, the prospects of the expedition showed signs of brightening. The health of the party had improved; the rainy season was at an end; and the local authorities at Muong Long were proving amenable. The King and the *Sena*, or governing body of Chieng Hong—the immediate objective of the explorers—threatened to create difficulties, however, and Alévy, the invaluable, was sent forward to make the rough paths smooth. De Lagrée and his whole band followed him on September 27th, permission to advance having been accorded to them. The way led through densely populated country, where the streams were crossed by bridges with convenient benches set upon them to invite the weary to repose. After passing the Nam Pui, hilly country was entered where the wooded slopes recalled to the exiles many well-remembered spots in *la belle France*. The track, however, led up and down hill unceasingly, and now and again lost itself in bogs, the flagged road having ended at a very short distance from Muong Long. The people of this district were mostly Khos tribesmen, a pale-skinned race whose presence in this European-looking country emphasised its resemblance to the dear home-land. The ending of the wet season had let loose the dammed-up trade of Chieng Hong, and numerous caravans of laden pack-bullocks, bearing stores of tea, lead, cotton, and tobacco, were met upon the road.

On September 29th the explorers emerged on to the great plain of Chieng Hong, *vià* the valley of a tributary of the Nam Ha, a river which falls into the Mekong at Chip Song Panna. Having passed across the plain, on which villages newly reared stood cheek by jowl with others which a ruthless war had ruined, and having crossed the Nam Ha by ferry-boat, the travellers camped in a pagoda without the walls of Chieng Hong, where

they were speedily joined by Alévy. He had failed to
obtain an interview with the King, or with either the
Chinese or the Burmese agent stationed at the Court of
this much administered monarch; but he had harangued
the *Sena*, and had bluffed that august body into grant-
ing permission to his employers to advance to Chieng
Hong. On the very morning of their arrival, after a
great discussion in the *Sena*, the Chinese agent had
left post-haste for Yun-nan, for what purpose was
unknown.

De Lagrée acted promptly, and called upon the *Sena*
to give him a formal refusal in writing to his request to
be allowed to proceed, or else to furnish the transport
necessary to enable him to continue his journey. The
Sena finally yielded, wherefore an audience with the
King was arranged, and the requisite transport was
promised. Garnier did not attend the interview, for,
finding himself once more close to the Mekong, he was
fain to visit it. It here measures about 400 yards across,
running between high banks, and Garnier followed it up
for some miles, though, as the trade-tracks lie at a considerable distance from the stream, the dense bamboo
jungle made walking somewhat difficult. What he saw
of it reminded him of the troubled reaches above Vien
Chan; for the Mekong flows towards Chieng Hong
through broken and mountainous country. The ruins of
the old town, destroyed by Maha Sai and completely
overgrown with jungle, were also visited by several
members of the expedition, and the remains of the palace
and of one pagoda proved to be of great interest, their
architecture and ornamentation surpassing in beauty and

originality anything seen by the travellers since their entry into the Laos country.

Leaving Chieng Hong on October 8th, the explorers crossed the Mekong upon a huge ferry-raft just above the town.

" *C'était la dernière fois que nous naviguions les eaux du Mékong,*" writes Garnier, with very genuine grief in his words; " *il fallait dire un adieu définitif à tous ces paysages imposants ou gracieux avec lesquels un long séjour sur ses bords nous avait familiarisés. Les fêtes sur l'eau, les courses de pirogues, les illuminations vénitiennes, les dangers et les plaisirs qui lui avaient fait une place à part dans nos souvenirs, tout cela allaient être remplacé sur la scène du voyage par des décors nouveaux et des impressions d'un autre genre.*"

The uncertain promise of the future, despite its mystery and its compelling interest, was powerless to console at least one heart among the adventurers for this parting with the great river which had borne them company for so long, and which had won so great a place in his affections. Still, Chieng Hong was the uttermost point to which McLeod had attained in 1837; now, after a lapse of thirty years, it was to fall to the lot of this little band of Frenchmen to penetrate into lands which had hitherto been hidden from the prying eyes of the West. In this thought there was magic, and a rich reward for privations passed and dangers yet to come.

Once across the Mekong, the explorers zigzagged up the hills, through sparsely populated country, to Muong Yang. On October 9th the valley of the Nam Yang was quitted and a mountainous region was entered. The party camped that night at a height of 4,500 feet above sea-level, and so passed on to Chieng Nua, the last important Shan village, which is regarded as "the portal of China." On October 12th the Frenchmen quitted the valley of the Nam Yot, in which Chieng Nua stands, by a narrow gorge which led them to Muong Pang, a village which, half hidden in a fold of the hills, 3,800 feet above sea-level, was found to be in some sort an integral portion of the Celestial Empire—the first outpost of the Promised Land. The population was partly Thai, partly Chinese, and huts built on the ground had replaced the houses perched on piles in use in the Shan States, while benches, tables, ploughs, winnowing machines, and the improved character of the tillage, all bore witness to the existence of a higher standard of civilisation. The immense energy of the Chinese, as evidenced even here on the outskirts of their empire, struck the explorers with admiration and surprise after their long sojourn among folk of a lesser breed. That night they were treated to a "musical" entertainment, in which certain athletic Thais performed gymnastic exercises with feet, knees, and hands, upon a number of gongs.

From Muong Pang the party made its way to Chu Chai, through country in which villages were perched on the caps of most of the hills, amid clumps of oak and pine, while maize had replaced rice crops on the higher levels, and plums, pears, peaches, and vegetables such as the Chinese love, were cultivated in great abundance. Chu Chai, reached on October 16th, was the first purely Chinese place met with, and Garnier noted that the peculiar power of the Chinese civilisation to mould all whom it influences into conformity with a single type was as plainly evident here as in the country between Tien-Tsin and Peking, which he had visited during the Franco Chinese war.

"*Nous retrouvions partout,*" he writes, "*ce cachet d'uniformité routinière qu'une civilisation, vieille de plusieurs milliers d'années, a su imprimer aux mœurs d'une immense population, malgré la diversité des origines et l'étendue d'un territoire qui réunit tous les climats.*"

The devastation caused by the Muhammadan rebellion was now becoming apparent; moreover the ravages of cholera had caused many homesteads to be deserted. The events of the insurrection were painted by the natives in lurid colours, and the prowess of the rebels and the marvellous weapons at their disposal were exaggerated fantastically. Passing through this land of roofless houses, deserted fields, and blackened ruins, the explorers came at last to an immense plain, in the centre of which is Se-Mao, the first Chinese city of Yun-nan. The goal towards which they had been struggling with such splendid endurance was reached. Here was China in very truth, and her portals had at length been forced upon the western side.

"*Ce ne fut pas sans une vive émotion que nous saluâmes cette première ville chinoise qui dressait devant nous ses toits hospitaliers. Après dix-huit mois de fatigues, après avoir traversé des régions presque vierges encore de pas humains, nous nous trouvions en présence d'une cité de l'Orient. Pour la première fois, des voyageurs européens pénétraient en Chine par la frontière indo-chinoise! A ce moment sans doute, notre enthousiasme dépassa la mesure: les souffrances dont nous l'avions payé nous exagérèrent l'importance du résultat, et, un instant, nous crûmes de bonne foi que la Chine se révélait enfin à l'Europe, represéntée par six Français!"*

It was a great achievement, and the victory was all the more precious because it had been bought at the price of so much toil and suffering, yet I make no doubt that the band of hardy adventurers felt, in this first moment of their triumph, that for all their pains they now received " an over-payment of delight."

The entrance of the explorers into Se-Mao, where they were received by genuflecting mandarins, an escort of soldiers, and huge crowds of curious spectators, was an occasion of some embarrassment to the travel-worn members of the expedition. Shoeless and with their clothes in tatters, they were conscious of cutting a despicable figure in the eyes of their punctilious and form-loving hosts, but for all that they were kindly treated by the Governor, and on October 30th they pushed on to Pu-ul-fu. Se-Mao was at this time an immense armed camp. Fighting was even then going on at Muong Ka and Muong Pan with the Kuitze, as the insurgent Muhammadans were called, and the local authorities had ceased to be practically controlled by the central Government at Peking. Having procured shoes at the shops of Se-Mao, the travellers passed with comfort over the paved road leading from that place to Pu-ul-fu, though the country all around was utterly devastated. Pu-ul-fu, which is the capital of a province of which Se-Mao, Tai-lang, and Uei-yuan are the principal towns, was under the charge of a prefect, "*melancolique docteur à bouton rouge*," who was suffering badly from funk, and entreated de Lagrée to abandon his project of further exploration of lands so troublous.

Garnier had been pestering his chief for permission to go alone across country to the Mekong, distant some seven days' journey from Pu-ul-fu, but after weighing all the chances, de Lagrée decided that the risks were too great, and his lieutenant had to resign himself to the abandonment of the object he had nearest at heart—the discovery of the sources of the great river.

From Pu-ul-fu the party crossed through hilly country into the valley of the Pa-pien, an affluent of the Black River, or Song Bo, which is one of the main branches of the Song Koi, or Red River of Tongking. New heights were scaled leading up to the plateau of Yun-nan, and after passing through the town of Tong Kuan and crossing the Pu-ku Kiang in boats, the travellers reached Tai-lang, a city somewhat smaller than Pu-ul-fu, on November 9th. Here potatoes were found for the first time for many long months, while the surrounding district yielded an abundance of European fruits. An extraordinary feature of this valley was that peaches, pears, and chestnuts were growing almost side by side with mangoes, guavas and other tropical fruits. Here too a new tribe of "wild folk" was met—the Ho-Nhi—a fine race, resembling the Khas Khos, in whom Garnier thought to detect specimens of the aboriginal people from whom the natives of Laos and the Shan States are descended. The important gold mines in the vicinity, in which as many as 10,000 labourers had been employed in peaceful times, were also visited.

On November 16th, climbing the heights to the east of Tai-lang, near the summits of which the first fields of the opium-poppy were seen, the explorers marched all day through pelting rain. After crossing a torrent by means of a very fine stone bridge, and breasting a steep ascent, they looked down upon the valley of the Ho-ti-Kiang, in which, amid verdure and cultivation of a semi-tropical character, is situated the town of Yuan-kiang. This place was ruled by the Thais until the Chinese finally possessed themselves of it in 1712, and large numbers of the "wild" people called Pa-i, who seem to be a branch of the Thai family, still live in its neighbourhood. Near Yuan-kiang large quantities of cotton and sugar-cane are grown, and Joubert visited the copper mines which are also a feature of the district. The town stands on the banks of the Ho-ki Kiang, which is here some 300 yards across. Lower down the stream narrows, but is navigable for some distance until its bed becomes impeded by rapids. Down the Ho-ki Kiang the expedition proceeded in boats to Pu-pio, whence a road leads to Che-pin. Here there is an impassable rapid, but Garnier obtained a boat below this obstruction and followed the river down for some distance. It ran through deep gorges pent between heights which sometimes attained an elevation of 3,000 feet, and very soon a rapid was reached which could not be negotiated. Garnier accordingly had to scale the cliffs, a matter of some difficulty, and to make his way to Lin-ngan across a great plateau, arriving there in advance of his chief. His coming caused immense popular excitement, and it was with great relief that Garnier hailed the arrival of de Lagrée and his party on the following day.

At Lin-ngan the explorers made the acquaintance of Leang Ta Jen, a remarkable man who, from humble beginnings, had by sheer force of character, skill in leadership, and courage, succeeded in raising himself to one of the foremost positions in this part of China. A man of herculean build and of vigorous manner, he presented a striking contrast to the poor dyspeptic of Pu-ul-fu, and while he treated the strangers with marked courtesy, did nothing to dissuade them from their enterprise. From him and others Garnier collected, while at Lin-ngan, a considerable number of data concerning the neighbouring provinces and the route to Tongking *viâ* the Red River—data which subsequently aided the Frenchman, Dupuis, to push his discoveries in this direction.

From Lin-ngan the party proceeded across the plain to Che-pin on the borders of a lake some 8½ miles in length, and on December 14th Tong-hai was reached, a town situated on the banks of a lake somewhat larger than that of Che-pin. Here the crowds again proved troublesome.

Tong-hai, like most of the towns of the province at this time, was a great armed camp, and on the heights above it was a fortified post named Tung-Kao, which was held by a band of Muhammadans who remained in possession until 1870, when, having refused the honourable terms of surrender offered to them, they died in a fashion which may fairly be termed heroic. On December 17th the lake of Kiang-Chuan was seen,—a patch of blue water between snow-clad mountains,—its borders tilled and densely peopled, the heights above it barren and covered sparsely with patches of rhododendron scrub.

Passing through an enormous grave-yard on the borders of the lake, the travellers climbed to the summit of a range some 6,000 feet above sea-level, and thence obtained a splendid view of the surrounding country. To the south lay Kiang Chuan with its plain and lake, and with Chin Kiang at its northern extremity; to the north rich valleys fell away to the plain of Yun-nan, in which the greatest of the lakes seemed a veritable sea. Having descended the range, the explorers reached Tsin-ning, at the entrance to the plain, on December 21st, and found that its neighbourhood presented a terrible picture of the devastation which Muhammadans can work in the name of their faith. From this point a paved road led to the town of Yun-nan, and as they passed along it the Frenchmen observed that the signs of ravage ceased, and the increasing traffic and the number and beauty of the wayside buildings showed that they were nearing the capital. Splendid stone bridges, similar to those which had excited the admiration of the travellers near Muong Long, were crossed at frequent intervals, and after long wanderings through countries peopled by weaker races, the innate greatness and energy of the Chinese civilisation struck the visitors with something akin to wonder.

Prairies on the Mekong

From Mission Pavie, by permission of M. Ernest Leroux, Paris

"*Jamais,*" writes Garnier, "*la puissante civilisation dont nous étions les hôtes ne s'était révélée à nous avec autant d'enchantment et sous d'aussi riches apparences. La nouveauté de ce spectacle, marqué dans tous ses détails de ce caractère étrange qui est spécial au Céleste-Empire, le souvenir des forêts et de la barbarie au milieu desquelles nous avions si longtemps vecus nous faisaient parfois croire à un rêve, et nous nous surprenions à rougir de nos allures misérables et de nos costumes informes et souillés, en croisant un palanquin ou en frôlant les robes de soie des bourgeois qui se pressaient sur le seuil de leur maisons pour voir passer les étrangers.*"

Yun-nan was sighted at mid-day, and presently a minor mandarin arriving from the city handed to de Lagrée a letter written in French! Coming now at the end of so long a period of exile and isolation, this missive was to the wanderers as a very breath of Home. They gathered round their chief and scanned the precious page with hungry eyes; it seemed to them, inconsequently enough, that they would now learn the tidings of France for which they were pining. They entered the city through its southern portal, and passing up the long street amid curious crowds took possession of the yamen which had been placed at their disposal. They were met by some of the officials of the place, and Père Protteau, the author of the letter, hastened to introduce himself to his compatriots. The town was in a state bordering upon panic caused by recent Muhammadan successes. It was a great rectangular place, enclosed by walls measuring 2 miles by 1¼, and its population of 50,000 souls were all professedly in the Imperial interest, although many of them were Muslims, the Muhammadans of Yunnan being divided at this time into two camps, the one loyal to Peking, the other paying allegiance to the Sultan whose capital was Ta-li-fu.

The insurrection had had its beginning more than ten years earlier, in 1856, when the Muhammadans of Yunnan city rose and pillaged that place. The Chinese authorities thereupon decided upon a general massacre of the Muslims, and in the city of Yun-nan alone some thousands perished. With the hour of the Muslims' need, however, came also the man,—one Tu-uan-si,— who taking the field with some forty of his coreligionists, was speedily joined by others who had escaped the general massacre. With 600 men this leader marched upon Ta-li-fu, the town of next importance to the capital in the province of Yun-nan, and here the garrison of 4,000 soldiers, many of them Muslims, surrendered to him without a blow being struck. The Chinese authorities immediately besieged Ta-li-fu, but their troops were routed, and the victorious Muhammadans promptly marched against Yun-nan. Pang, the governor of the province, succeeded in checking their advance, but he was assassinated shortly afterwards, and a Muhammadan Haji, styled Lao Papa, was proclaimed emperor. Ma Tien, who later assumed the title of Ma Ta Jen, a Muhammadan leader professedly in the Imperial interest, lost no time in deposing Lao Papa, who thereupon retired into obscurity, though as a great doctor of Muhammadan Law he continued to exercise considerable religious influence over all the Muslims of the province. Ma Ta Jen set up in his stead a governor on whom he conferred the title of Lao Ta Jen, though the actual power continued to be vested in the Muhammadan king-maker. In the south, Leang Ta Jen, the giant of whom mention has already been made, refused to obey either Ma Ta Jen or his puppet, and the two factions, both nominally Imperial, were soon at open warfare. In the encounters which resulted the giant had the best of it, and Ma Ta Jen was for a period a prisoner at Lin-ngan. Later an accommodation was come to, and Ma Ta Jen, being set at liberty, succeeded in driving the rebel Muhammadans out of Yun-nan. They then fell back upon Ta-li-fu, which they fortified, and which thenceforth became their capital and the centre of their power. The adventurer Tu-uan-si was there proclaimed Sultan in 1867. In the southern portion of the province Leang Ta Jen, the giant, continued to reign, practically without reference to Peking, while at the time of the Frenchmen's visit Ma Ta Jen was supreme in the north, Lao Papa, his dreams of temporal power laid aside, living peacefully in the city of Yun-nan. Throughout all these troubles Peking maintained an attitude of magnificent indifference, the fact being that the interest of the Imperial authorities in this outlying flange of the empire ceased to be active when the province itself discontinued the regular payment of tribute.

On the day following his arrival, de Lagrée hastened to pay a visit to Ma Ta Jen, and was well received; but the king-maker was powerless to further his guest's desire to proceed to Ta-li-fu, whence it would be possible to explore the upper reaches of the Mekong. Beyond

the confines of his immediate province, the authority of
this Muhammadan viceroy did not run, and the Ta-li-fu
district, as has been said, was in the hands of the rebel
Sultan. From the excellent Père Protteau, also, neither
aid nor information could be obtained. The good priest
was kindly, courteous, and devoted. Dressed in Chinese
costume, living on native food and in the native fashion,
he appeared to have become totally denationalised, and
he stood in great awe of the local authorities. He was
zealous in his religious work, however, and the Frenchmen had the curious experience of attending Midnight
Mass on Christmas Day in this distant Chinese city. On
January 2nd, however, another missionary arrived. This
was Père Fenouil, who, under his native name of Ko-
su-to, had been heard of by the explorers as a first-rate
fighting man and an indefatigable manufacturer of gun-
powder, ever since their arrival in Chinese territory.

" *Nous retrouvâmes en lui*," writes Garnier, " *un
homme qui pleurait à la pensée de sa mère, un Français
dont le cœur battait toujours au nom de sa patrie. Nous
admirâmes l'obscur dévouement du P. Protteau, nous
aimâmes le P. Fenouil.*"

Acting on the advice of this new-comer, de Lagrée
paid a visit to Lao Papa, the Muhammadan sage and
saint who for a day had played the proud rôle of emperor
in Yun-nan. The holy man was much interested in
astronomy, and had in his possession a fine telescope,
brought at much expense from Singapore. Over this in-
strument, which hitherto had defied his attempts to focus
it, a pact of friendship was presently sealed, Lao Papa

furnishing the explorers with letters recommending them
to all his coreligionists. Ma Ta Jen, for his part, advanced 5,000 francs to de Lagrée, saying that repayment
was quite unnecessary, but that if the Frenchman was
really concerned about such details, he might send him
the equivalent in rifles when he reached the coast. One
cannot but be struck with the extraordinary hospitality,
courtesy and kindness with which the strangers were
invariably treated by the authorities in China. From the
crowds collected to stare at them they occasionally suffered some inconvenience, but I greatly question whether
the first Chinese to penetrate to London would have
fared better at the hands of the English populace had
they ventured abroad in our streets.

Leaving Yun-nan on January 8th, the travellers descended into the valley of the Li-tang Ho, which falls
into the Blue River near Tong-Chuan, and passing
through forest country reached the village of Kon-chang
on the 14th. Here de Lagrée was attacked by fever, and
on the following day, when heights 7,800 feet above sea-
level had to be scaled, he was so ill that it became necessary to carry him in a palanquin. Descending from this
point to Tai-phu, the explorers followed the banks of
the river for a short distance and then embarked in boats
which carried them through desolate, woe-begone looking country to Tong-Chuan. De Lagrée's condition had
now become so critical that he was forced to abandon
all idea of continuing his journey, and deciding to keep
the doctor, Joubert, with him, he instructed the remainder
of the party, under Garnier, to make an attempt to reach
the Muhammadan stronghold of Ta-li-fu.

For this place a start was made on January 30th.
On the following day the waters of the Kin-sha Kiang,
the upper branch of the Yang-tse, were seen near their
junction with the Li-tang Ho, 1,800 feet below the track
cut in the mountain-side, and the explorers had the delight of thinking that, since the days of Marco Polo, no
white men had looked upon this river at a point so far
distant from the coast. On February 1st the Kin-sha
Kiang was crossed by ferry, and the province of Se-
Chuan was entered. The river was 200 yards in width,
but owing to big rapids lower down it was still quite
useless for purposes of navigation. Climbing heights on
the farther bank to an altitude of 3,600 feet, the party
made its way through mountainous country, amid frequent snow-storms, crossing the summit on February 3rd.
Descending to Tzan-hi-pa the travellers found some
native Christians, and leaving them, passed to Chang-chu,
beyond which place the country becomes less wild and
difficult. Thence they made their way to the plain on
which Hui-lu-chu, an important trading centre, stands,
and from there to Hong-pu-so, a visit being paid to the
point where the Ya-long Kiang joins the Kin-sha at a
distance of 8½ miles from the last named town. On
February 11th a young native priest, Père Lu, who had
been educated at the missionary college of Pûlau Tîkus
near Penang, arrived at Hong-pu-so, and consented to
accompany the party to Ma-chang. On the road thither
some coal-mines were visited. Coal was the fuel in general use in this district, and the chimneys with which
the houses were fitted struck the Europeans as objects at
once familiar and unfamiliar. On February 16th the

Yang-tse was crossed, and the night was passed in an isolated homestead 4,000 feet above sea-level. The country, covered with pine forests, was sparsely inhabited, but the great step had been taken—the borders of the Muhammadan kingdom had been crossed.

Switchbacking over hilly ground the explorers rejoined the direct track from Hong-pu-so to Ta-li-fu, which they had temporarily abandoned, and found a considerable traffic plying along it. The road led along the banks of the Pe-ma Ho, a considerable river, and here the flag of the insurgent Muhammadans was first seen. The valley of this river was quitted on February 20th,—mountains 9,000 feet in height having to be scaled,—and a descent was made into the valley of the Pe-yen-tzin. Following a left influent of that stream, the explorers crossed another divide into the plain of Pin-Chuan, where the devastation of the country was even more deplorable than in any of the districts previously traversed, the only inhabited places being miserable huts which were fortified against attack. At Pin-Chuan an inn was found, and the letter from Lao Papa had its desired effect upon the local authorities, who made no attempt to detain the travellers. Another climb brought the party to Pien-kio, where another native priest, Père Fang, also a Pûlau Tikus man, was found. By his aid a letter was despatched to Père Leguilcher, a French priest whose advice Garnier was anxious to obtain, and the morrow being Ash Wednesday, the explorers attended Mass and received the ashes upon their foreheads, with the reminder that "Man is dust, and unto dust he shall return." The fact was already patent to their imagination, for the country through which they were now travelling held its own terrible record of suffering and death. It had been raided again and again by the " Whites," or rebel Muslims, and by the " Reds," or Imperialists, while the tribesmen of the hills, plundering on their own account, had completed the tale of ruin.

The river which runs through the plain of Pien-kio was crossed by a fine stone bridge, and the same afternoon a summit, 9,000 feet in altitude, was climbed. From the top glimpses were caught of a few houses down below, surrounded by trees, and a cross surmounting one of the buildings showed that Père Leguilcher's mission had been reached. This devoted man, who in the face of all dangers had remained at his post in the heart of the Muhammadan country, placed himself unreservedly at the disposal of his countrymen, and consented to accompany them to Ta-li-fu.

After a day's rest the descent was continued to Kuang-tia-pin, and when the hills which lie beyond this little town had been scaled, the lake of Ta-li was seen, its blue waters, surrounded by villages and gardens, with great snow-clad mountains for a background, making one of the most beautiful and impressive sights upon which the explorers had looked during the whole course of their wanderings. Ta-li-fu stands on the margin of the lake and is enclosed on all sides by mountains, the only practicable passes at each extremity of the valley being guarded by the fortified towns of Hiang-Kuan and Hia-Kuan respectively. A paved road runs along the whole length of the valley, and over this the Frenchmen tramped on March 2nd. A great uneasiness fell upon the native portion of the cortège as the capital was neared, and Père Leguilcher's native Christians deserted one by one till not a single man remained. Ta-li-fu, however, was reached without incident, and was entered by the northern gate. Immense crowds had gathered in the main street, and the strangers were met by two mandarins and conducted to a yamen which had been prepared for their accommodation. Formal visits were paid to Garnier, and all appeared to be going so well that he had high hopes of once more visiting the banks of the Mekong, when quite suddenly Père Leguilcher was sent for by the Sultan, and was informed that the expedition must forthwith return by the way it had come. This was a terrible blow to Garnier, who attributed the abrupt change of attitude to the suspicions of the Sultan's military advisers. He also, quaintly enough, finds an additional reason in the supposition that he and his fellows must have been mistaken for Englishmen! The Muslim populations are in touch all the world over, he argues; those of India must of course hate Englishmen; therefore the Muhammadans of Ta-li-fu must hate Englishmen. The Sultan of Ta-li-fu having behaved with brutal rudeness to a band of Frenchmen, it follows that the nationality of the latter cannot have been known, and that they must have been mistaken for Englishmen. To the average Frenchman, seemingly, there is nothing ridiculous in accusing our countrymen of " filling the butchers' shops with large, blue flies! "

For twenty-four hours, during which the ill-will of the authorities became momentarily more and more apparent, Garnier remained at Ta-li-fu, and it was only after a bitter struggle that he abandoned all hopes of revisiting the valley of the Mekong. On March 4th he started back, passing rapidly through Hiang-kuan, and reaching Kuang-ti-pin after spending a night at Ma-cha. The authorities now evinced a disposition to persecute Père Leguilcher, but Garnier supported the good priest with so brave a show of force that he was suffered to go his way unmolested to the mission station at Tu-tui-tze. His position, however, had now become untenable, and greatly to his own regret and that of his native Christians, he was obliged to accompany Garnier out of the Muhammadan dominions.

The journey to Ta-li-fu was unquestionably the most hazardous exploit undertaken by the explorers during the whole course of their travels, a fact which was recognised by the Royal Geographical Society when, in May, 1870, they conferred upon Francis Garnier the Patron's Medal. Garnier begged that this distinction should be divided between him and his late chief, de Lagrée, but to this the Council would not consent, stating that such divisions were contrary to their rules, and adding that the medal was given more particularly for the journey to the Muhammadan capital.

At Ta-li-fu the Tibetan element in the population was strongly marked; pilgrimages from Tibet to the caves of The-Tong, to the south-east of Kuan-tia-pin, were made with frequency; and prior to the troublous times of the Muhammadan rebellion, commercial intercourse with both Tibet and Burma had attained to considerable proportions. On the eastern borders of the lake, tribes known as Min-kin and Penti were met with, who are said to be the descendants of the original Chinese settled in the valley by Kublai Kaan.

From Ma-chang Garnier and his party crossed the range to Kan-chu-tse, 7,500 feet above sea-level, whence they descended to Sen-o-kai. Leaving this place on March 18th they once more entered the valley of the upper Yang-tsè, and reached Mong-ku on the 31st, after Thorel had paid a visit to the copper mines of Tsin-chui-ho. From Mong-ku the river was explored by Garnier, who found it too much obstructed by rapids to be navigable. On April 2nd a letter was received from Joubert conveying the sad news of the death of Doudart de Lagrée on March 12th. The loss of the chief under whom all had been serving for nearly two years was a keen personal grief to every member of the expedition, and the tragedy of the event was deepened by the fact that death had come to him on the eve of the longed-for return to civilisation. De Lagrée lacked, it is probable, the initiative and the geographical instinct of Francis Garnier, but in appointing him to the leadership the Government had made a wise selection. His mingled gentleness and firmness, combined with his great natural aptitude for dealing with Orientals, had contributed enormously to the success of the expedition, and his wisdom and calm good sense placed a useful restraint upon the impetuosity of his ardent young lieutenant. At a later period the enemies of the latter were never weary of accusing Garnier of having filched from his dead chief the honour and glory of their common exploits, but nothing could be further from the truth. From first to last, in season and out of season, Garnier let no opportunity escape him of paying well-deserved tributes to the memory of the man who had been at once his leader and his friend. When the learned societies of Europe showered distinctions upon him, he pleaded, often with success, that they should be divided between himself and de Lagrée's widow, and though he suffered cruelly from the calumnies spread concerning him, he never made the slightest attempt to defend himself at the expense of the dead. The fact remains, however, that the exploration of the Mekong was an idea of which Garnier was the originator; that by far the greater part of the geographical results obtained represented his individual work; and that the success of the expedition was due in great measure to his untiring energy and shrewd advice, while the dangerous journey to Ta-li-fu was made under his sole leadership.

On April 5th the body of de Lagrée, which had been buried at Tong-Chuan, was disinterred in order that it might be conveyed to Saigon, and a rude monument was erected on the spot where it had lain. On the 9th the Ngian-nan, a tributary of the Kin-sha, was crossed at Kiang-ti, and next day the plateau of Kiang-ti was reached. Thence the party passed to Chao-tung, and crossing some low hills, finally quitted the plateau of Yun-nan, descending into the hot, moist valley of the Yang-tse. The party embarked on a big boat at Lao-ua-tan, on April 20th, and after spending a day or two with Mgr. Ponsot, the Bishop of Yun-nan, at Long-ki, proceeded down river to Kieu-long-tan, where boats were engaged for the journey to Su-chau. At this place, reached on May 5th, two junks were hired, and on May

27th the French Consulate at Han-kau was reached, and the remarkable journey was ended.

An American steamer, the *Plymouth Rock*, conveyed the travellers to Shanghai, whence after a week's stay they left for Saigon, which was reached on June 29th, 1868, after an absence of two years and twenty-four days.

The exploration of the sources of the Mekong, the main object for the attainment of which the expedition had been organised, had not been effected, and the valley of that river had not been visited at any point above Chieng Hong, to which McLeod had attained in 1837. Similarly, the dream of a trade-route from Yun-nan to Saigon *viâ* the Mekong had proved to be no more than a dream. Thus far, therefore, the great expedition may be accounted to have failed, but on the other hand it could lay claim to some remarkable achievements. A detailed survey of the valley of the Mekong had been made from Pnom Penh to a point a day's march above the rapid of Tang He, and the river had been frequently visited between that place and Chieng Hong. Most of the large tributaries below Luang Prabang had been explored in detail. A vast area in Laos and the Shan States, where no white man had hitherto set foot, had been carefully examined; China had been reached from the south; much of Yun-nan had been explored and surveyed for the first time; and finally, in circumstances of great difficulty, Ta-li-fu had been visited. In addition to this much information had been collected concerning not only the geography, but the social, commercial and political condition, of the countries traversed. Facts bearing upon the history and upon the difficult ethnological problems of this part of Asia had been assiduously noted and recorded, the whole being subsequently embodied by Garnier in his elaborate *Publication Officielle*. The expedition had the good fortune to be well received by the natives throughout almost the whole of its journey, a fact which was due in a measure to the tact of its members; but none the less the important results which it achieved were only obtained at the price of an immense amount of toil, of persistent effort, of suffering, and of patient endurance. Long months of exile in the wilderness, of complete severance from their kind, of privation and acute discomfort, never succeeded in disheartening the travellers, who, through so much individual sacrifice, were able to secure for France the honour of having penetrated, first of all the white nations, into the southern provinces of China by one of the great overland routes of south-eastern Asia.

CHAPTER XI

THE Burmese war of 1826 forced upon the attention of the Government of India a recognition of the perilously scant measure of knowledge at its disposal concerning the topography of the country lying beyond its borders. The only part of upper Burma which at that time was known to Europeans was the Irawadi River from Rangoon and Bassein to Ava, over which so many British envoys had travelled on humiliating embassies. Lieutenant Woods, who accompanied Symes to Ava in 1798, had made a survey of this part of the river, and Dr. Buchanan on the same occasion had collected a considerable amount of information relating to the districts traversed. Writing in 1835, Pemberton states that to the geographical and statistical facts ascertained by these officers no material addition had been made up to the time of the outbreak of the first Burmese war, and he mentions that the frontier officers had been blamed for this by the Government of India. It was forgotten that the attitude maintained by the British authorities in Calcutta towards the Court of Ava had fostered and flattered the natural arrogance of the Burmese; that the humiliations inflicted with impunity upon our envoys had brought us nothing but contempt; and that the Burmese frontier chiefs, sublimely conscious of their innate superiority to a mere white man, had resolutely declined to permit our officers to acquaint themselves with the districts beyond their jurisdiction. In these circumstances information gleaned from native sources—information of a notoriously inaccurate and unsatisfactory description—was the best that could be placed at the service of Sir Archibald Campbell when he assumed the command of our army in the field, and it is fortunate that the war was brought to a termination by the peace of Yandabu before the march upon Ava *viâ* Arakan, which he at one time contemplated, had been attempted. In the absence of all local knowledge such a venture might quite easily have ended in disaster, and realising this the Government of India determined to avoid having again to fight in the dark in this fashion— at any rate in so far as Burma was concerned. From this time forward, therefore, no opportunity of acquiring knowledge of the topography of Burma was suffered to escape, and the exploration of the country by Englishmen began in earnest.

Major Burney, as we have seen, was appointed British Resident at Ava on December 31st, 1829. Travelling *viâ* Rangoon he reached his post in the following April. Even after the defeat which it had suffered and the loss of Tenasserim, the Court of Ava had not learned its lesson, and its arrogance was unabated. Burney succeeded in obtaining his audience of the King on a day which was not a *Kodau*, or " beg-pardon day," and was the first of our envoys to do so and to avoid being paraded round the palace, bowing humbly to it, before gaining admittance to the presence chamber. None the less he was forced to unslipper at the entrance to the audience hall, and he owed it entirely to his own astuteness and firmness that he escaped being the victim of numerous other impertinences. In spite of his inauspicious beginning, Burney gradually won a considerable influence at the Court, and during the eight years that he resided at Ava the British were more free than ever before to come and go through the country under Burman jurisdiction.

In August, 1830, Lieutenant Pemberton, who had been serving in Manipur, travelled overland to Ava, and in company with Burney succeeded in settling certain outstanding boundary disputes. He came over the mountains by the Akui route to Kindat, and so through the valley of the Chindwin, the great right tributary of the Irawadi, to the mouth of that river and thence to Ava, thus filling in a large blank upon the then existing map of north-western Burma. On January 20th of the following year Dr. Richardson left Ava, in obedience to instructions given to him by Burney, and made his way overland to Shwebo, then a town of less than 1,000 houses, surrounded by a dilapidated wall and a dry ditch, and containing a large pagoda and the ruins of a once royal palace. Shwebo, which lies some five and sixty miles to the north-west of Mandalay, is now the first station of importance on the railway line from that place to Katha. Richardson reached Shwebo on January 23rd, and thence went in a westerly direction to a small jungle village called Benthi, where the track turned abruptly to the north. The Chindwin, or Ningthi, River was struck at Thun-buk on January 28th, and Maukadau was reached on the following day. From this place the track lay

through jungle, and after passing several villages of
trifling importance, Kendat was reached on February
2nd. Here Richardson was able to procure specimens of
the lignite found in the vicinity, and he also heard of the
amber mines of the Hukong valley, some " forty days up
the Chindwin from Kendat," which were subsequently
visited by Captain Hannay. At Kendat Richardson was
joined by Captain Grant, who had come thither from
Manipur. His journey was the first made by a white
man over the Angochin hills and along the banks of the
Chindwin from Mulfu to Kendat, and supplemented the
geographical information collected by Pemberton during
his trip from Manipur to Ava in the preceding year.

In a valuable report furnished by the latter officer to
the Government of India in 1835, a detailed account is
given of the whole of the eastern frontier of India as it
then was. Pemberton begins by describing from personal
observation the mountain system to the north and east
of Manipur, and gives details of three routes from that
State into Burma territory,—those by Akui, by Kala
Naga, and through the Koki villages. He next, still as
the result of personal exploration, gives a detailed account of Arakan and of its communications with Chittagong, passing on to a description of the footpaths over
the Yoma mountains from Arakan into Burma. The
best of these was that by the Aeng Pass, first traversed
by Captain David Ross with a small military force in
March, 1826. In 1830 this route was explored to the
summit from the Arakan side by Captain White, and in
September of the same year Pemberton travelled by river
from Ava to Mimbu, on the right bank of the Irawadi,

and thence tramped to Aeng, whence he crossed the range into Arakan. In March of the following year, accompanied by Captain Jenkins, he examined this pass in detail and reported upon it to the Government of India. Pemberton was thus able to furnish an exact account of the Indian borders from Assam and Manipur to Arakan, and of the routes leading therefrom into Burma, all of which was mainly the result of his own explorations; further, in the same report, he attempts some description of the country lying between India, Burma, and Yun-nan, collected from native sources.

In 1835–36 Captain S. F. Hannay made an important journey from Ava to the Hukong valley. The occasion for this was furnished by a dispute between the chiefs of two tribes of Singfos which had led to a raid, headed by one Dupha Gam, into which a Burmese commission was appointed to inquire. Burney seized the opportunity to send an officer with this commission, and Hannay accordingly left Ava by river in November, 1835. Up to this time the valley of the Irawadi above Ava had been completely unknown to Europeans. In the seventeenth century the British certainly, and possibly also the Dutch, had had a factory at Bhamo, but that was not the age of exact survey or precise information, and though the name of the place was familiarly known to Europeans from that time forward, it was virgin soil for the explorer when Hannay visited it.

Owing to the existence of a practical monopoly of the trade with the upper districts of the Irawadi, which was held by the Chinese traders in Ava, no foreigner, and only Burmese who had obtained special authorisation,

were permitted to ascend the river above the Choki of
Tsampaynago, wherefore when Hannay passed above
this point he entered country which had long been closed
to all save the natives inhabiting it and a very few men
from districts farther south. At Yedan the first " *kiuk-
dwen*," or rocky defile, was entered. Below it the river
varied in breadth from a mile to two and a half miles;
in the defile itself the river narrowed down and in places
was not more than 150 yards from bank to bank. Great
bamboo rafts, similar to those observed by Garnier in
Laos, were here met with, their freight consisting of
pickled tea. The defile was entered on November 30th,
eight days after leaving Ava, and the water, which attained a great depth, was described by Hannay as being
" almost as still as a lake." Tsampaynago was reached
on December 1st, and here the direction of the famous
ruby mines was pointed out to the traveller, who judged
them to lie some thirty or forty miles away behind a
conspicuous peak called Shueu Tung. At Tagaung Myu,
reached four days later, Hannay found the crumbling
remains of walls, all that was left of the city said to
have been founded by a king from western India, whose
descendants afterwards founded kingdoms at Prome,
Pagan and Ava. The old fort of Tagaung had been
built of brick, and what could still be seen of it convinced Hannay that its architecture was peculiar and
was distinct from that of the Burmese. A mile to the
south Hannay reported the existence of the extensive
ruins of Pagan, which he described as stretching away
" as far as the eye can see." It was in this neighbourhood that teak trees first began to appear on the banks

On the Irawadi River, in the First Defile

From a hill 800 feet high

of the river. From Tagaung Hannay also took a cross-bearing to the ruby mines, which he placed some 45 or 50 miles to the east of his point of observation.

At Yebuk Yua boats bringing Chinese merchants from Bhamo were passed, and on December 13th Katha was reached. The river here ran between high banks which were about a quarter of a mile apart, and Hannay estimated its volume and velocity at 52,272 cubic feet per second, which would be about two-thirds of that of the Ganges at the same season. Katha was at this time a town of only some 400 houses, that is to say about 2,000 souls. By December 17th the traveller had entered the great curve of the Irawadi from east to west which leads from Bhamo to Katha, and soon the increasing number of villages upon the river's banks showed that the neighbourhood of the former town was reached. The island of Kywundo, upon which stand a hundred pagodas, was passed just below the entrance to the second *kiuk-dwen*, a defile which is pent between hills averaging some 400 feet in height; in one place where the height is 500 feet, the side of the defile is described as being " as perpendicular as a wall." This defile is some four miles in length, and the cliffs on either hand are composed of sandstone upon a base of blue limestone veined in places by streaks of white marble.

On December 20th Kungtun was reached, and here Hannay met people of the " wild " tribe called Kakhyens who belong to a type which is clearly not Tatar, and nearly resembles that of the Caucasian races. The next day the traveller arrived at Bhamo itself, the " largest place in Burma except Ava and Rangoon," consisting at the time of Hannay's visit of about 1,500 houses, or 2,000 including its immediate environs, and having a population of some 9,000 souls. The Chinese quarter was composed of 200 houses, and from the Chinese traders Hannay obtained some valuable information concerning the passes from Bhamo into Yun-nan. The best route lay, as does the highway now in use, up the valley of the Ta-ping River to Ta-li-fu *viâ* Yung-Chang, the river itself being crossed by a ferry. Geographers had for a long time been of opinion that the Ta-ping was identical with the Tsangpo, the course of which after its disappearance in Tibet was then not known. The information which Hannay collected concerning the size of the Ta-ping, and the fact that it falls into the Irawadi on the left bank of that river, disposed once for all of this opinion, the Tsangpo being, as a matter of fact, the name borne in its uppermost reaches by the Brahmaputra. None the less, the identity of the Tsangpo with the upper course of the Irawadi was advanced by Mgr. de Mazure, Vicar Apostolic of Tibet, and received a qualified endorsement from Yule, as late as 1861.

After leaving Bhamo Hannay found the country through which the Irawadi ran far more hilly than any hitherto traversed. The third defile was entered at Thaphan Beng, and here the river was sometimes not more than eighty yards across. At a village above this defile a new tribe of " wild " folk was met with—the Phwongs—who built their long houses on piles and placed the thatch upon the roofs in such a fashion that it nearly touched the ground on either side. On December 26th the part of the Irawadi in which navigation

The Bazaar at Bhamo

becomes most dangerous was reached, the stream being beset with rapids and the country around showing obvious traces of volcanic disturbance. At Tshenbo, a point some ten miles below the mouth of the Mogaung River, the boats which had brought the party from Ava were exchanged for others of smaller size and more shallow draught, but it is noticeable that as far as this, that is to say some 400 miles above Ava, the Irawadi had been proved to be navigable for large native boats.

The mouth of the Mogaung was reached on December 31st, exactly 40 days after the start from Ava, and Hannay fixed the latitude of this point by astronomical observation at 24° 56′ 53″, which, however, puts it in a position somewhat more to the south than that which it really occupies. He here quitted the Irawadi, which he described as " still a fine river a mile broad," flowing at the rate of about two miles an hour and having a depth of from two to three fathoms.

The Mogaung River, which Hannay now entered, was found to be barely 100 yards in width, its bed much impeded by rapids, its banks smothered in dense jungle. Above the village of Tapoh, the rapids having been passed, the river widened out to about 200 yards in breadth, and on January 5th, after five and forty days of almost uninterrupted travelling, Hannay reached Mogaung. This place, situated at the junction of the Nam Yun and Nam Yong Rivers with the Nam Kong, or Mogaung River, was found to be a town of some 300 houses, containing a population of about 1,500 souls. It is to-day the terminus of the railway from Katha, which is still under construction. At the time of Hannay's visit it was defended from attack from the lawless tribes in its vicinity by a timber stockade.

At Mogaung Hannay was forced to wait for several days before he was able to start upon his projected trip to the amber mines of the Hukong valley, but on January 19th some of the escort crossed the river and sacrificed a buffalo to the Ngatgyi, or spirits of the " Three Brother Tsanhuas," at that time a necessary preliminary ceremony without which no expedition could march from the town. Three days later a start was made, and for two days the travellers trudged through hilly country, the way leading amid defiles through the spurs of the Shuedung Gyi range on the east and irregular broken country on the west. On January 30th a descent into the Hukong valley was made, the valley itself being, in Hannay's opinion, the ancient bed of an Alpine lake, its greatest length from north to north-east being about 50 miles, its width varying from 15 to 45 miles. The Chindwin River, the lower portion of which had already been explored by Pemberton in his journey from Manipur, and by Richardson and Grant, ran through this valley, and the district was peopled by Singfos and their Assamese slaves, one Shan colony being established at a village called Meingkhwon. Salt and gold were found in the valley, but the only traffic of importance was in amber which the Singfos worked and sold to the Chinese.

Hannay obtained some information concerning the routes from this valley to eastern Singfo, one being through a pass in the Shuedung Gyi range, another round the base of the Lye-guepbhum mountain. From Meingkhwon he located a hill, distant some 25 miles

from that place and lying 35° to the west, as the source
of the Uru River, one of the principal tributaries of the
Chindwin or Ningthi. On March 21st he visited the
amber mines, but saw no amber of any value, the miners
having prudently hidden any that they possessed through
fear of the Burmese who accompanied him. Later he
made a trip to the banks of the Chindwin at a point five
miles north of Meingkhwon, and found the river measuring three hundred yards from bank to bank. On April
12th he returned to Mogaung. Here he obtained information concerning the serpentine mines which lay some
two days' journey above Mogaung, and learned that
about 1,000 men were at work in them. He had no
opportunity, however, of visiting these mines, as he immediately afterwards started for Ava, where he arrived
on May 1st, having accomplished the journey from
Meingkhwon, including the trudge across the hills to
Mogaung, in eighteen days.

Hannay's achievement was of considerable importance,
because the Irawadi from Ava to Bhamo and the mouth
of the Mogaung had now been explored by him for
the first time, no accurate record of its course having
been left by the European traders of the seventeenth century. Through him, too, Bhamo had become something
more than a name to the geographers of Europe. He
had further visited and determined the position of the
Hukong valley and its amber mines, and had fixed with
a fair approximation to accuracy the latitudes of all the
principal towns of the Irawadi valley between Ava and
Meingkhwon. In addition to this he had added a great
deal of information to the knowledge then possessed of

the course of the Chindwin River, filling in blanks which had been left by Wilcox working on the Assam boundary, and by Pemberton in his journeys from Manipur, though he had not actually cut the routes of either of these officers. The information which he brought back concerning the Ta-ping River also disposed of the attempts which had been made to identify it with the Tsangpo of Tibet, and his account of the Irawadi rendered the hypothesis that the Tsangpo was a continuation of the Irawadi very improbable, though the identification of the Tibetan river with the Brahmaputra was not made until more than thirty years later.

In March of 1837, the year after that in which Hannay's journey was made, Griffiths crossed the Naga hills from Assam and visited the Hukong valley, thus joining up Wilcox's explorations and those of the explorer whose travels we have just been following. Wilcox, whose work lies beyond the scope of our inquiry, had been employed from 1825 to 1828 in making a survey for the Indian Government of the country of Assam and its neighbouring States, and had succeeded in the course of his work in determining the western sources of the Irawadi. Between December, 1836, and May, 1837, the journey from Ava to the frontiers of Assam was made by Dr. G. T. Bayfield, who returned to the capital in the latter month. Burney had taken the opportunity of attaching him to a Burmese commission which was being sent from Ava to Assam, and he travelled over the same route as that followed by Hannay as far as Meingkhwon. From this point he travelled north-west to Lamung, and at Maguegun effected a meeting with Hannay and Griffiths, who had come across the hills from Assam and who returned with him to Ava.

Meanwhile, British explorers were also busy farther to the south and east. On December 11th, 1829, Dr. Richardson left Maulmain on his first journey to Chieng Mai, the important town at the head of the valley of the Menam. He ascended the Salwin to the mouth of the Yam Byne, which he reached on December 14th, and landing here made his way across hills into the valley of the Me Gnau and thence into that of the Mein-lung-hi, both of which streams belong to the drainage-area of the Salwin. The frontier station of Mein-lung-hi, near the junction of the stream of that name with the Thung-yin, was at this time an important place, since all traders from Maulmain and the Shan States *en route* for the Karin country passed through it. Richardson reached this place on January 1st, 1830, and did not resume his march until the 6th. On the 10th, after climbing over a huddle of hills for four days, he at last sighted the Me-ping River, the great western branch of the Menam upon which Chieng Mai is situated. The next day the descent into the valley of the Me-ping was made, the river being struck at Muong Haut, or Muong Hal, where the Me-ping measures 747 feet in width. The country traversed between the Salwin and the Me-ping was described by Richardson as " one succession of mountains; nearly all of the primitive series, principally gneiss, trap, lime and sandstone." The inhabitants of these hills were mostly Karins, and the population was sparse and scattered. From Muong Haut Richardson ascended the valley of the Me-ping, passing over level country and grassy plains, until on January 15th he reached Labong, or Lampun. He was not permitted, however, to proceed to Chieng Mai, and after remaining nearly a month at Labong, where he contrived to establish very friendly relations with the Laos Governor, he began his return journey on February 9th. On his way back he struck south from Yembing to the Gyne River, and returned to Maulmain in boats, arriving at his journey's end on March 10th.

In 1834 Dr. Richardson was again despatched on a mission to Chieng Mai, the object of which was to inquire into the causes of the cessation of the cattle trade between the Shan States and Maulmain. He left the latter place on March 6th, and followed the route which he had passed over in 1829–30 as far as Labong, where he arrived on April 1st. On April 15th, having at last procured permission to visit Chieng Mai, he left Labong and reached his destination after a march of five and a half hours. He remained at Chieng Mai till April 24th, when he once more returned to Labong. On April 29th he started on his return journey to Maulmain, where he arrived by his old route on May 21st. The rainy season had begun before he left Labong, and the march had to be made through an incessant downpour which greatly tried the endurance of the party.

So far as can be ascertained, Dr. Richardson was the first European to visit Chieng Mai from the Bay of Bengal, though the unhappy trader Samuel, who was carried off to Ava from that town in 1618, as has already been related, may possibly have traversed the route followed by Richardson as far as Mein-lung-hi on his com-

Plain, South of Bhamo

pulsory journey to the Burmese capital. Richardson's
main object in these two journeys, and in the third which
he made to Chieng Mai in 1834–35, was the establishment of trade between the Shan States and the newly
acquired British territories of lower Burma. Concerning the condition of the districts traversed he brought
back a great deal of valuable information, and he also
collected a considerable amount of geographical data
concerning a hitherto unexplored region. In the December following his return to Maulmain he again started
for Chieng Mai, travelling by the now familiar route *viâ*
Mein-lung-hi and Labong, and on his arrival on January
26th, 1835, he had the good fortune to meet a big caravan
from China, consisting of some 200 mules and pack-
horses, while a second still larger caravan was reported
to be at Muong Nan. The information which he collected from these Chinese merchants on the subject of
the trade-route to Yun-nan *viâ* Chieng Tong and Chieng
Hong on the Mekong, led directly to McLeod's being
entrusted with the mission to which we have already
referred. On this journey, too, Richardson visited Lakon, a town on the Me-wang, the great left influent of
the Me-ping, this being the first occasion upon which the
place had been visited by a white man from the Burmese
side. From Lakon he returned to Labong, which he left
on March 25th, reaching Mein-lung-hi on the last day
of that month. From this point he passed through magnificent teak forests towards the Salwin, crossing the
divide on April 5th, and striking the great river at
Banong on the 9th. The Salwin was here found to be
400 yards in width, running rapidly through a narrow

valley. Crossing the river, Richardson penetrated into
the Karîn country as far as Dwom Tulve, and was fairly
well received by the Karîns, the almost barbarous hillmen who had contrived to maintain their independence
and whose predatory raids in search of Shan slaves were
at this time the terror of the little States owing allegiance
to Ava. After spending nearly a month at Dwom Tulve,
Richardson returned by his original route to Mein-lung-
hi, and thence made his way down to Maulmain by the
trade-track over which he had now so often passed.

In December, 1836, Richardson again left Maulmain,
this time in company with McLeod, and proceeded up
the Gyne River. On the fourth day the travellers landed
at the last village in British territory, and thence proceeded on elephant-back, crossing the boundary between
British and Siamese territory on December 25th, twelve
days after their departure from Maulmain. Next day
McLeod branched off, following a track to Chieng Mai
somewhat to the south of the route by which Richardson
had reached that place; from Chieng Mai he hoped to
enter China *viâ* Chieng Tong and Chieng Hong. With
the details of McLeod's journey we are already acquainted. Richardson, having other plans, went on to
Mein-lung-hi, where he arrived on New Year's Day,
1837, and which he left on 6th January. The Mein-
lung-hi being too deep to ford at this season of the year,
he departed by a route which is only used during the
monsoon. This passed through uninhabited country,
and brought him to the Salwin in 18° 16′ N. Lat. on
January 16th. Having crossed the river, Richardson
made his way as before to Dwom Tulve in the Karîn

country, where he arranged with the Pha Pho, the
Chief of the hillmen, to grant him a free passage
through the Karîn territory. On February 6th he again
started, journeying through country which had never
before been traversed by a white man. The first two
days led through mountains, and the country next entered was found to be hilly and treeless, but very carefully and completely cultivated. Seven days' steady
marching through this hilly region brought Richardson
from Dwom Túlve to Ka-du-gyi, the first Burmese village on the Ava side: the country of the Red Karins
had at last been traversed by a white man. It was discovered to be at once more extensive and more thickly
populated than had hitherto been suspected, but of the
trade of the district Richardson entertained no very
great hopes. Tin and stick-lac were both obtained in
abundance, but the one was too heavy, the other too
bulky, to be exported with ease, with the means of
transport then available. Moreover, the Red Karins
"entertained the most rancorous enmity to the Burmans," and the people—with whom, however, Richardson had established good relations—were little removed
from savagery.

"Theirs," he writes, "is the first and rudest stage of
an agricultural population; their habitations are miserable and destitute of everything that conduces to the
comfort of human beings, to which they are scarcely
allowed by the Burmans to belong. Nearly all their
present limited wants are supplied within themselves.
They only traffic in stick-lac which is produced in great
quantities, and slaves which they capture from the Shan

villages subject to the Burmans lying along their frontier. From three hundred to four hundred are annually
bartered with the Siamese Shans for black cattle, buffa-
loes, salt and betel-nut."

On February 13th Richardson reached Kudu, on the
borders of Karini and Burma, and continuing his journey on the 15th, he three days later reached Mok-mai, a
stockaded town of 300 or 350 houses, where his appearance was greeted by riotous and insulting crowds of
sightseers. The superior civilisation of the Shans, as
compared with their Karin neighbours, did not manifest
itself in improved manners or in a power to curb their
curiosity.

On February 20th Richardson left Mok-mai for Monai,
another Shan State under the rule of Ava. The first day's
march brought him to Lome, the first place met with that
" considered itself fairly safe from the forays of the
Kareens, which they compare to the swoop of a hawk."
Even at Mok-mai the natives did not dare to wander far
from their stockade, so lawless and ubiquitous were the
hill slave-traders, and so utterly inefficient the Burmese
Government whose duty it was to protect its subjects.
At Monai Richardson was detained 42 days, awaiting
the authorisation to proceed which Burney was trying to
obtain for him at the Court of Ava; but on April 6th a
start was made, Hai-pek being reached on the following
day. Thence the track led through hilly and undulating
country where the soil was exceedingly poor, and on
April 16th news of the revolution at Ava, whereby
Tharawadi made himself master of Burma, reached the
travellers. On the morrow the escort from Monai beat

Second Defile of the Irawadi River

a hasty retreat, having no desire to get nearer to the
scene of trouble, but Richardson pushed on to Neaung
Shewai, where he spent an anxious month of inactivity.
On May 13th, however, he received orders to proceed to
Ava, which had been procured for him by Burney, and
on the 18th he resumed his march. He made his way
across the mountains, descending the Nat Tike pass—
" the longest and most laborious pass in the Burmese
dominions "—into the valley of the Irawadi. Here he
found himself on a great plain called the Lap-dau, or
royal elds, which extends to the hills east and north of
Mandalay and away to the mountains of the Manipuri
frontier. Four days' trudge across this plain brought
Richardson, on May 28th, to the British Residency at
Ava. His was the first journey ever made by a European from Maulmain to Mandalay, and in the course of
it he had explored the hitherto unknown country of the
Karins, and the Shan States lying between that country
and Ava. Richardson's journey served to link up the
British possessions in lower Burma with the region explored under Burney's auspices farther to the north and
west. At the same time McLeod's journey had added
to the map many details of the eastern Shan States between the Salwin and the Mekong.

In December, 1838, Richardson once more left Maulmain upon one of his venturesome journeys, travelling
this time on elephants over the main range of mountains
which divides Tenasserim from Siam, and making his
way to Bangkok *via* Kanburi on the Me-klong River.
This journey will be described more fully in the chapter
which deals with the exploration of Siam. It was the

last of a series of remarkable explorations, many of which
had been made by Richardson himself, which were undertaken during the decade following Burney's appointment
to the post of British Resident at Ava. The Burmese
revolution of 1837 led to the withdrawal of our Resident,
and from that time until the war of 1852 little official
intercourse was held with Ava, and the work of exploration necessarily ceased for a space. After the war Major
Arthur Phayre, who had been appointed Governor of
Pegu, the province annexed by Great Britain, was sent
to Ava on an embassy in 1855, and Captain Henry Yule
—afterwards so well known as Colonel Sir Henry Yule,
the Orientalist and the editor of the Book of Messer
Marco Polo—accompanied the party and acted as its
chronicler. Yule's own contributions to the study of
Burmese history and topography are considerable, though
they represented comparatively little in the nature of
original research, most of his information having been
collected by others. In 1856, however, he devoted himself to the production of a map of Burma, in so far as
the country was then known to Europeans, and published it in the Journal of the Asiatic Society of Bengal
with a long commentary from his own pen. This map
embodied the results of all the explorations with which
we have already dealt, and further profited by the surveys made by Captain Rennie and Lièutenant Heath-
cote, who also had accompanied Phayre on his mission
to Ava in the preceding year. In Burma proper below
Ava, the interior towns and districts, Yule tells us, had
been filled in from native information by Major Grant
Allen of the Madras Army, and this part of the map

Colonel Sir H. Yule, K.C.S.I., C.B.

was, therefore, confessedly inaccurate. For the rest the country lying between the Salwin and the Me-ping Rivers is blank, as also is the large tract north of Chieng Mai and south of the Salwin valley. Similar blanks occur between Tungu and Yemethin, points which to-day are joined to one another by a line of railway leading from Rangoon to Mandalay; between the Arakan Yoma range and the Chindwin River; and again in the northern districts between the Chindwin and the Irawadi. This map, however, in spite of all its deficiencies, was in 1856 by far the best that had ever been put together of these regions, and a glance at the copy of it here reproduced will show the reader how substantial was the progress which had been made during the period that elapsed between the first and second Burmese wars.

By the peace concluded at the end of 1852, not only had Pegu been ceded to Great Britain, Rangoon becoming from that time forward the capital of British or lower Burma, but agencies were opened at Ava and Tungu. The territory ceded after the war of 1826 had already been surveyed by the British Government with more or less detail and accuracy, while Richardson had not only explored the main range between Tenasserim and the Me-klong valley in 1838–39, as has already been mentioned, but in company with Captain G. B. Tremenheere had walked across the Isthmus of Kra from Pakchan to Chimpohun, within a few miles of the coast of the Gulf of Siam. Tremenheere, who drew up a report on this trip, which was undertaken in 1843, considered that the Kra canal scheme, of which since that date so much has from time to time been heard, was " reasonably

practicable," the difference of level never exceeding 450
feet, and a rough estimate for a canal 100 feet wide of
rectangular shape giving 3,556,640,000 solid feet of ex-
cavation. In 1856, by which time the surveys of Pegu
were fairly advanced, Mr. Edward O'Riley was sent
from Tungu to look for a trace across the Panglong, or
Pegu Yoma, range into the Karin country, and crossing
these mountains made his way to Ngwai Tung and Nung
Belai, two important Karin villages in the heart of the
hills peopled by these tribesmen. He returned to Maulmain by the trade-route which had already been famil-
iarised by the explorations of Richardson, and thence
made his way back to Tungu by the To-lo-hi villages.
He estimated the Karin population of the Pegu Yoma
range at between 55,000 and 60,000 souls; he was able
to determine the altitudes of several peaks and passes,
and his surveys formed a considerable addition to our
knowledge of the Karin country.

But much the most interesting journey of exploration undertaken in the neighbourhood of Burma, during the period between the war of 1852 and that of
1855, was that of Captain Sladen, and its story is told
by the leader of the expedition with an amount of
humour, good temper, and high spirits, which presents
a great contrast to the dry-as-dust records of travel
which reach us from most of our British explorers in this
region. Sladen's objective was Ta-li-fu, the capital of
the rebel Muhammadan Sultan in Yun-nan, which Garnier succeeded in visiting from Tong-Chuan in March,
1868. The object of the mission was to re-establish the
trade between Burma and Yun-nan, which had long been

Forest Scenery, Burma

interrupted owing to the protracted disturbances in the latter province. A start was made from Mandalay on January 13th, 1868. The journey from that place to Bhamo was only remarkable because it was performed for the first time in a shallow-draught steamer, the property of the King of Burma, and was accomplished without difficulty by January 21st. The Irawadi above Mandalay was thus proved to be navigable for steam-vessels of this description as high up its course as Bhamo, and Captain Bowers, who accompanied Sladen, was the first to make a chart of its bed between these two points.

The expedition had been launched with the consent and approval of the Burmese King, but from the outset, after his arrival at Bhamo, Sladen found that the influence of native officialism was being used in every insidious way that could suggest itself to frustrate his plans. The way from Bhamo into the provinces of western China led necessarily through the hills peopled by Kakhyen tribesmen, beyond whose country lay a fringe of Chinese Shan States. The first step, therefore, was to obtain the co-operation and goodwill of the Kakhyen chiefs; but the Burmese officers at Bhamo did their best to prevent these gentry from visiting Sladen, and it was not until January 31st that the chief of Ponlyne at last came in.

" Half Burman, half Chinese, as regarded his externals, the hang-dog expression of his countenance (different in every respect from the Kakhyen type, or from any type I had ever seen) was an ugly feature in the proceedings, which did not augur well for the results of our proposed conference," writes Sladen.

Torn in twain by his dread of incurring the anger of the Burmese on the one hand, and his reluctance to let so excellent an opportunity of enriching himself escape him on the other, this man temporised and procrastinated, but at last promised to procure the necessary mule transport, and to convey Sladen and his party as far as Manwyne, the first Shan town on the Yun-nan side of the hills. This pledge, it subsequently transpired, was only given with a view to getting the expedition into the hills where it could be plundered at leisure, the Burmese officials and the Chinese traders at Bhamo, who regarded with extreme disapproval any attempt to infringe their monopoly of commerce with Yun-nan, seeing in this device the most convenient way of putting an end to a troublesome business.

On February 26th Sladen at last shook the dust of Bhamo from off his feet, and marched to a point on the banks of the Ta-ping River at which the mules collected by the Kakhyen chief of Ponlyne were in waiting to convey the party into the hills. Immense difficulty was experienced with the mule-drivers, each of whom was " a sort of irresponsible agent, demanding separate recognition in all that related to the hire and use of his particular property." Most of the Kakhyens, chiefs and peasants, were drunk, " but this," said Sladen cheerfully, " seemed to be of no consequence, as drunkenness is the normal condition of Kakhyens when on duty, and is not regarded by them as any real interruption to love or business." Owing to these and other difficulties the expedition did not get away from Sitkaw, the village where the mules had been met, until 2 P.M. on March 2nd, Pon-

lyne village being reached at dusk. From this point
Sladen succeeded in pushing on to the village of Pon-si,
but here he was deserted by his mules and mule-men,
the latter not even waiting to receive the hire that was
due to them. At a subsequent date Sladen learned that
the mule-men had been told from the first that as soon
as the expedition was trapped in the hills it would be set
upon by the tribesmen, when all who had aided would
receive a share of the spoil. Relying upon this arrangement they did not wait to receive their hire, but deserted
hastily, so that the fighting which was to enrich them
might begin with as little delay as possible.

During its long sojourn at Pon-si the party was unquestionably in a position of great danger. Sladen could
neither move forward nor retreat; he refused absolutely
to pay the blackmail which was repeatedly demanded by
Ponlyne and the other Kakhyen chiefs; and he owed it
only to his own calm temper, resource, and to the bold
face which he consistently presented to his persecutors,
that he was at length able to extricate his party from
so critical a situation. His great stroke of policy was
the opening up of direct communications with the " Pan-
thai," as he called the rebel Muhammadan authorities in
Yun-nan, and as soon as the Kakhyen chiefs learned that
he had stolen this march upon them, their whole attitude
towards the Englishmen changed. The rebels were more
feared than the Burmans, and the travellers had displayed a considerable ability to take care of themselves
and to make friends with the rank and file of the tribesmen, who were further much impressed by the fact that
Sladen's escort possessed guns which would actually go

off! Accordingly when it was made known that the Muhammadan Government was favourable to the advance of the expedition, difficulties vanished like smoke.

The Muhammadan Governor of Mo-mein, however, urged Sladen to remain at Pon-si for the present, this official having determined to dislodge the Chinese robber chief, Lis-hi-ta-hi, who held a position commanding the line of march and had been honourably received by the King of Burma when he paid a visit to Ava. Mau-phu was the name of the place occupied by this ruffian and his followers, and the Muhammadans presently attacked and took it with considerable slaughter, thus clearing the way for the British expedition. Captain Williams, the engineer of Sladen's party, unfortunately elected to return from Pon-si to Burma, a decision which robbed the expedition of some of the detailed topographical results which it might otherwise have obtained, but Sladen and the officers who remained with him left Pon-si on May 11th, and resumed their long-interrupted march through the Kakhyen hills. The Shan town of Manwyne was reached the same day, and on May 14th the party moved on again to Sanda. On the way the expedition, which had already been the object of futile demonstrations of hostility between Sitkaw and Pon-si, was treated to another exhibition of the kind, an armed band of wildly gesticulating Shans keeping parallel with the travellers on the opposite bank of the Ta-ping River, and even firing a few shots over their heads. The object of this farce, though it was doubtless connected with an attempt to " save the face " of some robber chieftain, was never satisfactorily explained, but the Shans who were accom-

Burman Family Group

panying Sladen treated the demonstration as something
of no account, as indeed it proved to be. On their own
side of the Ta-ping the travellers were received with
open arms by the natives, who looked forward to the
re-establishment of trade between Yun-nan and Burma
with the keenest expectation. After their long captivity
at Pon-si—for indeed their sojourn there deserved no
other name—the delight of the travellers at finding themselves upon the march again was great, and this was
enhanced not only by the kindliness of the welcome
afforded to them, but also by the magnificence of the
country through which they were journeying.

" The monotonous grandeur of this endless valley,"
writes Sladen, " with its sublime ridges towering up on
either side to a height of 5,000 feet, and running in
straight parallels into boundless space, was in itself a
source of infinite admiration. But to this estimate of
its interest and sublimity I may add the fact that the
valley area teemed with villages, and was alive with a
population which had laid out and conjoined every available acre into one vast garden of fertility and wealth."

Half-way between Manwyne and Sanda, the Chinese
town of Karahokha was reached. This place was curious because it was an entirely Chinese centre of trade
situated in a district otherwise peopled only by Shans.
The broad road running through the town was not
only flanked by Chinese shops, but on market-days was
crammed with temporary booths and sheds in which
merchandise was displayed for sale. Sanda itself was
found to be a poor and insignificant place, containing

about 800 houses, and it had not recovered from the Muhammadan invasion of five years earlier, when, after it had been scientifically looted by the " Pan-thai " soldiers, it was handed over to their Kakhyen allies. The Shan king of the place, however, received the travellers very kindly, and insisted upon Sladen adopting his grandson, certain astrologers having declared that the youth would never prosper unless the Englishman would consent to undertake this purely formal charge. Sladen won his heart by his ready acceptance of this commission, and the travellers quitted Sanda on the 16th May, leaving staunch friends behind them.

From Sanda the way led through rice-fields for a couple of miles to the foot of a red spur, whence a descent was again made into the Ta-ping valley. A road leading up the centre of the valley brought the party to Mynela, on the left bank of the river, a town of some eight or ten thousand inhabitants and some 1,200 houses. Like Sanda it was built upon rising ground and was surrounded by a loop-holed brick wall.

" The temples of Mynela are costly stone buildings, and the interior decorations have been carried out with a lavish expenditure of gold-leaf and labour which proclaims the wealth of the people at large, and is evidence also of their artistic attainments."

Like their brethren in Laos and the Burmese Shan States, the Shans of the Chinese frontier were found to be greatly given to the erection of Buddhistical temples; but Sladen noted how deeply they had taken the impress of the Chinese civilisation, and how unorthodox was

their religion contrasting with the pure Buddhism of
Burma. One curious element in the population was the
Buddhist nuns, all of whom were of a peripatetic habit,
many having wandered in pious pilgrimage as far afield
as Rangoon. They had brought back with them the
most favourable accounts of that portion of Burma which
had already fallen under the rule of Great Britain, spoke
"in rapturous and familiar strains of Colonel Phayre,"
and had been instrumental in teaching their countrymen
to regard Englishmen with feelings of friendship.

While at Mynela, Sladen collected a considerable
amount of information relative to the Chinese Shan
States, the population of which he estimated at not less
than 250,000 souls. He also had an interesting interview
with the dowager-regent of the place and with her heir,
by whom he was kindly received, before leaving for Mau-
phu on May 23rd. This latter place, it will be recalled,
was the stronghold of the robber chieftain, Lis-hi-ta-hi,
whom the Governor of Mo-mein had routed a few weeks
earlier.

" Mauphoo itself," writes Sladen, " is insignificant both
as a town and fortification, but its position had been
well chosen as a safe and convenient place of retreat and
rendezvous on account of natural defences and general
inaccessibility. The Panthays for some years past had
either tolerated or submitted to the presence at Mauphoo
of an enemy who intercepted their communication with
Burmah and disputed with them the sovereignty of the
northern Shan States. It is now evident that this submission originated in a fear of offending against Bur-

man scruples by direct interference with one who was
known to be the secret agent of the Burmese Government. It was not therefore until my letters had reached
Momein, and the Governor had been led to believe that
we were supported and countenanced by the Burmese
Government, that the Governor undertook the work of
reducing Mauphoo and of opening out communication
with ourselves at Ponsee. He argued rightly that either
Mauphoo must cease to be a Chinese garrison, or the
British expedition must fail in gaining access to the
Chinese frontier."

The Governor had invested the robber stronghold with
a force of 5,000 men, and finally took it by assault after
a large part of the garrison, failing to cut their way out,
had submitted. Lis-hi-ta-hi lost several hundred of his
followers during these operations, and the air was sick-
ened by the exhalations from still unburied corpses at
the time of Sladen's visit.

From Mau-phu the travellers pushed on to the Nan-
tin valley. The heights were guarded by bodies of
friendly natives, and the Englishmen, as those who had
been the indirect means of freeing the district from the
tyranny of the Chinese robber, were everywhere greeted
with noisy acclamations of pleasure. Again the country
traversed was magnificent.

"How superbly quiet and picturesque," exclaims
Sladen, " is the view which is disclosed during the descent from the Mau-phoo heights ! At our feet lies the
Ta-haw, now a smooth, quiet stream, flowing between
deep precipitous banks of alternate rock and vegetation,

and spanned by a veritable suspension bridge, the first of a series which assures us that we have passed the confines of the celestial empire. Six miles in advance (though apparently at our feet) may be descried the towns of Mynetee and Nantin, the former Shan and the latter Chinese, though at present under the rule of a Panthay Governor. In the distance the valley stretches away into space, with a dark background of lofty mountains which tend northerly far into Yunan. The average width of the valley did not exceed three miles, and the well-defined terraces or gradations of terraces at corresponding heights on either side were evidences of a lacustrine period during which a gradual outlet was being forced through the Mauphoo gorge. The lake itself had silted up and formed the present rich alluvial expanse of plain and valley. There is reason to believe that the other Shan valleys we have thus far visited owe much of their present formation to a lacustrine origin, and that their unusual fertility and elevation are due as much to former sedimentary lake deposits as to a continual accession of productive matter which is being incessantly superadded by periodical floods, as well as by the descent of *débris* from the adjoining slopes towards their several valley centres."

Nan-tin was reached at dusk, and shortly after the travellers had taken up their quarters in the half-ruined Chinese temple assigned to them, a visit was paid to them by the Pan-thai Governor of the place and by his colleague, the Muhammadan Kazi. Next day the visit was repeated, and this time the Governor was also accom-

panied by Thong-wet-shein, a noted Chinese robber
chieftain who had submitted to the Muhammadan Government after the fall of Mau-phu. This worthy, says
Sladen, "evidenced in his outward exterior an impressive realisation of the living brigand," for in a wild
country such as this, a man does not rise even to the
position of leader of a band of outlaws unless he stand
possessed of unusual qualities of mind and person.

From Nan-tin Sladen pushed on to Mo-mein, which
is situated on the lower slopes of a plateau whose
highest point is crossed about half-way between the
two places. The volcanic origin of this plateau and
of the whole surrounding region is plainly indicated,
and in one place hot springs were found in which the
temperature of the water was a trifle above boiling-point.
The chief incident of the march, however, was the sudden attack delivered by a band of Chinese *dakaits* upon
the Pan-thai escort,—an attack in which one or two of
the Muhammadan officers lost their lives, while several
of the leading baggage-mules were carried off. Sladen
and his companions were far at the rear at the moment
when this ambush was revealed, but they succeeded in
rallying and steadying their little force, and reached
Mo-mein that evening without further interruption.

"The approach to Momein," writes Sladen, "is very
grand and beautiful. We had been descending for some
time the eastern side of the high ridges which intersect
to some extent the main valley of the Tahaw. The road,
after passing down a long series of grassy undulations,
led round the southern slope of a tumulus-shaped hill,

1,000 feet in height, crowned on its summit by a high
Chinese tower pagoda. It is at this point that the city
of Momein is suddenly brought into view in a hollow
basin, enclosed on all sides by hills of every shape and
altitude, which slope down apparently to its very walls.
In reality they are at some distance, and the intervening
valley spaces are either under cultivation or mark the
remains of large Chinese towns, now for the most part
in ruins and deserted. Beyond the city, from our present
point of view, the Tahaw and Momein valleys have
formed a junction, and a narrow plain extends for about
five miles in a northerly direction along the banks of the
Tahaw, until limited in the distance by the gradual con-
vergence of the lateral hill ranges. On the extreme north
the horizon was bounded by a dark rugged outline of
black mountains, with an apparent north and south direction, which form, as far as it is allowed to deduce facts
from observation and inquiry, a portion of the main central Himalayan chain, which is continued far south into
Burma and the Malay Peninsula."

The Governor of Mo-mein was waiting to receive the
travellers without the walls of his city, having come out
in full state for that purpose. The attitude of this Governor, as indeed of all the " Pan thai " authorities encountered by Sladen, presents an interesting contrast to
that of the men of the same clan who had dealings with
Garnier during his flying visit to Ta-li-fu. It will be
remembered that the French traveller ascribed his failure
to obtain permission to proceed to the fact that the Muhammadans of Ta-li-fu must have mistaken him for an

Englishman, all Englishmen, in Garnier's opinion, being necessarily hateful to the followers of the Prophet. This contention is not sustained by the reception everywhere accorded to Sladen in the territory under Muhammadan jurisdiction. By no stretch of imagination could the following words have been written of the welcome extended to Garnier, armed though he was with letters of recommendation to the rulers of Ta-li-fu from Lao Papa, the great Muhammadan doctor and priest.

" The reception," writes Sladen, " was flattering and courteous to excess, and as such produced feelings of special gratification in those who had come as strangers to an unknown government, and after three months of obstruction and annoyance, suddenly found themselves amongst powerful friends and raised to the position of well-favoured guests."

None the less Sladen was not destined to visit Ta-li-fu or to travel farther into Yun-nan. He had already seen his caravan attacked by *dakaits*, and he became convinced, after a protracted stay at Mo-mein, that he could pursue his journey only at the cost of causing great trouble and danger to the authorities who had treated him with so much hospitality. The road to Ta-li-fu was infested by armed parties of brigands, and the strangers could get to that town only by fighting their way thither. To do this would have been contrary to his instructions, and Sladen therefore reluctantly decided to abandon the attempt. On July 13th the party left Mo-mein and began its march back to Bhamo. Passing through Nan-tin, Sladen pushed on to Myne-la, whence he purposed travelling to Burma *viâ* the Hotha route, which lies somewhat farther to the south than that previously traversed by way of Sanda. After long conferences with the Shans, Sladen was forced to abandon a portion of his project, and had to follow the old route as far as Manwyne. Leaving this place on August 10th, he crossed into the Hotha valley, visited that town, and thence despatched a Burmese surveyor to examine the route to Bhamo *viâ* Myne-wan. Sladen himself passed near the town of Latha, and thence followed the valley of the Ta-ping, journeying through the Kakhyen hills to the south of that river, and so to Bhamo, which was reached on September 5th.

At Myne-la Sladen had been joined by Mr. Robert Gordon, an engineer who had been sent to replace Williams, and this officer was subsequently able to supply the Government with some valuable surveys of the country between that place and Bhamo, together with detailed reports concerning the merits of the several routes into Yun-nan. Moreover, as engineer in charge of the river works, he added largely to our knowledge of the Lower Irawadi, and published a valuable report on the river, 1879-80. So late as 1885 he was an ardent advocate of the theory—then generally believed, and almost immediately afterwards demonstrated, to be erroneous—that the main source of the Irawadi was to be found in the Sanpo of Tibet. In 1868, both this officer and Sladen fell into the error of supposing that, once the difficulties of the Kakhyen hills had been surmounted and Mo-mein had been reached, no serious obstacles remained in the way of the traveller to Ta-li-fu. Their reports, therefore, induced the belief that an admirable route, whereby the trade of Yun-nan might be tapped, had been discovered, and this gave to the results obtained by the expedition an air of importance which was not rightly to be claimed for them.

On January 4th, 1868, Mr. T. T. Cooper left Han-Kau and made his way to Batang, on the south-eastern borders of Tibet. From this point he travelled south, chiefly following the valley of the Lan-tsang, as the waters of the Mekong are here called. At Tse-ku, just within the Yun-nan boundary, he found French Roman Catholic missionaries established on the left bank of the river, and he calculated that this place was distant only some 80 miles from the upper portion of the Irawadi in the Khanti country which had been visited from Assam by Wilcox, though this estimate was not sufficiently liberal. Proceeding south he was stopped before he could reach Ta-li-fu, and was forced to retrace his steps.

In October, 1869, however, he returned to the charge, this time making Assam his starting-point. Leaving Sadiya he passed up the line of the Lohit, that is, the Brahmaputra, and reached Prun, a village 20 miles from Rima, the first Tibetan post. But again he was turned back.

In 1874 the Muhammadan, or as Sladen erroneously called it the " Panthai," rebellion, of which in these pages such frequent mention has been made, came to an end, Ta-li-fu falling at last into the hands of the Chinese Government. In January of the following year Lord Salisbury appointed a British Mission, under Colonel Browne, to cross China from Bhamo to Shanghai, and in order to obviate difficulties Mr. Augustus Raymond Margary, of the Consular Service in China, was instructed to proceed overland to Bhamo, there to join the mission after having prepared the way for its advent. This young Englishman is the type of those of his race who have built up our world-wide empire, and the hazardous duty assigned to him filled him with pride and with delight.

"Is it not a splendid mission?" he writes in a letter addressed to the lady whom he hoped to make his wife. "What wonderful things I shall see! I shall hope to have grand sport in the forests and mountains which teem with wild life. It is impossible to say when you may hear from me. . . . All sorts of rumours may arise as to my fate. Let me beg of you not to believe one; rest assured I will make my way there and back, by God's help, as safe as a trivit."

It is a fine thing truly to be possessed of youth, and health and high spirits, to be vouchsafed that golden gift—an opportunity—and to be endowed above your fellows with a special mission that promises so great a measure of adventure and of romance. So doubtless thought young Margary when, on August 23rd, 1874, he set out from Shanghai to traverse China. He ascended the Yang-tse to Han-Kau, and thence, to use his own words, "plunged into the Dark for six months." Travelling over a route similar to that followed by Garnier six years earlier, he reached Ta-li-fu, and thence passed on to Bhamo *viâ* Mo-mein and the Kakhyen hills, arriving at the Burmese city on January 17th, 1875. He

was thus the first to traverse the country between Ta-
li-fu, which had been visited by Garnier, and Mo-mein,
which as we have seen was the point to which Sladen's
expedition had attained. He was, moreover, the first
white man to make his way into Burma from Shanghai,
and when he joined Colonel Browne at Bhamo his arrival caused a tremendous sensation, not only among
the Europeans, but also among the natives in that place.

Early in February Browne's mission left Bhamo, and
began its march to Shanghai, but on the fringe of the
Kakhyen country rumours of trouble reached the travellers, the hill-tribes, instigated it was reported by the
mandarins of Serai and Manwyne, being said to be preparing to resist the advance of the Europeans. Margary, who had come single-handed through China, and
had made friends with the authorities, laughed at these
rumours, and leaving the rest of the mission, pushed
on ahead to make inquiries and to reassure the natives.
He crossed the frontier on February 19th, taking no
escort with him, and on the following day letters from
him reported his safe arrival at Serai. On February
21st Browne moved forward and reached Serai, and
next day the mission-camp was surrounded by hostile
natives. The same day news was received from Manwyne that poor young Margary had been murdered on
February 22nd. After a hard day's fighting, Browne
was able in the evening to draw off his people, and to
recross the frontier into Burmese territory with all his
baggage. The mission had failed on the very threshold
of its enterprise, and one more youngster of high promise had fallen, as so many Englishmen have fallen, in

Augustus R. Margary

From his "Journey from Shanghai to Bhamo." By permission of
Macmillan & Co.

the foremost skirmishing-line of the Empire. The man who had crossed China from the sea to Burma without any armed escort, and had thus accomplished something the memory of which will never be forgotten, was not quite nine and twenty years old at the time of his premature death.

On November 5th, 1875, a mission under the command of the Hon. T. Grosvenor left Han-Kau for the purpose of inquiring into the circumstances of poor young Margary's assassination. The mission reached Yunnan-fu on March 6th, 1876, and Ta-li-fu on April 11th, and thence passed on to Mo-mein, thus again traversing the country between the regions explored by Garnier and those visited by Sladen in 1868. Mr. Colborne Baber, of the British Consular Service in China, who was attached to the mission, made a careful examination of the country traversed by the Grosvenor mission, and in February, 1877, forwarded from Han-Kau copies of the surveys which he had made. Of these the most important was the survey of the route from Ta-li-fu to Teng-yue, as Mo-mein is called by the Chinese, for Margary's death had robbed the Government of the detailed information concerning this area which he had collected. Bhamo was placed by Baber's survey in topographical communication with Shanghai and Saigon, for it was now linked to the areas surveyed by Garnier. In other respects, however, the results of Baber's investigations were not so satisfactory to Englishmen. Sladen, as we have noted, had imagined that the difficulties of the route from Burma into Yun-nan ended at Mo-mein, the point reached by his expedition. Baber now corrected this misapprehension, and added that it was precisely at Mo-mein that the greatest difficulties began.

"The valleys, or rather abysses, of the Salwin and Mekong," he wrote, "must long remain insuperable difficulties, not to mention many other obstacles."

And again he writes,

"Loath as most Englishmen are to admit it, the simple and evident approach to Eastern Yun-nan is from the Gulf of Tongking. But it by no means follows that the same holds true of the western part of the province. The object should be to attain some town of importance south of Yung-chang and Ta-li-fu, such as Shun-ning, from which both these cities could be reached by ascending the valleys instead of crossing all the mountain ranges, as must be done if the T'eng-yueh (Mo-mein) route is selected."

Baber, moreover, threw much light upon the route described by Marco Polo in the fifth chapter of his book, and established the identity of Yachi and Carajan with the modern Yun-nan-fu and Ta-li-fu. His careful and accurate investigations added largely to the stock of information at that time in the possession of Europeans concerning western China,—a region which only indirectly comes within the scope of our inquiry,—and in May, 1883, his labours were rewarded by the bestowal on him of the Patron's Medal of the Royal Geographical Society.

In August, 1877, Mr. McCarthy, of the China Inland Mission, reached Bhamo, having come across Yun-nan *viâ* Yun-nan-fu and Ta-li-fu. Eight months later the journey from Ta-li-fu to Bhamo was also performed by

Captain William Gill, R. E.   Edward Colborne Baber

From "The River of Golden Sand." By permission of
Mr. John Murray

Captain William John Gill, who in 1877–78 made some important explorations in China, the most interesting of which were undertaken in the valley of the "River of Golden Sand," the Kin-sha-kiang, which is the name borne by the upper waters of the Yang-tse. Gill explored this valley to the south-eastern confines of Tibet, and traversed the country between Batang and Ta-li-fu. From the latter place he made his way to Bhamo, and later recorded his experiences in an interesting book of travel, a subsequent edition of which had the good fortune to be edited by Colonel Henry Yule. In September, 1877, the journey from Ta-li-fu to Bhamo had been made by another missionary, Mr. Cameron, and on February 13th, 1880, Count Bela Széchenyi, a young Austrian noble, after traversing China and trying vainly to force an entrance into Tibet, arrived at Bhamo from Ta-li-fu. In 1882 Mr. Archibald Colquhoun, accompanied by Mr. Charles Wahab, ascended the West River of Canton to Pe-se, and travelled through southern Yunnan to the frontier town of Sze-mao—so long known to our officers in Burma under the name of Esmok—the once suggested terminus of the Burma-Chinese railway which Sprey had so persistently and vainly advocated in the sixties. Here Mr. Colquhoun was stopped, and was forced to turn north, eventually reaching Bhamo *viâ* the Ta-li-fu route. His journey was interesting and important since it covered an area which had never previously been scientifically explored and surveyed. Moreover, it was made by one who could use his pen as well as his limbs, and the result was a delightful book, "Across Chryse," published in 1883. A study of this journey, however, does not come within the scope of the present work.

By this time the relations between the British and the Burmese Governments had become greatly strained, the position having become critical after the accession of Thibaw, who came to the throne in 1878, and celebrated the occasion by having a number of his relatives murdered in a singularly cold-blooded manner. In 1879 our Resident had been withdrawn from Mandalay, his position having become untenable since he was the impotent witness of horrors which he had no power to prevent. A large amount of British capital, however, had been invested in Burma, the Irawadi Flotilla Company possessing all the shipping on the great river, and being engaged on a large scale in the export of teak. France, too, had realised the importance of Burma, and Thibaw's persistent coquetting with foreign intriguers caused acute anxiety to the Government of India. At last in 1885 the King inflicted a huge fine upon the Flotilla Company, and threatened to confiscate its property unless his demands were immediately satisfied. This led to war. The Flotilla Company's fleet was chartered, and in November a force of 9,000 men was moved up the Irawadi. After a stubborn fight at Minhla on November 17th, the flotilla made its way to the vicinity of Ava, and as it drew near to the ancient capital it was met, on November 26th, with an offer of surrender. Thibaw was deposed; Burma was annexed; and the first stage of the last Burmese War had ended ere it had well begun.

Many thousands of Burman soldiers, however, had not come into collision with our troops, and these pres-

ently formed themselves into bands of *dakaits* by whom
a guerilla warfare was carried on for a protracted period.
The second phase of the struggle upon which the British
army now entered has rightly been described as " a
subaltern's war." That is to say, the force was split
up into innumerable tiny detachments, each of which
had for its duty the tranquillisation of a particular area.
By this means upper Burma was overrun by white men
in a fashion which defies detailed description. After
the conclusion of the war followed the work of administration and survey, and to-day it is hardly too much
to say that almost every cranny of the Burmese empire,
from which of old Europeans were so rigidly excluded,
has been visited and explored by British officers. Where
so many explorers, acting for the most part in official
capacities, have done such excellent work, it is somewhat invidious to refer to individuals, but mention may
perhaps be made of one or two expeditions from the
side of India which made important contributions towards
the solution of the problem of the sources of the Irawadi.
Two native explorers were despatched by the Indian
Government in 1879 to locate the sources of the river,
and though they did not succeed in accomplishing this
task, they brought back much interesting information
derived from the natives with whom they came into
contact. In 1884–85 Colonel R. G. Woodthorpe and
Major C. R. Macgregor conducted an expedition from
Sadiya, on the upper waters of the Brahmaputra, to the
Kampti Shan country on the western branch of the Ira-
wadi—the Nam-kiu—returning over the Pathoi range.
Just above the point where it is joined by the Nam-lung

($27°$ $15'$ $30''$ N., $97°$ $38'$ $30''$ E.) they found the Nam-kiu to be only about 85 yards broad and nowhere more than 5 feet deep. Its source was stated to lie among hills immediately to the north. In 1885–86 Mr. J. F. Needham followed the Brahmaputra up to Rima, and disposed of the theory that the Sampo River of Tibet was the upper Irawadi, while seven years later, in the season of 1892–93, Mr. Errol Gray, a tea-planter of Assam, in attempting to make his way from that province to Western China, penetrated farther east than any previous traveller who had explored upper Burma from the west, and though unable to complete his programme, crossed the Nam-kiu and reached the valley of the Tisang, a tributary of the Irawadi ranking in importance with the Nam-kiu branch of the river. An account of the contribution made by Prince Henri of Orleans to our knowledge of the headwaters of the Irawadi must be reserved for the next chapter. Finally, in connection with the general exploration of upper Burma, special mention must be made of the work of Mr. J. G. (now Sir James) Scott, who, both as an administrator and as a member of the various boundary commissions that have been engaged in settling the frontiers, has added largely to the sum of our information about the country, with which he has, perhaps, a more intimate acquaintance than any living European. Of the results obtained by all these incessant efforts to open up Burma and the Shan States under Burmese rule, more will have to be said in the concluding chapter of the book.

Lao Town, Muang-Nan

CHAPTER XII

THE comparatively meagre knowledge possessed
by Europeans concerning the geography of
Siam up to the middle of the last century is
well exemplified by a paper on the subject which was
read before the Royal Geographical Society in London
on December 10th, 1855, by Mr., afterwards Sir, Harry
Parkes, who at that time occupied the position of British
Consul at Bangkok. The only surveys of the country
then available, he declared, were those which had been
made in the course of their professional journeys by Dr.
S. R. House and his fellows of the American Missions.
These journeys had always been made by boat, and the
surveys were taken by the somewhat primitive system
known as "time and compass." The map thus compiled, however, contained, Sir Harry Parkes wrote, "all
the authentic geographical information we possess on
that most important part of the Siamese dominions, the
great valley of the Menam." Yet when we come to examine it, the area delineated is very meagre and circum-
scribed. It is covered by barely as much as two degrees
of latitude, and embraces nothing beyond the lower
valleys of the Menam and Meklong Rivers. Bishop
Pallegoix, whose important work on Siam appeared in
1852, had penetrated somewhat farther into the interior,

though Sir Harry Parkes believed that his explorations only extended on the Menam as far as Pakprian, a distance of 30 miles from the point at which the American survey terminated, on the Meklong for a distance of about 120 miles from its mouth, and on the Tachin as far as Supanburi, a matter of 180 miles or so from its outfall. For the rest, the latitude of Ayuthia, the ancient capital of Siam, and of Lopburi, a town somewhat farther up the valley of the Menam, had been fixed by Captain Davis, the commander of a merchantman, who had accompanied the King to these places a year or two before the time of which Parkes was speaking.

Topographical and statistical information on the subject of Siam, albeit of a character of only approximate accuracy, was not, however, lacking. Merchants and missionaries were now residing in Siam in fair numbers, and in 1852 Frederick Arthur Neale, an Englishman who had spent many years in Siam, published an account of the country. His personal knowledge of it does not appear to have extended much beyond a few trade-centres, and in the same year Bishop Pallegoix's far more important work made its appearance. The Roman Catholic missionaries in south-eastern Asia have made good their claim to be regarded as among the most adventuresome of their kind, and Pallegoix, from his position as head of their organisation in Siam and from his intimate knowledge of the natives and of their language, had been able to collect a remarkable amount of reliable information concerning Siam and its inhabitants. His book, therefore, represented by far the most important contribution to European knowledge of Siam that had then been made. It is, on the whole, wonderfully accurate, and even to-day it ranks as a standard work upon the Siam of half a century ago. He knew, chiefly through native reports, the names and relative positions of all the provinces of Siam; he described each of these with a fair amount of detail, from Chieng Mai on the Meping, and Luang Prabang on the Mekong, to the Malay States of the Peninsula; and his estimates of the total population of the country, 6,000,000 souls, and its division into races, were fairly correct so far as can now be judged. Of the Mekong he possessed no personal knowledge, and he merely repeated information supplied to him by natives, but he had obtained a fair idea of its size and of the direction in which it flows from Luang Prabang through Laos.

In 1855 Sir John Bowring was sent to Bangkok on a special mission, and in his published account of his visit a considerable amount of information is given concerning the past history of Siam and Siamese relations with the West. Bowring, however, had no opportunity of materially adding to the facts collected by his predecessors.

In 1856 Mr. D. O. King returned to Bangkok after nearly a year spent in Eastern Siam and in Kambodia. He had ascended the Bang Pa Kong from Bangkok to Pachim and Muong Kabin, and thence had made his way over a "military road," which had been constructed five and twenty years earlier, to the Tasawai River. He had spent some time at Batambang, and thence had paid visits to Chantabun and to the gold mines situated between Batambang and the Menam valley. Leaving

Batambang he had passed completely round the shores of the great lake of Tonle Sap, visiting Siam-reap and Angkor (which he spelled " Nakon "), subsequently descending the branch of the lake to Udong and Pnom Penh. Thence he eventually passed through Cochin-China to the sea. He made no surveys, and his account of his journey, written in a style which has nothing to recommend it to the reader, is curiously barren of interest. In 1859 the Angkor ruins were visited and described by Dr. James Campbell, a medical officer of the Royal Navy.

In the previous year, Henri Mouhot, the story of whose wanderings and death near Luang Prabang has been told in an earlier chapter, landed in Siam, and between that time and 1861 explored the lower Menam valley, the greater part of Chantabun and Batambang, the lake of Tonle-Sap and its vicinity, the ruins of Angkor, much of the hill country of Kambodia inhabited by primitive tribes, and finally the land-route between Korat and Luang Prabang. Mouhot, as we have seen, did not live to edit his own notes, and his latitudes were inaccurate, his instruments having suffered in the course of the rough overland journey from the Menam to the Mekong. He was thus robbed of the best fruits of the labours which cost him his life; but none the less, to Henri Mouhot belongs the distinction of being, so far as is known, the first white man to traverse the country lying between Korat and Luang Prabang, and his delightful book, to which so melancholy an interest attaches, threw the first light upon what had hitherto been one of the dark places of the earth.

Bangkok

Nearly twenty years before Mouhot's time, however, a similar service had been rendered to the upper districts of western Siam by Richardson, who, in addition to playing the part already described in the history of Burmese explorations, had made his way overland from Maulmain to Bangkok. He was intrusted, as usual, with a commercial mission, and he left Maulmain by boat in December, 1838. At the end of a few days he exchanged his boats for elephants, and followed the Zimi River up into the hills. The extension of these hills towards the south, it may be noted, forms the range which is, as it were, the backbone of the Malay Peninsula. The road was difficult, the country sparsely peopled by rude tribes, and rain fell incessantly, but he wormed his way through the highlands with his accustomed doggedness, and on January 14th, 1839, found himself upon the eastern slope within a journey of "five or six days of Tavoi, as the Kareens travel." From this point he descended into the valley of the Meklong, reaching Kanaburi on the 25th January, and descending the river from that place, cut across to the Menam, which he reached some distance below Bangkok. In the course of his journey he obtained a good general idea of the mountain system between Tenasserim and Siam, added to the information then possessed on the subject of the Meklong and its tributaries, but otherwise achieved no very important results; for his commercial mission led to nothing. The mountains with their uncivilised inhabitants presented a serious barrier to trade between Siam and Tenasserim.

In 1859 Sir Robert Schomburgk, F.R.S., during his

tenure of office as British Consul at Bangkok, undertook
a long and arduous journey, of which, however, he has
left us only a meagre record. Starting from Bangkok
on December 12th, he reached Raheng, the most southerly
of the Laos cities on the Me-ping, the great western
branch of the Menam, on January 9th, 1860. Here he
sent his boats back to Bangkok, and continued the journey on elephants, reaching Chieng Mai *viâ* Lampun—or
Labun, as Richardson and his fellows always called it—
on 11th February. From Chieng Mai he made his way
to Maulmain by the trade route which had already been
explored more than once by British officers from the Burmese side. Schomburgk was certainly among the earliest,
if not the very first, European to reach the Gulf of Bengal from the Gulf of Siam, *viâ* Chieng Mai, since the
time of the ill-fated factor, Samuel, at the beginning of
the seventeenth century. From Maulmain Schomburgk
proceeded by steamer to Tavoi, whence he crossed the
mountain range on elephants, and in eight days reached
the junction of the Me-nam-noi with the Meklong.
Descending the banks of the latter stream as far as
Kanburi, he next struck across to Bangkok, where he
arrived after an absence of 135 days, 86 of which had
been occupied in actual travelling. He made no surveys
of the route followed, and the information which he
gathered was of a general and statistical rather than of
a geographical character. The same remark applies with
equal force to other consular journeys made in Siam
during the next twenty years, and unofficial visitors to
the country, who were either missionaries or traders,
were more concerned with their own immediate interests

than with the duty of adding to the sum of geographical knowledge. The scientific mapping and exploration of Siam did not begin until 1881, when Mr. James Mc-Carthy, of whose work more will be said presently, entered the Siamese service, began a series of interesting journeys, and gradually brought into being an efficient State survey department.

In the meanwhile in other parts of the Indo-Chinese peninsula European explorers had been busy. M. J. Dupuis, a French merchant, had met Garnier at Han-Kau in May, 1868, and though he claimed originality for his idea, there seems to be little doubt that the notion of opening up a trade-route between Yun-nan and the Gulf of Tongking by means of the Song-Koi was suggested to Dupuis by the discoveries made by the French mission. Be this how it may, Dupuis travelled in the province of Yun-nan in 1868 and 1869, but the disturbed state of the country consequent upon the Muhammadan rebellion, prevented him from proceeding beyond Yunnan-fu. In 1871, by which time he had become a contractor for the Chinese army, he left Yun-nan-fu on February 25th bound for Tongking. Travelling overland in a southerly direction, he struck the Song-Koi at Mang-hao, and navigated it from that point to the sea. He was under contract to bring a cargo of arms and ammunition up the river into Yun-nan, and this he succeeded in doing in 1872, in spite of the opposition of the authorities in Tongking and the difficulties of the river route which he had selected for his operations. At Yun-nan-sen he purchased a cargo of tin and copper, and undertook to bring back a return cargo of salt from

Tongking. On his arrival at Hanoi, however, the local mandarins declined absolutely to permit him to purchase and carry salt to China, salt being their own precious monopoly. Dupuis appealed to the French Government at Saigon, and our old friend Francis Garnier was sent with a small force to arbitrate between the French merchant and the mandarins of Hanoi.

Garnier arrived at the capital of Tongking on November 5th, 1873, and ten days later issued a proclamation declaring the Song-Koi open to general commerce. This determined, but perhaps over-hasty, action led to immediate hostilities, and on November 20th Garnier seized the citadel of Hanoi by assault. For one backed by so tiny a force, Garnier's policy was audacious to the point of recklessness, but for the moment it succeeded so well that in the course of a few weeks he had made himself master of five native strongholds, and seemingly had the whole of lower Tongking in his grip. The Annamese, who saw their possession slipping from their grasp, now called in the Black Flags, the lawless bands of marauders who had effected a lodging in northern Tongking during the prolonged disturbances in Yun-nan. These new enemies forthwith attacked Hanoi, and on December 21st Francis Garnier was killed while leading a sortie against them. Impetuous, eager, strenuous, and fearless to the last, he fell far in advance of his men, and by his death France was robbed at a critical moment of one of the few of her sons who have won for themselves great reputations while engaged in building up her empire beyond the seas.

The man who was next sent to Hanoi was of another

River Scene, Bangkok

type. This worthy, M. Philastre, lost no time in issuing
a proclamation in which he not only repudiated all the
doings of Garnier, but went out of his way to insult publicly the memory of his great predecessor. He ordered
the evacuation of Tongking, and losing his head at a
critical moment, mistook some harmless native trading-
ships for pirates, fired upon and sunk them, and hanged
their captains. As for poor M. Dupuis, his vessels were
sequestrated, and the withdrawal of the French was followed by a massacre of their native allies. In March,
1874, a treaty was concluded between France and Annam whereby Kui-nhon, Haiphong, and Hanoi were
thrown open to commerce and French consuls were stationed in these towns. The position of these officers,
however, was the reverse of enviable, for their country
had for the moment fallen into contempt, and they were
subjected to the greatest indignities.

Dupuis had none the less succeeded in accomplishing
something, for he had explored the course of the Song-
Koi. Above Mang-hao he found that the stream passed
through long defiles, with almost perpendicular mountains rising abruptly from its banks, and even he owned
that it was doubtful whether the stream was navigable
for any save small canoes in this portion of its course.
Below Mang-hao, however, at which point it is already
about 100 yards across, he considered the Song-Koi an
excellent waterway, and he placed the distance from
Mang-hao to Hanoi at 304 miles, or 414 miles from
the sea at the mouth of the Thai Binh branch of the
delta. That the Song-Koi was navigable Dupuis proved
past any doubt, since he actually carried his cargo of

warlike stores up river, and returned with tin and copper; but his desire to create a new trade-route led him to underestimate its difficulties, and above Tuan-kuan it is impracticable except from April to November. As a trade-route the Song-Koi must therefore be regarded as of little value, and if the commerce of southern China is ever to be brought to the Gulf of Tongking it must be not by water but by railroad.

A few years later the French were once more engaged in active warfare in Tongking, their enemies being the redoubtable Black Flags, who were now in possession of upper Tongking and had made numerous descents into the valley of the Mekong. It is at this point that explorations in Siam begin to join on to the explorations of French officers in the " Empire of Annam," as Annam and Tongking are collectively named, and we must turn for the moment to the journeys of Mr. James McCarthy, which are the first link in the chain.

It was in 1881 that Mr. McCarthy, who, it has been noted, was in the service of the King of Siam, began to prepare the way for a map of that country. His first undertaking was an examination of the route for a telegraph line between Bangkok and Maulmain, viâ Raheng and Tak. Mr. McCarthy fixed the position of Raheng by a small series of triangles in connection with the Eastern Frontier series of Surveys made by the Government of India, and ran a traverse with chain and compass from Kampangpet to Nakon Sawan, a distance of 90 miles, but was then compelled to return to Bangkok owing to a bad attack of fever. He next employed himself in making a large scale survey of Sampeng, the most thickly populated quarter of Bangkok, and made this a training-ground for the Siamese youths whom he was educating to become his assistants. After this he again ascended the Menam, and entering the Me-ping surveyed and mapped the country between Raheng and Chieng Mai, in order to facilitate the settlement of a dispute as to boundaries; but fever, which, as he cheerfully says, had now become his "annual companion," once more forced him to return to Bangkok. In 1883 Mr. McCarthy made a tour in the Malay Peninsula in connection with a boundary dispute which had arisen between the State of Pêrak, which was under British protection, and Raman, a portion of the ancient kingdom of Pĕtâni. Touching first at Champon—which had been visited a few months earlier by a party of French engineers, who desired to report upon the possibility of cutting a ship-canal through the isthmus of Kra—he passed on to Sĕnggôra, and thence to the mouth of the Pĕtâni River. The French engineers, it should be noted, had found a point at which the highest hill was only 250 feet above sea-level, which was 200 feet lower than the pass crossed by Richardson and Tremenheere in 1839. Passing up-stream, McCarthy reached Raman; Sir Hugh Low, the British Resident of Pêrak, had a conference with the Siamese Commissioner sent to meet him; and McCarthy then made a survey of the disputed territory, including the upper reaches of the Pêrak River. He returned to Bangkok *viâ* Singapore, which he reached by steamer.

In January, 1884, he again left Bangkok, and after ascending the Menam to Saraburi, quitted his boats and marched to Korat through the "Dong Phia Fai," or

Forest of the Lord of Fire, a region which is notorious as a terrible fever-trap. He crossed the Pi-mun,
on the banks of which is the town of Ubon, at Muong
Pi-mai, whence he proceeded to Kunwapi, and after
traversing forest country emerged into the populous district in which Nong-Kai, the new city erected close to
the ruins of Vien Chan, is situated. Here for the first
time McCarthy saw the waters of the Mekong, and sending his assistant, Mr. Bush, up that river, he himself
crossed over into the country which had been ravaged by
the Haws, or Black Flags. It will be remembered that
the country lying between Tongking and the Mekong had
at one time been entirely under the control of Annam,
but later the Siamese laid claim to it, and after they
had suffered defeat, returned to the charge, and by
transporting the entire population across the river left
the armies of Annam nothing to fight for. Later, Siam
quietly reoccupied the abandoned territory, and it was
not until France had won ascendency over Annam that
the rights of that kingdom to the region in question
were at last enforced, and the Mekong became the
boundary-line between French Indo-China and the Laos
States under Siamese control. At the time of McCarthy's visit, this beautiful country was practically deserted,
the troubles caused by the Haw being in full swing; but
crossing the Nam Tang, he ascended into a plateau,
some 60 square miles in extent, at an elevation of 3,500
feet above sea-level. Thence he passed on to Chieng
Kwang, or Muong Puan, as it is variously called, the
capital of the district, and found it under the sway of
the Haw, the robber stronghold of Tung-Chieng-Kam

On the Mon River

being within three days' march of it. From Chieng
Kwang he passed on in a south-easterly direction to
Muong Ngan, which lies at an elevation of 4,800 feet.
Here he found that two French priests had shortly
before been living in the place, which had also been
visited by M. Neiss, a French traveller and political
agent. The latter had endeavoured to obtain an acknow-
ledgment of the sovereignty of Annam from the people
of Muong Ngan, and after his departure the Haw had
come down and looted the little town. At Ta Tom, the
place next reached, the Nam Chan, a tributary of the
Mekong, was found to be navigable for rafts, and on May
14th McCarthy reached Pachum, where the Nam Chan
falls into the great river, and passed on to Nong Kai.
Starting again on May 16th he made his way up-stream
to Luang Prabang, where he arrived on May 29th.
Heavy rains now began to fall, and the party suffered
severely from fever, Mr. Bush dying of it on June 29th,
adding yet one more name to the long roll of those who
have given their lives in the cause of exploration in
south-eastern Asia. On July 5th McCarthy left Luang
Prabang, and dropping down the river to Pak-Lai, a
short distance below which the Mekong turns abruptly to
the east, landed and marched across the divide to
Muong Wa, striking the Menam at Yandu. The pass
from the Mekong to the Menam valleys is here traversed
by a very easy track. From Yandu McCarthy returned
to Bangkok down the Menam River.

In November he again started for the Mekong valley,
ascending the Menam to Nakon Sawan, and thence to
Pak-nam Po, at the junction of the Me-ping. Continu-

ing the ascent of the Menam he reached Utaradit, where
the boats were finally quitted, Mr. D. J. Collins and Lieutenant Rossmussen, a Dane, who had accompanied him,
leaving him at Nan and proceeding to Luang Prabang
via Muong Hung. McCarthy, on the other hand, went
by Tanun on the Mekong, visiting *en route* the crater
of the volcano called the Pu Fai Yai, or Great Fire Hill,
which had disappointed the expectations of the members
of the French mission deputed by de Lagrée to examine
it. From Tanun McCarthy, who had traversed from
Nan a considerable stretch of unexplored country, went
down river to Luang Prabang, halting on the way to
see the great cave opposite to the mouth of the Nam
Hu, which had also been visited by Garnier and his
companions. McCarthy, Collins and Rossmussen next
marched to join the Siamese army which had been sent
into the districts to the east of the Mekong to subdue
the Haw; they took part in the fighting, and witnessed the beginning of the investment of the robber
stronghold at Tung-Chieng-Kam. Seeing that the siege
was likely to be a protracted business—in the end the
Siamese were obliged to raise it—McCarthy presently
started on a tour in a northerly direction. From Ban
Le he despatched Rossmussen and the Siamese sick and
wounded to Luang Prabang, and went on with Collins
to Muong Son and Muong Kao, intending to visit Muong
Sop Et, where the Nam Et falls into the Song Ma, the
more southerly of the two great rivers of Tongking.
At Muong Kao rafts were made, and the river was
descended as far as Sop Pon, but McCarthy's native
companions contrived to prevent him from proceeding

Auguste Pavie

farther down the Nam Et, and the explorers were obliged to regain the valley of the Mekong, striking the Nam Hu at Muong Ngoi. Collins thence ascended the Nam Hu as far as Muong Hahin, within a measurable distance of its source, and so added the valley of that important tributary of the Mekong to the map of the region. McCarthy meanwhile marched over very rough country north-north-east to Muong Teng, which is situated in a magnificent plain some 60 square miles in extent at the head of the valley of the Nam Nua, a left-bank tributary of the Nam Hu. On May 26th he started down this river on rafts, which he later exchanged for boats, and on June 1st arrived at Luang Prabang, where he found Collins already awaiting him. The travellers then returned to Bangkok by McCarthy's former route.

The siege of the Haw stronghold of Tung-Chieng-Kam by the forces of Siam had beeen raised in 1885, after the place had been invested for three whole months, and in the following year the Government at Bangkok decided to make a final effort to suppress the Haw. By this time a treaty had been concluded between Great Britain and Siam, under the provisions of which a British consul was appointed to reside at Chieng Mai. The French followed suit by apppointing a consul at Luang Prabang, though not a single French subject lived in that city or the neighbouring district. The officer selected for this latter post was M. Auguste Pavie, whose name was destined to become more intimately associated with the work of exploration in the valley of the Mekong and its neighbourhood than that of any other living European. Shortly after the time of the Garnier mission, M. Harmand had made some detailed explorations in Kambodia and in the neighbouring provinces of Batambang and Siam-Reap. These had been supplemented by M. Pavie, who while in the service of the King of Siam had surveyed the telegraph line from Bangkok to Batambang. He now set off, towards the end of 1885, to take up his appointment at Luang Prabang, starting from Bangkok in the company of McCarthy, who had with him Collins and Louis du Plessis de Richelieu, all three being in the service of Siam. At Pak-nam Po McCarthy and Pavie separated, each going on independently to Luang Prabang. McCarthy, who did not wish to interfere with the transport arrangements of the Siamese army, which was making its way from the valley of the Menam to fight against the Haw across the Mekong, ascended the Me-ping to Chieng Mai, and thence struck off in a northerly direction to Chieng Rai on the Nam Kok, a right-bank tributary of the Mekong. Descending this river, he struck the Mekong at Chieng Hsen, and so reached Luang Prabang. Thence he immmediately set out for Muong Teng, where he joined a wing of the Siamese army on December 16th, 1885. It had been his intention to make for Muong Lai and to survey the natural boundary between the valley of the Mekong and Tongking, but Phia Surasak, the Siamese general, preferred to send him to Sop Et on the Song Ma, whence he was to survey the boundary of the district known as Hua Pan Tang Ha Tang Hok, eventually making his way to Nong Kai on the Mekong. De Richelieu, falling sick, was sent back to Luang Prabang, Collins going with McCarthy. An attack of his old enemy, fever, interfered, however, with McCarthy's plans and he was forced to return to Luang Prabang and Bangkok. Shortly afterwards, the Haw, having got the better of the Siamese troops, swooped down upon Luang Prabang, their advance meeting with no opposition, and sacked that city.

In 1887 the French in Tongking made a final effort to subdue the outlying provinces, and attacked the Haw before the Siamese army under Phia Surasak had quitted the valley of the Menam. It was now that Pavie began a series of journeys through the country lying between the Mekong and Tongking, eventually effecting a junction with the French troops in the latter kingdom. In 1888 he was joined by Captain Cupet and Lieutenant Nicolon, who met him near Luang Prabang just after his return from his first journey into Tongking. Nicolon was left at Luang Prabang to survey the district, and Pavie and Cupet once more set off for Tongking, their objective being Tak-Khoa on the Song-Koi. From this place Cupet returned to Luang Prabang by a new route, and in 1889 he surveyed the country to the eastward of the Mekong farther to the south, and explored the whole of it from Laos and Kambodia to Annam and the China Sea, covering in his journeys across and across the country more than 5,500 miles in all. He also in 1888 travelled on the left bank of the Mekong from Pak Lai to Pit Chai on the Menam, surveying the intervening country, and in 1893 he, in conjunction with Captain Friquegnon and Captain de Malglaive, was appointed to edit the great map of Indo-China which has been prepared under the auspices of M. Pavie.

Captain de Malglaive, who was also attached at a

somewhat later period to the " Mission Pavie," undertook an important series of explorations in 1890 and 1891 between the coast of central Annam and the Mekong, his object being to discover the best means of communication through the country. M. Harmand, whose name has already been mentioned, had partly explored this region between 1875–77, his principal journey in the former year being up the Mekong to Khong, and thence through the Siamese provinces of Melu-prey, Tonle Repu, and Kompang Soai, which had never previously been traversed by a European. From the slopes of Dongrek to near Prea-khan, he found few Kambodians, almost the entire population being composed of Kui tribesmen. In 1877 Harmand explored the southern basin of the Se-mun, went from Pnom Penh to Siam-Reap, and thence cut across to Bassak and the country between that place and the Se-Dom. He next explored the valley of the Se-Dom as far as Atopeu, a piece of work already accomplished to some extent by de Lagrée, and later made his way from Pnom Penh to Lakon, and thence to Nghe An and Binh-Dinh, succeeding in the course of his journeys in making some important rectifications in the map of the delta of the Mekong. This was the work which Captain de Malglaive now completed, crossing the divide between the Mekong and the sea no less than five times, and carrying a line of survey over this rough tract of country by four separate routes. The fruit of his labours was the discovery of an excellent route from the coast into the interior by the passage of Ai-Lao.

In 1890–91 Captain Rivière completed some interesting

The Great Rapid. Red River, Lukay to Manhao

explorations under Pavie in the upper basin of the Mekong, especially in the district to the south-east of Luang
Prabang, and in 1894 he was attached to the Pavie mission for the examination of the upper Mekong in connection with Sir J. G. Scott's Mekong Commission.
Rivière, like Henri Mouhot before him, sacrificed his
life in the cause of exploration, and though his reports
have since been published by M. Pavie, they do scant
justice to the work which he performed. Another officer
attached to the Mission Pavie was M. Lefèvre-Pontalis,
who accompanied M. Pavie on many of his journeys and
was afterwards attached to the Mekong Commission of
1894, in the course of which he explored the middle valley of the Nam Hu, in conjunction with Lieutenant
Thomassin and Dr. Lefèvre, a district which, as we have
seen, had already been visited and mapped by McCarthy
and Collins. Other important explorations have also
been made under the auspices of M. Pavie, but at the
time of writing the results obtained have not yet been
published, though all will eventually appear in the monumental work on French Indo-China edited by M. Pavie,
five huge quarto volumes of which have already been
given to the public. The fruit of all these explorations is
the magnificent large-scale map of Indo-China which has
now been published by the French Government under
the editorship already named. It is a monument of
accurate and patient labour, and not only surpasses anything of the kind that the British have done for Malaya,
but compares favourably with the great maps produced
by the Survey Department of India.

In 1895 an expedition under Prince Henri of Orleans

explored the greater portion of the long stretch of the
Mekong River that lies within the Chinese province of
Yun-nan, and then turning west made important contributions to our knowledge of the headwaters of the Irawadi. The European members of the party included,
besides Prince Henri, M. Roux, who superintended the
cartographical work, and M. Briffaud. After penetrating
to the interior by way of the Red River, the expedition
struck westwards from Isse, a town north of the French
frontier, and made its way through unexplored country
to the Mekong, which was reached at a place called
Ti-an-pi in 22° 38′ N. lat. " The river here," says
Prince Henri, " is from 350 to about 500 feet wide." It
flows partly between wooded hills whose slopes are less
steep than those which form the valley of the Red River.
Rapids render navigation impossible in some places.
Striking the river from time to time, the expedition
journeyed northward through the country on the right
bank of the Mekong as far as 24° 45′ N. lat. Here a
crossing was effected, and the travellers pushed on to
Ta-li-fu. After a rest at this now well-known stopping-
place, the expedition again turned west to the Mekong,
which was reached at Fei-long-kiao, in 25° 50′ N. An excursion was made still farther west, to the Salwin River,
and then the expedition ascended the valley of the Mekong, following the course of the river more or less
closely as far as Tseku, on the Tibetan frontier, north
of the 28th parallel. During this part of the journey
the scientific instruments were stolen, and henceforward
the route could only be laid down by compass. North
of Tseku the course of the Mekong has been followed

Village Road, Anam

by French missionaries, and at that place the exploration of the river by Prince Henri's expedition practically came to a close, though a trip was made three days' journey farther north, to Atense. Once more turning west, the expedition made an important journey through difficult country to Sadiya, situated at the great bend of the Brahmaputra. The passage of this stretch of country entailed severe hardships on all concerned, but as a result of the journey Prince Henri was led to more than one interesting conclusion. In the first place he found the Salwin to be, on the same latitude as Tseku, "a large, fairly deep river, coming from a long distance," and affirmed that missionary and native evidence, coupled with the observations of his own expedition, showed the Oi Chu of Tibet, the Lu-tze-kiang, and the Salwin, to be sections of one and the same river. In the second place he reported that the headwaters of the Irawadi comprised three main streams, the Kiu-kiang and the Telo in the east, and the Nam-kiu in the west. Of these the Kiu-kiang has the largest volume of water, "and its source is farther north in a well-known mountain in Tsarony, two days' journey from Menkong, i.e., 28° or 29° lat. north. The Telo issues from a mountain that we had seen farther south. The mountain out of which the Nam-kiu has its source can be seen from Khamti, and is well known to the English." On the north the whole of the basin of the Irawadi is bounded, Prince Henri further declared, by a chain of mountains, forming apparently a continuation of the Himalaya. These mountains are intersected by openings through which flow the Dibong and the Lohit. As to the great volume of the Irawadi in its upper reaches, a feature of the river which had been of great weight in inducing some geographers to support the view that the main sources of the Irawadi were to be found far away to the north, in the San-po River to Tibet, Prince Henri pointed out that this was due to the comparatively wide extent of the valley of the Upper Irawadi, the width of which, where crossed by the expedition, he set down as 115 miles, while in the same latitude the width of the Salwin valley was not more than 25 miles. If this evidence may be accepted, and there is no reason to doubt its accuracy, Prince Henri may justly claim that his expedition practically solved the problem of the sources of the Irawadi.

To return for the moment to McCarthy and his work in Siam, we find him in 1887 and 1888 engaged upon the trace for the now completed railway from Bangkok to Korat *viâ* Ayuthia, and on a similar trace to Chieng Mai *viâ* Utarit, on the Menam, and Muong Pre, a Laotine town on the Nam Yom. In 1890 McCarthy took up survey work on the north-west, to delimit the boundary between Siam and Burma, but the fact of his nationality made him suspect, and he quitted this unpleasant task as soon as possible. At the end of 1890, aided by Siamese surveyors whom he had himself trained to the work, he made a series of valuable surveys in northern Siam, fixing the height of Doi Intanon (8,450 feet), a mountain to the west of Chieng Mai, which is the highest peak in Siam, and later making a trigonometrical station on Pahom Pok, a peak on the range which divides Siam from Burma, the summit of which was reached after great labour on February 24th, 1891.

Kachin Village

This peak had been fixed by the Indian surveyors in 1889–90, at which period an Anglo-Siamese Commission, on which Great Britain was represented by Sir James Scott, the Superintendent of the Northern Shan States, had delimited the boundary between Burma and Siam. McCarthy therefore took this as his starting-point, and from it made his triangulations which were the beginning of a trigonometrical survey of northern Siam. McCarthy, with a few European assistants, the most prominent of whom was Mr. Smiles, yet another victim to the work of exploration in these regions, continued to push his surveys forward until the middle of 1893, much help being rendered to him by the native surveyors whom he had trained. Shortly after that date he was able to publish the first really reliable map of the kingdom, which, up to the present time, has received no material additions that have been made public. An examination of this map shows that northern Siam, Mr. McCarthy's especial sphere of labour, has now been carefully and fully explored, as also have a narrow area along the valley of the Menam and its branches, and the mountain ranges which divide British territory from Siam. Eastern Siam, between the lower Menam and the Mekong, is far less fully mapped, though all places of real importance have been visited and their positions fixed. The valley of the Meklong is fairly well known, but the rest of lower Siam, south of the Tenasserim, is still very imperfectly known, McCarthy's surveys in Raman, made in 1883, being the most accurate work of the kind yet done in this region.

It has already been pointed out that, after the war of

1885 had at last drawn to a close, the systematic survey
of Burma and the Shan States under Burmese rule was
begun. Thus the close of the nineteenth century saw the
trained surveyor penetrate to the heart alike of the British, the French, and the Siamese spheres. Indeed it may
be said that the Anglo-Siamese Boundary Commission
of 1889–90, the Anglo-French Mekong Commission of
1894–96, and the Burma-China Boundary Commission of
1898–1900—of all of which Sir James Scott was a member—practically completed the work of exploration in
those regions wherein we have watched the gradual
growth of discovery from its primitive beginnings. The
labours of these Commissions cannot be here followed in
detail. In many cases ground was traversed which had
already been explored and described by travellers whose
journeys we have examined; for the rest these Commissions linked up individual and independent explorations,
and did the work with an accuracy which had been beyond the reach of earlier geographers. With the era of
Boundary Commissions much of the adventure, the
glamour and the romance of exploration inevitably van-
ishes. Discovery, in the old sense of the word, is at an
end, and the work, for all its geographical and political
importance, assumes the more sombre tinge of prosaic
business, done with comparative ease and comfort in a
dull, methodical fashion, as business should be done.
The achievements of these Commissions are best appreciated by a study of the recent maps of the Indo-Chinese
Hinterland, which disclose an almost bewildering wealth
of detail in all the regions under effective European
domination, that is to say, in every part of it with the

exception of portions of China and Siam and a few uninhabited or sparsely peopled tracts.

But we have still to review the progress of exploration in the Malay Peninsula during the past quarter of a century. It has been noted that up to 1874 the interior was practically unknown to Europeans, though Newbolt, Crawfurd and Logan had collected a vast quantity of information concerning it from native sources. In 1874 the Sultan of Pêrak applied for advice and assistance to the Governor of the Straits Settlements, and Mr. J. W. Birch, Colonial Secretary in Singapore, was sent to reside at his Court. Shortly afterwards the Sultan and the rival claimant to the throne settled their differences on the grounds of common detestation of the white men, and Mr. Birch was treacherously murdered. Upon this British troops were landed in Pêrak, and after a short war the Sultan Abdullah was exiled to the Seychelles, and his relative Râja Mûda Jusuf was made Regent. Sir Hugh Low, an officer of great experience of the Malays, who had imbibed from the first Râja Brooke sound principles on the subject of European responsibilities towards and methods of governing natives, was appointed Resident of Pêrak, and under his wise and tactful guidance complete tranquillity was speedily restored.

Prolonged civil war and acts of piracy and aggression led to the adoption of a similar policy in Sĕlângor and Sûngei Ujong—two Native States farther to the south, on the western shore of the Peninsula—and in 1887 a treaty was entered into with the Sultan of Pahang, on the east coast, whereby a British agent, the present writer, was appointed to reside at Pĕkan, the capital, and was invested with consular powers. During the following year a British subject, a Chinaman, was murdered at Pĕkan in very unequivocal circumstances, and the British Government, considering that the presence of a British Resident in Pahang was the only sufficient guarantee for the safety of life and property, induced the Sultan to place his country under British protection. In 1891 disturbances broke out in the State, which lasted for something over a twelvemonth, by which time the rebel leaders had been driven to seek refuge over the border in the independent States of Trĕnggânu and Kĕlantan. A raid into Pahang headed by these outlaws occurred in 1894, and in the following year an expedition, composed of irregular native levies under European leadership, was sent into Kĕlantan and Trĕnggânu for the purpose of effecting their capture. The ringleaders subsequently fell into the hands of the Siamese commissioners sent from Bangkok to aid in their arrest, and after one of them had been treacherously murdered by Siamese officials, the survivors were carried off to Siam. Since that time the peace of the British protectorate has not been broken.

It was after the wars in Pêrak and Sûngei Ujong, and the bombardment of Kuâla Sĕlângor by a British ship, that the task of exploring the interior began in earnest. During the Pêrak war British troops had ascended the river as far as Kôta Lâma, but though an Italian, Mr. Bozzolo, in the service of the Pêrak Government, who had been engaged in mining operations in Pĕtâni, explored the country from that point to the little State of Raman between 1880 and 1883, it was not until the latter year that the Pêrak River, which had been ascended by the late Sir William Maxwell in 1875, was mapped almost to its source, partly by M. St. George Caulfield and partly, as we have seen, by Mr. McCarthy. A few years prior to this the Peninsula had been crossed from Sûngei Ujong to the mouth of the Pahang River by Messrs. Daly and O'Brien, who had followed the route leading over the mountains to the Bra, a right-bank tributary of the Pahang. In 1884–85 Mr. William Cameron, an explorer in Government employ, made his way from the Kinta valley in Pêrak over the main range into the valley of the Tĕlom, one of the upper branches of the Pahang River, descended the Tĕlom to its junction with the Jĕlai, and the latter stream to Kuâla Tĕmbĕling. At this point the united waters first take the name of Pahang, and Cameron continued his descent of that river to the sea, making a time and compass survey of his route.

In 1884 Mr., now Sir Frank, Swettenham, who at that time was acting for Sir Hugh Low as Resident of Pêrak, crossed the Peninsula to the mouth of the Pahang with Captain Giles, R.A., and the Hon. Martin Lister. The route followed was up the Berman River, a stream which had been first explored by Sir Frank Swettenham some years earlier, and then up its tributary, the Siam. From this point the party was conveyed overland by elephants to the headwaters of the Lĭpis, the main right-bank tributary of the Jĕlai. The two rivers flow together some twenty miles above Kuâla Tĕmbĕling, and from their confluence the party descended the Pahang River to its mouth, and returned to the west coast by sea.

Captain Giles somewhat improved upon the time and compass survey which had already been made by Mr. Cameron.

A few years before this, a Russian, Baron Mikioucho-Maclay, had made his way up the Pahang River to Kuâla Těmběling, and up that stream to Kuâla Sat, whence he had walked over the divide into the Lebir valley, one of the main branches of the Kělantan River. Such surveys as he made, however, were very inexact and added little to the knowledge of this region which had already been obtained from native sources.

Between 1884 and 1887 a number of speculators were busy obtaining concessions from the Sultan of Pahang, and the Peninsula was crossed by several of their employees from the mouth of the Klang River to the mouth of the Pahang, *viâ* Kuâla Kûbu, Raub, and the Lĭpis valley, the line of country over which the Sělângor railway and the Pahang trunk road now pass. In 1887 the present writer followed in the steps of Sir Frank Swettenham, crossing the Peninsula by the Siam route and descending the river to the sea, and in the following year he undertook an extensive journey through the districts lying on the eastern slope of the main range in Pahang territory, rejoining the Pahang River *viâ* its right-bank tributary, the Sěmantan. About the same time the Peninsula was crossed from Kědah to the mouth of the Pětâni River by several gentlemen interested in mining, the first of whom to make a survey of the route was the late Mr. H. M. Becher, who in 1895 lost his life while attempting to make the ascent of Gûnong Tâhan, which is believed to be the highest peak in the Malay Peninsula.

View of River from Belida, Kechau, Pahang

Meanwhile in Pêrak, Sĕlângor, and Sûngei Ujong, the work of detailed survey and exploration was going forward steadily under the auspices of the local Governments, and in 1887 our protectorate was extended to the Nĕgri Sĕmbilan, or Nine States, which form the *Hinterland* of Malacca. Little by little the whole of the country on the west coast, from the boundaries of Kĕdah to the Mûar River, which is under the jurisdiction of Johor, was mapped with considerable accuracy, and this region has since been opened up by means of railways and excellent roads. On the east coast a similar service was performed for Pahang, and in 1895 the present writer, while leading an armed expedition over the British borders, traversed and mapped the whole of the Trĕnggânu valley from the mountains to the sea, being the first white man to cross the Peninsula by this route. Mr. R. W. Duff, who accompanied the expedition, added to the map the valleys of the Stiu and Bĕsut, two rivers which fall into the sea north of Kuâla Trĕnggânu, and on the same occasion the Lebir and a large part of the Kĕlantan River were roughly surveyed. Three years earlier Mr. W. W. Bailey had crossed the divide between the upper waters of the Jĕlai and those of the Gâlas, the main branch of the Kĕlantan, and had descended and roughly surveyed the latter river to its mouth. In 1896 the late Mr. D. H. Wise, while acting as Resident of Pahang, reached the divide between the Pahang and Kinta Rivers, following in an opposite direction the route which twelve years earlier had been traversed by Mr. William Cameron. The Kĕlantan River has since been explored in some detail by Mr. R. W. Duff and the gentlemen associated with him in the exploitation of the mines of Kělantan.

This brief summary will suffice to convey an idea of the extent to which exploration has been carried up to the present time in the Malay Peninsula. In the western States under British protection the work of survey in its rougher stages may be said to have been completed, though the trigonometrical work begun in 1883 in Pêrak has made slow progress. On the eastern side, Pahang has now been fully, and Trěnggânu, Kělantan, and Pětâni partially, explored, though even in the first-named State there are still large areas of forest which have never been penetrated by a white man, and others where it is probable that no Malay has ever set foot. The areas which have been least adequately explored are the districts under the rule of the Sultan of Johor, which include the whole of the southern portion of the Malay Peninsula, though the country between the Ěndau and the Pahang Rivers has been visited severally by Mr. H. B. Ellerton in 1897, and Mr. E. Townley in 1900. Similarly on the north, from Kedah to the Isthmus of Kra, and on the east coast above the Pětâni River, the knowledge which we possess of the interior is very imperfect, though the area in question is not great and the coast-lines have been determined by Admiralty surveys. The Skeat expedition of 1899–1900, though its objects were mainly ethnological, added considerably to the details in our possession relating to Kělantan, Pětâni, and the neighbouring districts; but on this occasion comparatively little new ground was broken.

Gûnong Tâhan, which, as already stated, is believed to

On the Tenasserim River

be the highest mountain in the Malay Peninsula, is situated in the range from which many of the rivers of the Jĕlai and Lebir valleys take their source. Several unsuccessful attempts were made to reach its summit before the feat was accomplished by Mr. Waterstradt in 1901. Messrs. Davidson and Ridley tried to effect its ascent from the Tĕmbĕling side by means of the Tâhan River in 1893, but they were forced to turn back, owing to want of sufficient provisions, at a very early stage of their journey. Mr. H. M. Becher repeated the attempt, following the same route, in 1894, but he was unfortunately drowned in a sudden freshet of the Tâhan River before he had done more than obtain a distant view of the peak. Mr. Skeat made a solitary dash for Gûnong Tâhan in the course of his journey, but he too failed. Mr. Waterstradt approached Gûnong Tâhan from the north, and had some difficulty in identifying the mountain. He first attempted the ascent from the Pahang side, but after climbing 4,000 feet was brought to a stop by a sheer wall of rock, down which poured an enormous volume of water into the Tâhan River. Success, however, finally crowned his efforts on the north or Kĕlantan side of the mountain, where the most serious obstacle to progress was the dense jungle which is characteristic of the surrounding country. According to Mr. Waterstradt, Gûnong Tâhan is less lofty than it was thought to be, attaining only from 7,500 to 8,000 feet in height.

In this chapter we have surveyed the progress of exploration in Indo-China, in Siam and in the Malay Peninsula, during the concluding years of the nineteenth century. Space has often forbidden a more detailed examination of work, here described in outline, which from its intrinsic interest merits more elaborate treatment; but it is hoped that sufficient has been said to enable the reader to obtain a fair general idea of what has been accomplished in these regions. In every case the supremacy of Europeans or the extension of European influence, whether in the realm of politics or of ideas, has been a necessary prelude to the advancement of knowledge. The lands in question have been the homes of men of the brown or yellow races, but in every case the geographical work done therein has been inspired, if not actually executed, by Europeans alone. Science is, for the moment, the exclusive possession of the white races, and while in many lands men of European breed are bringing law and order, peace and plenty, into troubled places, that other task of advancing the knowledge of the world proceeds apace, and yearly more and more light is made to pierce the darkness which has so long obscured our view of the less accessible parts of Asia. Precisely what that light has so far revealed will be the subject of our next and concluding chapter.

CHAPTER XIII

THE story of the exploration of south-eastern Asia by Europeans—and Europeans, for our purposes, are the only true explorers—has now been told. We have seen the first dim dawning of the idea that the Gangetic Valley was not in truth the most easterly limit of the habitable world—that beyond it lay other lands, to which distance lent the glamour of mystery and of romance. We have seen how Chryse the Golden, the earliest conception of which was an island of paltry extent lying over against the mouths of the Ganges, began at last to find a place upon the maps of the ancient geographers; how later this germ of truth developed into the Golden Chersonese of Ptolemy and Marinus of Tyre. Thereafter we have watched the growth of knowledge of south-eastern Asia, fostered first by the adventurous Arabian and Persian traders, who so long held the commercial empire of the East after the rise of the Power of Islâm, then extended little by little by the tales brought home to Europe by the mediæval wanderers of Italy. Next, with the dawning of the sixteenth century, came the invasion of the East by the Portuguese, the events of which, in so far as they affect Chyrse the Golden, have been examined in so much detail in a section of this work. After that period of adventure, lawlessness and rediscovery of ancient lands came the age of the great trading companies of Britain and of Holland, an epoch which, though trade reigned supreme and political supremacy was sought after as merely a road to riches, has a romance of its own because of the mighty over-seas empires of which these commercial ventures were the beginning. Lastly we have traced the gradual extension of European influence throughout the lands of south-eastern Asia—in Burma, in Malaya, in Siam, and in French Indo-China—of all of which to-day Siam alone retains its ancient independence, though it too has had its administrative system materially altered and improved by contact with the nations of the West. It is to this last period—the nineteenth century, and more especially the concluding half of that century—that the detailed exploration of Chryse the Golden belongs, and it now remains for us to take a rapid survey of the information acquired and of the work which remains to be accomplished.

The coast-line of the great Indo-Chinese peninsula, from the mouths of the Ganges to the boundary between Tongking and China, has now been surveyed and charted with an accuracy that leaves nothing to be desired, and the same may be said for almost the whole of the neighbouring archipelago of Malaya. The outline, as it were, has been traced with the utmost exactitude: what is the extent to which that outline has been filled in?

The most important geographical feature of these lavishly watered lands is their immense river-systems, and it will be convenient, in the first place, to see what is the state of our present knowledge with regard to these.

The Red River of Tongking, commonly called the Song-Koi, but named Song-tao by the Tongkingese, was, as we have seen, first descended from Yun-nan by the Frenchman Dupuis, who afterwards ascended it with a cargo of warlike stores from Hanoi. Its navigability for anything bigger than native poling-boats was long disputed, but in August, 1890, the steam-launch "Yun-nan," drawing 70 centimetres, was taken up as far as Laokai, thus proving the practicability of using vessels of shallow draught upon the river. As a trade-route, however, the Song-Koi is admittedly unsatisfactory, and the French Government has decided that railways, not rivers, are to be regarded as the only possible means of opening up communication with the southern provinces of China. The actual sources of the Red River have not been located with accuracy, though the main branch is believed to take its rise in the mountains to the east of King-tung, in Yun-nan, in approximately 24° N. lat. and 103° E. long. The eastern branch rises partly in the mountains between Tongking and Kwang-si, and partly in the latter province, while the western branch, the Song-Bo, or Black River, has its source in the hills to the westward of Tsu-hiung, in Yun-nan. Beyond the Tongkingese boundary none of these branches has been explored or surveyed in detail for any great portion of its course.

The Song-Ma, the next important river to the south, has been traced to its source in the mountains of Uei-bak, which divide its basin from that of the Nam U, a left-bank tributary of the Mekong which falls into that river above Luang Prabang; this was part of the work performed by M. Pavie's mission. Similarly the Song Ka, still farther to the south, has been traced to its rise in the mountains which divide Tongking from the valley of the Mekong.

We come now to the Mekong itself, the immense river with the exploration of which we have been so much engaged in the pages of this work. Garnier, it will be remembered, arrived unwillingly at the conclusion that the Mekong was impracticable for navigation by steam-launches above the Khong rapids, but since his day the construction of shallow-draught river-craft has undergone an immense development, such as he may well be excused for having failed to foresee. The most formidable obstacle in the Sombor flight of rapids was the fall known as Preatapang, which Garnier himself had made two several attempts to examine, and had pronounced impossible for steam-launches. In 1883, however, Captain Réveillère succeeded after much difficulty in forcing a launch up the flight, and in the course of examinations made during 1891 and 1892, Lieutenant Robaglia discovered a channel some six metres in width which is practicable for steam-launches at all seasons of the year. He further discovered that the island of Khon is in fact a cluster of small islands, and in one of the channels dividing these it has been found possible to dig a canal, protected by locks, which gives easy access to the river above the falls. Steam communication between Saigon and the reaches immediately above Khon is thus at last assured. In 1893 an expedition under the command of Lieutenant Simon and Ensign Le Vay was sent with three steamers, the *Ham Luong*, the *Massie* and the *La Grandière*, to attempt the navigation of the Mekong as far as Luang Prabang. A start was made from Khon, and after a short halt at Bassak, Simon and Le Vay reached Vien Chan in 15 days with the *Ham Luong* and the *Massie,* arriving at the ancient capital of Laos on November 27th Two years later, in August and September, 1895, Simon took the *La Grandière* up-stream to Luang Prabang without mishap, and thence proceeded as far as Keng Hoi. This rapid fairly beat him, and he was forced to return to Luang Prabang, but on October 15th he returned to the charge, and after five days of incessant struggle succeeded in reaching Chieng Khong, having counted no fewer than forty-seven rapids on the way, many of which he describes as exceedingly dangerous. From Chieng Khong he pushed on to Chieng Hsen, above which point he found the stream shallow, but much easier to navigate, and on October 25th he arrived at Tang-Ho, which is distant one day's march from Chieng Lap. In 1898 Ensign Mazeran explored the reaches above Tang-Ho for a distance of about five and thirty miles, and it appears to be probable that launches may yet be conveyed up-stream as far as Chieng Hong, the highest point on the river attained by McLeod and by the De Lagrée-Garnier expedition. Up to the present time, the distance up stream which steam launches have been taken by French officers—from the mouth of the Mekong to a point five and thirty miles above Tang-Ho —is 1,600 miles. The fact should not be lost sight of, however, that this is a feat that cannot be regarded as of much practical utility. Even below Luang Prabang the navigation of the river is fraught with immense difficulty; above that point it is excessively dangerous; and therefore it may safely be averred that there is little probability of the trade of the *Hinterland* of Indo-China being diverted from its ancient channels by means of a steam flotilla plying upon the waters of the Mekong.

The actual sources of the Mekong are still to some extent in doubt, though the upper reaches of the river have been explored in some detail by Prjévalsky, by the Pundit Krishna who was sent on an exploring expedition by the Government of India, by Dutreuil de Rhins in 1893, and by Prince Henri of Orleans and Lieutenant E. Roux in 1895. The best information at our disposal leads to the belief that the main or western branch of the river rises on the slopes of Dza-Nag-Lung-Mung in about 33° N. lat. and about 93° E. long., at an altitude of 16,760 feet above sea-level, close to the point indicated by Prjévalsky. This stream is called the Lung-Mung until it unites its waters with that of the Nor-Pa-Chu, when it assumes the name of Dza-Nag-Chu and flows through deep ravines, the surrounding country being sparsely inhabited by Tibetan Gejis, a wild tribe in a primitive state of civilisation. Lower down it receives the waters of the Dza-Gar-Chu and is called the Dza-Chu, the name by which it is known throughout the remainder of its Tibetan course. Immediately below this point of junction it forms a rapid of tremendous force, its waters flowing so swiftly that even in winter no ice is able to form upon them. It is none the less an insignificant stream, for lower down, just above the monastery of Tachi-Gonpa, the Dza-Chu measures barely thirty yards from bank to bank and is less than three feet deep. Its altitude above sea-level at this point is 14,400 feet.

Fifty miles lower down the Dza-Chu is joined by a torrent called the Pur-Dong-Chu, and thence to Aten-tze the river has only been visited by French missionaries; it seems probable that its general trend is in a south-easterly direction. Dutreuil de Rhins followed its tributary, the Dze Chu, for a distance of between ninety and a hundred and fifteen miles, to its source on the slopes of a mountain 13,660 feet in height above sea-level; his way led through dense forest.

From Aten-tze, in about 28° 30' N. lat., to Fei-long-kiao, in 25° 50' N., the course of the river was explored by Prince Henri of Orleans and M. Roux. It is described as broader but very rapid, running through poor country with which the Chinese do little or no trade, although the region on the left bank is reputed to be rich in minerals. At Fei-long-kiao the river-bed is still 4,000 feet above sea-level. This place is distant only some thirty or forty miles from Sa-yang or Sha-yang, near where the river has been crossed by several explorers, among them the Pundit Krishna. From Loma, again,—situated some forty or fifty miles below Sa-yang, on the left bank of the river, in 24° 45' N. lat., at an altitude of 3,600 feet above sea-level—to Ti an pi—a place fifty miles from Chieng Hong, in 22° 38' N. lat., where the river-bed is 2,550 feet above sea-level—Prince Henri has furnished us with some account of the river. In the course of this section of his journey, the French explorer struck the Mekong six times. On each occasion the river was found flowing through a deep and narrow valley, the banks on either hand rising to a height of nearly 4,000 feet. The current was slack, but there were numerous difficult rapids, and the stream was crossed by two suspension bridges and by a dozen ferries between Fei-long-kiao and Ti-an-pi, at each of which a custom-house was set for the collection of *li-kin*. The banks of the river were uninhabited and unexplored even by the natives of the country, and were only touched by the tracks leading to the various ferries and bridges. The explorers published a map of this portion of the river, according to which the Mekong flows from N. to S. from Yerkalo to Sa-yang, with a slight inclination to the S.E. below that point, until opposite Loma it is nearly W. and E. This part of the map, however, is only approximately accurate, having been compiled from information gathered from natives of the valley. A little below Loma the Mekong turns sharply to the south, and at the ferry at Kali, in 24° N. lat., it is still running from N. to S. with a slight inclination towards the S.S.W. From Kali it flows S.S.E. to Chieng Hong.

"This section of the Mekong," writes M. Vivien St. Martin, "must be considered not as a trade-route but as a barrier to commerce, since each crossing of the river necessitates a descent and an ascent of from 3,300 to 4,400 feet each."

Here, of course, the river, flowing through Yun-nan, is completely Chinese, the only alien element in the region being a few Pa-i tribes living in some of the richer valleys, and some Lo-lo, called Lo-kai locally, dwelling in some of the hills.

Forest in Anam

Photo by J. Thorson

Between Fei-long-kiao and Chieng Hong the Mekong receives numerous tributaries, the Pi-kiang above Sa-yang, the Tze-kiang below; the Yang-pi-kung, which falls in near Loma, and the Tong-eul-ho, which flows by the town of Pu-cul-fu, a place famous for its teas. All these are left-bank tributaries of the river, and on the right are the Lau-cho-ho, which joins the Pe-hsiao and falls in below Loma opposite to Yung-cheu, the Nam-pi-ho or Se-kiang, and the Heu-ho.

The Mekong—"the Captain of all the Rivers," as Linschoten called it—stands revealed to us as the third or fourth longest river in Asia and the seventh or eighth longest river in the world, flowing from the mountains of Tibet, gathering to itself the highland torrents of that country and of Yun-nan, running through the Shan States and Laos, receiving at each step the waters of great streams, and finding the sea at last through the mazes of its extensive delta. The length of the river may be roughly computed at about 2,800 miles, of which some 1,600 flow through French territory, and 1,200 through portions of the Chinese empire and Tibet. Its exploration, as we have seen, is mainly a French achievement, and it is moreover a work which has been accomplished during the last fifty years. The first steps—and the first steps are proverbially the most costly—were taken by Henri Mouhot and by de Lagrée and Francis Garnier, but to the roll of fame upon which these names find so high a place many others must be added—names frequently mentioned in these pages, among which, perhaps, none have a better right to be remembered than that of

M. Pavie, who still lives to carry on his great work of revealing to Europeans the secrets of Indo-China.

The Menam, the great river of Siam, takes its rise in the mountains which form the northern boundaries of that State. It is no mystery to us, as is still to some extent the Mekong in its uttermost reaches, and of its two main branches, the Menam and the Me-ping, enough has already been said incidentally in the chapters relating to the exploration of Siam. Similarly the rivers of the Malay Peninsula, fine and imposing though they be as they flow majestically through vast regions of forest, call for no special attention. They all have their sources in the main range of mountains which forms the backbone of the Peninsula, and though the sources of the streams on the eastern slope have not yet been adequately examined, their approximate positions are known with a fair approach to accuracy.

The next river which demands examination is the Salwin, which falls into the Gulf of Martaban near Maulmain. Like the Mekong it takes its rise in Tibet, but its course is not as thoroughly known as is that of the more easterly river. According to Pundit Nain Singh, who was sent on an exploring expedition by the Indian Government, and to Prjévalsky, it begins as the Nap-chu or Nak-chu, which has two branches, the one on the west flowing through the province of Gnari, the other from the south running through the province of Khat-shi. It changes its name with bewildering frequency, being called the Nap-chu or Nak-chu in Tibet, the Khara-Ussu, the Om-chu, Uir-chu, Ghiama Nu-chu, Ngeu-kio, Nu-kiang or Nu-chu in Yun-nan, and later the Lu-kiang or Lu-tze-kiang and Li-kiang, and finally the Salwin! The identification of the Lu-tze-kiang with the Salwin was established by Desgodins, who followed the valley of the river for a distance of 250 miles, and was also, as stated in the previous chapter, affirmed by Prince Henri of Orleans, who further pronounced himself in favour of the identification of the upper reaches of the river with the Oi-chu of Tibet. Sprye and other Englishmen surveyed the river from its mouth to a point some six hundred miles by river from the coast, and the portion of it which flows through British territory is now familiarly known. But of its upper reaches no very exact data are forthcoming, and it is humiliating to have to acknowledge that the work which Frenchmen have done for the Mekong has not been accomplished in like measure by Englishmen for the Salwin.

The Irawadi was supposed at the beginning of the eighteenth century to be identical with the Lu-kiang of Yun-nan, which, as we have seen, was subsequently proved to be the upper portion of the Salwin, and in 1731 D'Anville promulgated the opinion that the Tsang-po of Tibet was the upper part of the Irawadi. Buchanan and Dalrymple in 1797 added the weight of their opinion to this theory, and more than fifty years later, when the same view was advanced by the Roman Catholic missionaries in Tibet, it received the qualified approval of Colonel Henry Yule. The German Kalproth maintained this theory with great insistency, that learned sinologue placing undue reliance upon Chinese authorities, but as early as 1872 it was traversed by Major Rennell, who based his disagreement with the accepted view upon the bulk of the waters of the Brahmaputra, which, he held, proved that the river must have its rise somewhere beyond the limits of the mountain boundaries of Assam. In 1827 Wilcox, while engaged in exploring the Brahmaputra, crossed the mountains to the south, and located the western sources of the Irawadi, striking the river at a point where it was little more than eight yards across. He was unable to visit the eastern branch of the river, but his statements as to its source were subsequently confirmed by a planter named Lepper, who had obtained a considerable amount of native information on the subject. Wilcox's opinion, however, was not immediately accepted, and in 1879–80 the Government of India sent two native pundits to seek the true sources of the Irawadi. These men failed in their object, for they did not reach the sources, but they brought back with them a mass of information collected from natives, all of which tended to confirm Wilcox's opinion and to discredit that of D'Anville and Kalproth. It is now known that the Tsang-po of Tibet is the upper part of the Brahmaputra and has no connection with the Irawadi. The sources of the Irawadi, which like those of the Salwin are still far from being adequately explored, are generally held to be situated in the eastern extension of the Himalaya, between Assam and the frontiers of China. The valley of the Irawadi and those of its principal tributaries in British territory have now been explored and surveyed with considerable accuracy.

The mountain system of the Indo-Chinese peninsula, as it is now revealed to us, is found to be an extension of the great Himalaya range. On the north this forms

Valley of the Upper Donnai

From Courtellement's "Indo-Chine."   By permission of
M. M. Firmin-Didot & Cie., Paris

the range which separates Burma from Assam and Manipur, and extends southward in the Yoma-Arakan range, which divides Burma from the coast districts of Arakan; the Yoma-Pegu range to the south of Mandalay, including the Karini hills; and the main range of mountains which runs down the centre of the Malay Peninsula. Eastward the extension of the Himalayas stretches away through the highlands of Yun nan, across which Garnier and his fellows laboured and trudged, to the Gulf of Tongking, one great offshoot dividing Tongking from the valley of the Mekong. There is also an isolated range which runs parallel to the shores of French Indo-China, while an offshoot of the mountains of the Malay Peninsula forms the northern boundary of Siam. The majority of these mountains average some three or four thousand feet above the level of the plain, running up into peaks which in some instances are as much as 13,000 feet in height. In the southern portion of the great peninsula the mountains are covered from foot to crest by dense forest, but farther north this is exchanged for oaks and pines, and many of the hills of the far interior are barren of vegetation and are strewn with immense boulders.

The old theory that the rivers of Indo-China had their sources in an immense lake has long ago been discredited, in spite of the fact that the excellent Mendez Pinto went out of his way to declare that he had himself visited this lake. The lakes of Yun-nan and Tibet are, however, a remarkable feature of south-eastern Asia, and those of the latter province still remain inadequately explored. In Indo-China proper the great lake of Tonle

Sap, near the ruins of Angkor, stands without a rival. According to Mr. J. S. Black, of the British Consular Service in Siam, " this great sea of fresh water, which measures nearly 100 miles in length and 20 at its greatest breadth, rises no less than 21 feet during the rainy season, and floods all the adjoining country for miles. In the dry season it is not more than 4 or 5 feet deep, and it is at this time, during the months of March, April, and May, that the surrounding population flock to its shores to catch the numerous fish." It is now recognised that the formation of the lake is of comparatively recent date. Observations prove that the process of silting all along the coast of Indo-China has been effected with extraordinary rapidity, and that the whole of the low-lying coast-lands to the south of the hills has been formed within historical as opposed to geological times. The traveller on the Menam River can see, at a point some miles above the present capital of Bangkok, unmistakable signs of a river-bar which once existed at that spot, where the stream formerly had its outfall into the sea. Similarly the entire delta of the Mekong is of recent formation, and there is some reason to believe that Angkor Thom itself, when first it was founded, was a fort.

Another geographical feature of interest in these regions is the Isthmus of Kra, which joins the Malay Peninsula to Siam and Tenasserim. The mountain chain which, extending in a southerly direction from the Himalaya, bisects the Malay Peninsula through its entire length, is here broken, and the surveys made by the French Government in 1883 disclosed the fact that

Saigon

From Salaun's "L'Indo-Chine." By permission of the French Minister of the Colonies

the greatest elevation above sea-level amounted to only 250 feet. The possibility of cutting a canal across the isthmus is therefore rendered possible, but the construction of such a work would be very costly, and it is certainly altogether opposed to British interests, since it would deal a severe blow to the prosperity of Singapore. With the British in Tenasserim, therefore, it is highly improbable that such a work will ever be allowed to be put in hand.

Mention should here be made of yet another geographical feature of Indo-China which deserves attention—the great plateau which lies between Korat and the valley of the Mekong. A full description of this has already been given in dealing with the journeys of Mouhot, Garnier and others, but it may here be noted that this high land, with its abrupt " drops " into the flat plains of the coast-regions, marks, in all probability, an ancient sea-board whence the waters have receded as more and more land was won by the action of the rivers.

Our task is now completed : the tale is told, and Chryse the Golden stands revealed to us, robbed of its magic and its mystery, just a common fragment of the earth upon which we also tread. It has still a few, a very few, secrets left for discovery by the adventure-some—the actual sources of the Salwin and the Irawadi among the number; but for the rest it has been traversed again and again by alien explorers, and a man must go far afield indeed if to-day he would break new ground. The geographer has done his work, and has done the most of it in less than a century of time; and it remains for the scientist and the ethnologist—above all the ethnologist—to complete the task. More than this, Chryse is held to-day almost wholly by the nations of the West: by Great Britain and by France; the welfare of its peoples are in the keeping of strangers, who have already done much to bring peace and plenty to these troubled lands. Much more, however, still awaits the doing, for the white nations have not yet discovered the secret whereby the subject peoples may be preserved from the action of that swift degeneracy which too often follows on the heels of civilisation. In the past the East has suffered much at the hands of Europeans, and the burden of our sins should press sorely upon us. The age of frank brutality has passed away for ever, and has been replaced by an age of philanthropy and humanitarianism. Of old, white men wrought greatly and meant ill; now the position is reversed,—we work on a smaller scale and with a host of the best intentions. The future alone can decide whether the nations of Europe, England, France, Holland, and now also the United States —the white peoples who have assumed the responsibility for ordering the destinies of the East—will prove themselves equal to the task of making full amends for all the evil that was done in Asia by folk of their blood in centuries which have passed away.

APPENDIX

LIST OF THE PRINCIPAL PUBLICATIONS RELATIVE TO FURTHER INDIA

PURCHAS HIS PILGRIMES. 4 vols. (Parts.) Map and illustrations. Folio. London, 1625.

PINTO, FERNAND MENDEZ. The Voyages and Adventures of Fernand Mendez Pinto, a Portugal, during his Travels for the spaces of one and twenty years in the Kingdoms of Ethiopia, China, Tartaria, Cauchin-China, Calaminham, Siam, Pegu, Japan, and a great part of the East-Indaes. 4to. London, 1653.

VOYAGE DE SIAM, des Pères Jesuites; avec leurs observations Astronomiques, et leurs remarques de Physique, de Géographie, d'Hydrographie, et d'Histoire. Plates. Sm. 4to. Paris, 1686.

DAMPIER, CAPT. WILLIAM. A New Voyage round the World, describing particularly the Isthmus of America. Maps. 8vo. London, 1697.

HARRIS, JOHN. Navigantium atque Itinerantium Bibliotheca; or, a Complete Collection of Voyages and Travels. 2 vols. Maps, portraits and plates. Folio. London, 1705.

RENNEVILLE, R. A. CONSTANTIN DE. Recueil des Voyages qui ont servi à l'Establissement et aux Progrez de la Compagnie des Indes Orientales, formée dans les Provinces-Unies des Païs-Bas. Nouvelle édition. 10 vols. Plates. 12mo. Rouen, 1725.

HAMILTON, CAPT. ALEXANDER. A new Account of the East Indies. 2 vols. Maps and plates. 8vo. Edinburgh, 1727.

ASTLEY, THOMAS. New General Collection of Voyages and Travels. 4 vols. Maps and plates. 4to. London, 1745–47.

A GENERAL COLLECTION OF VOYAGES AND DISCOVERIES MADE BY THE PORTUGUESE AND THE SPANIARDS DURING THE FIFTEENTH AND SIXTEENTH CENTURIES. Map and plates. 4to. London, 1789.

SYMES, MAJOR M. Account of an Embassy to the Kingdom of Ava in 1795. Maps and plates. 4to. London, 1800.

PINKERTON, JOHN. A General Collection of the best and most interesting Voyages and Travels in all Parts of the World. 17 vols. Maps and plates. 4to. London, 1808–14.

FITCH, RALPH, the long, dangerous, and memorable Voyage of, by the way of Tripolis in Syria, to Ormuz, Goa in the East Indies, Cambaia, the River Ganges, Bengala, Bacola, Chonderi, Pegu, Siam, etc., begunne in 1583 and ended in 1591. (Hakluyt, R., "The Principal Navigations," etc., Vol. 2.) London, 1809.

FREDERICK, CESAR. Voyage of Master Cesar Frederick into the East India and beyond the Indies, 1563. (Hakluyt, R., "The Principal Navigations, etc., Vol. 2.) London, 1809.

LAHARPE, J. F. Abrégé de l'Histoire Générale des Voyages. 24 vols. 8vo. Paris, 1816.

COX, CAPT. H. Journal of a Residence in the Burmhan Empire, and more particularly at the Court of Amarapoorah. Plates. 8vo. London, 1821.

FINLAYSON, G. The Mission to Siam, and Hué, the Capital of Cochin-China, in 1821–22. From the Journal of the late G. Finlayson; with a Memoir of the Author by Sir T. Stamford Raffles. Plate. 8vo. London, 1826.

CRAWFURD, JOHN. Journal of an Embassy from the Governor-General of India to the Court of Ava in 1827; with an Appendix containing a Description of Fossil Remains, by Professor Buckland and Mr. Clift. Map and plates. 4to. London, 1829.

Ibn Batuta, The Travels of, in Asia and Africa, 1324–25. Translated from the abridged Arabic MS. copies preserved in the Public Library of Cambridge; with Notes illustrative of the History, Geography, Botany, Antiquities, etc., occurring throughout the work. By the Rev. S. Lee. 4to. London, 1829.

Rémusat, J. P. Abel. Nouveaux Mélanges Asiatiques, ou Recueil de Morceaux de Critiques et de Mémoires relatifs aux Réligions, aux Sciences, aux Coutumes, à l'Histoire et à la Géographie des Nations Orientales. 2 vols. Map. 8vo. Paris, 1829.

Lives and Voyages of Drake, Cavendish, and Dampier; including an Introductory View of earlier Discoveries in the South Sea, and the History of the Buccaneers. Portraits. 16mo. Edinburgh, 1831.

Wilcox, Lieut. R. Memoir of a Survey of Assam and the Neighbouring Countries, executed in 1825–6–7–8. Map. 4to. Calcutta, 1832.

Richardson, Dr. D. Journal of a March from Ava to Kendat, on the Khyen dwen River, performed in 1831 under the orders of Major H. Burney, the Resident at Ava. (Journal of the Asiatic Society of Bengal, Vol. 2, p. 59.) 8vo. Calcutta, 1833.

Sangermano, Rev. Father. Description of the Burmese Empire, compiled chiefly from Native Documents; translated from the MS. by W. Tandy. (Oriental Translation Fund.) 4to. 1833.

Grant, Capt. F. T. Extract from a Journal kept by Captain F. T. Grant, of the Manipur Levy, during a Tour of Inspection of the Manipur Frontier, along the course of the Ningthee River, etc., in January, 1832. (Journal of the Asiatic Society of Bengal, Vol. 3, p. 124.) 8vo. Calcutta, 1834.

Burney, Lt.-Col. H. Notice of Pugan, the Ancient Capital of

the Burmese Empire. (Journal of the Asiatic Society of Bengal, Vol. 4, p. 400.) 8vo. Calcutta, 1835.

PEMBERTON, CAPT. R. BOILEAU. Report on the Eastern Frontier of British India; with an Appendix; and a Supplement by Dr. Bayfield on the British Political Relations with Ava. Maps. 8vo. Calcutta, 1835.

RICHARDSON, DR. D. An account of some of the Petty States lying north of the Tenasserim Provinces; drawn up from the Journals and Reports of D. Richardson. By E. A. Blundell. (Journal of the Asiatic Society of Bengal, Vol. 5, 1836, pp. 601–625, 688–707.) Map and plate. 8vo. Calcutta.

BURNEY, LT.-COL. H. Some Account of the Wars between Burmah and China, together with the Journals and Routes of three different Embassies sent to Pekin by the King of Ava; taken from Burmese documents. (Journal of the Asiatic Society of Bengal, Vol. 6, pp. 121, 405, 542.) 8vo. Calcutta, 1837.

McLEOD, CAPT. T. E. Abstract Journal of an Expedition to Kiang Hung on the Chinese Frontier, starting from Moulmein on the 13th December, 1836. (Journal of the Asiatic Society of Bengal, Vol. 6, p. 989.) 8vo. Calcutta, 1837.

HANNAY, CAPT. S. F. Abstract of the Journal of a Route travelled by Capt. S. F. Hannay, of the 40th Regiment Native Infantry, from the Capital of Ava to the Amber Mines of the Húkong Valley on the south-east frontier of Assam. By Capt. R. Boileau Pemberton. (Journal of the Asiatic Society of Bengal, Vol. 6, p. 245.) 8vo. Calcutta, 1837.

RICHARDSON, DR. D. Abstract Journal of an expedition from Moulmein to Ava through the Kareen country, between December, 1836, and June, 1837. (Journal of the Asiatic Society of Bengal, Vol. 6, 1837, pp. 1005–1022.) 8vo. Calcutta,

MALCOLM, REV. H. Travels in South-Eastern Asia, embracing

Hindŭstan, Malaya, Siam, and China; with Notices of numerous Missionary Stations, and a full account of the Burman Empire. 2 vols. Map. 8vo. London, 1839.

NEWBOLD, CAPT. T. J. Political and Statistical Account of the British Settlements in the Straits of Malacca, viz.: Pinang, Malacca, and Singapore; with a History of the Malayan States of the Peninsula of Malacca. 2 vols. Maps. 8vo. London, 1839.

RICHARDSON, DR. D. Journal of a Mission from the Supreme Government of India to the Court of Siam. (Journal of the Asiatic Society of Bengal, Vol. 8, p. 1016; 9, pp. i, 219.) 8vo. Calcutta, 1839–1840.

LAFOND DE LURCY, CAPT. G. Voyages autour du Monde, et Naufrages célébres. 8 vols. Portrait and plates. Rl. 8vo. Paris, 1844.

WOOD, B. Extracts from a Report of a Journey into the Naga Hills in 1844. (Journal of the Asiatic Society of Bengal, Vol. 13, p. 771.) 8vo. Calcutta, 1844.

REINAUD, J. T. Relation des Voyages faits par les Arabes et les Persans dans l'Inde et à la Chine dans le 9e Siècle. 2 vols. 16mo. Paris, 1845.

ABOULFÉDA, GÉOGRAPHIE DE. TRADUITE DE L'ARABE . . . par M. REINAUD. Vol. 1, and Vol. 2, Part 1. 2 vols. Maps. 4to. Paris, 1848.

———— Ditto. Tome 2. Seconde partie. 4to. Paris, 1883.

LOGAN, J. R. Sketch of the Physical Geography and Geology of the Malay Peninsula. (Journal Indian Archipelago, Vol. 2, pp. 83–138.) 8vo. Singapore, 1848.

LOGAN, J. R. Journal of a Voyage to the Eastern Coast and Islands of Johore. (Journal Indian Archipelago, Vol. 2, pp. 616–624.) 8vo. Singapore, 1848.

FAVRE, REV. P. A Journey in Johore. (Journal Indian Archipelago, Vol. 3, pp. 50–64.) 8vo. Singapore, 1849.

FAVRE, REV. P. A Journey in the Menangkabau States of the Malay Peninsula. (Journal Indian Archipelago, Vol. 3, pp. 153–161.) 8vo. Singapore, 1849.

O'RILEY, E. Rough Notes on the Geological and Geographical Characteristics of the Tenasserim Provinces. (Journal Indian Archipelago, Vol. 3, pp. 385–401.) 8vo. Singapore, 1849.

O'RILEY, E. Notes on the Tract of Country lying between the head of the Zimmi River and the Source of the Kaundran, adjacent to the Siamese border Province of Ryout Raung. (Journal Indian Archipelago, Vol. 4, pp. 164–168.) 8vo. Singapore, 1850.

NEALE, F. A. Narrative of a Residence at the Capital of the Kingdom of Siam, with a Description of the Manners, Customs, and Laws of the Modern Siamese. Map and illustrations. London, 1852.

EARL, G. W. Contributions to the Physical Geography of Southeastern Asia and Australia. (Journal Indian Archipelago, Vol. 6, pp. 243–277; N. S., Vol. 2, pp. 278–286.) Maps. 8vo. Singapore, 1852, 1858.

DRAKE, SIR FRANCIS. The World Encompassed; being his next Voyage to that to Nombre de Dios. Collated with an unpublished Manuscript of Francis Fletcher, with Appendices illustrative of the same Voyage, and Introduction, by W. S. W. Vaux. (Hakluyt Society's publications, Vol. 16.) 8vo. London, 1854.

PALLEGOIX, MGR. Description du Royaume Thai ou Siam, comprenant la Topographie, Histoire Naturelle, Mœurs et Coutumes, Législation, Langue, etc. 2 vols. Map and plates. 12mo. Ligny, 1854.

CRAWFURD, J. A. Descriptive Dictionary of the Indian Islands and adjacent Countries. Map. 8vo. London, 1856.

PARKES, H. Geographical Notes on Siam, with a New Map of

the Lower Part of the Menam River. (Journal of the Royal Geographical Society, Vol. 26, 1856, pp. 71–78, map.) 8vo. London.

SMITH, DR. WILLIAM. Dictionary of Greek and Roman Geography. 2 vols. Wood cuts. 8vo. London, 1856–7.

YULE, COL. SIR HENRY. Narrative of Major Phayre's Mission to the Court of Ava; with Notices of the Country, Government, and People; and Notes on the Geological Features of the Banks of the River Irawadee, and of the Country north of the City of Amarapoora, by Thomas Oldham. Maps and plates. 4to. Calcutta, 1856.

BOWRING, SIR J. The Kingdom and People of Siam, with a Narrative of the Mission to that country in 1855. Map, facsimiles, and plates. 2 vols. 8vo. London, 1857.

INDIA IN THE FIFTEENTH CENTURY; being a Collection of Narratives of Voyages to India in the Century preceding the Portuguese Discovery of the Cape of Good Hope, from Latin, Persian, Russian, and Italian sources, translated into English. Edited, with an Introduction, by R. H. Major. (Hakluyt Society's publications, Vol. 22.) 8vo. London, 1857. Contains, among other matters, Nicolò Conti's "Travels in the East, in the early part of the Fifteenth Century."

YULE, CAPT. H. On the Geography of Burma and Its Tributary States, in illustration of a New Map of those Regions. (Journal of the Royal Geographical Society, Vol. 27, pp. 54–108.) Map. 8vo. London, 1857.

YULE, COL. SIR H. Narrative of the Mission sent by the Governor-General of India to the Court of Ava in 1855; with Notices of the Country, Government, and People. Maps and plates. 4to. London, 1858.

O'RILEY, E. Journal of a Tour to Karen Nee for the purpose of opening a trading-road to the Shan Traders from Mobyay and the adjacent Shan Territory direct to Toungoo. (Journal of the Indian Archipelago, N. S., Vol. 2, pp. 391–457.) 8vo. Singapore, 1858. (Also Journal of the Royal Geographical Society, Vol. 32, pp. 164–216.) Notes. Map. 8vo. London, 1862.

TICKELL, LIEUT.-COL. S. R. Itinerary, with Memoranda, chiefly Topographical and Zoological, through the southerly portions of the district of Amherst, province of Tenasserim. (Journal of the Asiatic Society of Bengal, Vol. 28, p. 421.) 8vo. Calcutta, 1859.

CAMPBELL, JAMES. Notes on the Antiquities, Natural History, etc., etc., of Cambodia, compiled from Manuscripts of the late E. F. J. Forrest, and from information derived from the Rev. Dr. House, etc., etc. (Journal of the Royal Geographical Society, Vol. 30, 1860, pp. 182–198.) 8vo. London.

KING, D. O. Travels in Siam and Cambodia. (Journal of the Royal Geographical Society, Vol. 30, 1860, pp. 177–182, map.) 8vo. London.

DES MAZURES, VERY REV. THOMINE. Memorandum on the Countries between Thibet, Yunân, and Burmah. With Notes and a Comment by Lieut.-Col. H. Yule. (Journal of the Asiatic Society of Bengal, Vol. 30, p. 367.) 8vo. Calcutta, 1861.

SCHOMBURGK, SIR R. H. Boat Excursion from Bangkok, in Siam, to the Pechaburri, on the Western Shore of the Gulf of Siam. (Journal of the Royal Geographical Society, Vol. 31, pp. 302–321.) 8vo. London, 1861.

SPRYE, CAPT. R., and R. H. F. SPRYE. Communication with the South-West Provinces of China from Rangoon in British Pegu. (Proceedings of the Royal Geographical Society, Vol. 5, pp. 45–47.) Map. 8vo. London, 1861.

SCHOMBURGK, SIR R. H. Travels in Siam. (Proceedings of the Royal Geographical Society, Vol. 5, pp. 118–119.) 8vo. London, 1861.

MOUHOT, H. Notes on Cambodia, the Lao Country, etc. (Journal of the Royal Geographical Society, Vol. 32, pp. 142–163.) Map. 8vo. London, 1862.

THE TRAVELS OF LUDOVICA DI VARTHEMA IN EGYPT, SYRIA, ARABIA DESERTA AND ARABIA FELIX, IN PERSIA, INDIA, AND ETHIOPIA, 1503 to 1508. Translated from the Italian edition of 1510, with a Preface by J. Winter Jones, and edited, with Notes and an Introduction, by G. Percy Badger. (Hakluyt Society's publications, Vol. 32.) Map. 8vo. London, 1863.

SCHOMBURGH, SIR R. H. A visit to Xiengmai, the principal city of the Laos or Shan States. (Journal of the Asiatic Society of Bengal, Vol. 32, p. 387.) 8vo. Calcutta, 1863.

STEVENSON, CAPT. J. F. Account of a visit to the Hot Springs of Pai in the Tavoy District. (Journal of the Asiatic Society of Bengal, Vol. 32, p. 383.) 8vo. Calcutta, 1863.

MOUHOT, H. Travels in the Central Parts of Indo-China (Siam), Cambodia, and Laos during 1858–60. 2 vols. Map and plates. 8vo. London, 1864.

WILLIAMS, DR. C. Extract from Journal of a Trip to Bhamo. (Journal of the Asiatic Society of Bengal, Vol. 33, p. 189.) 8vo. Calcutta, 1864.

WILLIAMS, DR. C. Memorandum on the Question of British Trade with Western China viâ Burmah. (Journal of the Asiatic Society of Bengal, Vol. 33, p. 407.) 8vo. Calcutta, 1864.

BASTIAN, DR. A. A visit to the Ruined Cities and Buildings of Cambodia. (Journal of the Royal Geographical Society, Vol. 35, pp. 74–87.) Map. 8vo. London, 1865.

PARISH, REV. C. Notes of a Trip up the Salween. (Journal of the Asiatic Society of Bengal, Vol. 34, pt. II, 135.) 8vo. Calcutta, 1865.

WILLIAMS, J. M. Memorandum on Railway Communication with Western China and the intermediate Shan States from the Port of Rangoon in British Burma. Map. Folio. London, 1865.

A DESCRIPTION OF THE COASTS OF EAST AFRICA AND MALABAR IN THE BEGINNING OF THE SIXTEENTH CENTURY, by Duarte Barbosa, a Portuguese. Translated from an early Spanish Manuscript in the Barcelona Library, with Notes and a Preface, by the Hon. Henry E. J. Stanley. (Hakluyt Society's publications, Vol. 35.) 8vo. London, 1866.

CATHAY AND THE WAY THITHER; being a Collection of Medieval Notices of China. Translated and edited by Col. H. Yule . . . with Essay on the Intercourse between China and the West previous to the Discovery of the Cape Route. (Hakluyt Society's publications, Vols. 36 and 37.) 2 vols. 8vo. London, 1866.

KENNEDY, H. G. Report of an Expedition made into Southern Laos and Cambodia in the early part of the year 1866. (Journal of the Royal Geographical Society, Vol. 37, pp. 298–327.) Map. 8vo. London, 1867.

THOMSON, JOHN. The Antiquities of Cambodia: a series of Photographs taken on the spot, with Letterpress description. Oblong 4to. Edinburgh, 1867.

WILLIAMS, J. M., and C. H. LUARD. Copies of the Survey Report, dated the 15th June, 1867, and of the Journals, Maps, Sections, etc., attached thereto, respecting Rangoon and Western China, etc. Folio. London, 1867.

THE PHILIPPINE ISLANDS, MOLUCCAS, SIAM, CAMBODIA, JAPAN, AND CHINA, AT THE CLOSE OF THE SIXTEENTH CENTURY, by Antonio de Morga. Translated from the Spanish, with Notes and a Preface, and a Letter from Luis Vaez de Torres describing his Voyage through the Torres Straits, by the Hon. Henry E. J. Stanley. (Hakluyt Society's publications, Vol. 39.) Maps and plate. 8vo. London, 1868.

PUNDIT ——. Report of a Route-Survey made by Pundit ——,

from Nepal to Lhasa, and thence through the Upper Valley of the Brahmaputra to its Source. By Capt. T. G. Montgomerie. (Journal of the Royal Geographical Society, Vol. 38, pp. 129–219.) Map. 8vo. London, 1868.

WILLIAMS, CLEMENT. Through Burmah to Western China; being Notes of a Journey in 1863 to establish the practicability of a Trade-Route between the Irawaddi and the Yangtse-Kiang. Map and plates. 8vo. London, 1868.

COOPER, T. T. Letter from, on the Course of the Tsan-po and Irrawaddy and on Tibet. (Proceedings of the Royal Geographical Society, Vol. 13, pp. 392–393.) Map. 8vo. London, 1869.

JENKINS, H. L. Notes on the Burmese Route from Assam to the Hookoong Valley. (Proceedings of the Royal Geographical Society, Vol. 13, pp. 244–248.) 8vo. London, 1869.

MACLEOD, W. C., and RICHARDSON, DR. D. Copy of Papers relating to the Route of Capt. W. C. Macleod from Moulmein to the Frontiers of China, and to the Route of Dr. Richardson on his Fourth Mission to the Shan Provinces of Burmah, or Extracts from the same. Map. Folio. London, 1869.

DIRECT COMMERCE WITH THE SHAN STATES AND WEST OF CHINA, BY RAILWAY FROM RANGOON TO KIAN-HUNG, ON THE UPPER KAMBOJA RIVER, ON THE SOUTH-WEST FRONTIER OF CHINA. Memorial from the Wakefield Chamber of Commerce to the Lords of Her Majesty's Treasury. 8vo London, 1869.

THE THREE VOYAGES OF VASCO DA GAMA AND HIS VICE-ROYALTY, from the Lendas da India of Gaspar Correa. . . . Translated from the Portuguese, with Notes and an Introduction, by the Hon. Henry E. J. Stanley. (Hakluyt Society's publications, Vol. 42.) Portrait, plate, etc. 8vo. London, 1869.

ANDERSON, DR. J. The Irawady and its Sources. (Journal of the Royal Geographical Society, Vol. 40, pp. 286–303.) 8vo. London, 1870.

ANDERSON, JOHN. A Report on the Expedition to Western Yunan *viâ* Bhamô. Royal 8vo. Calcutta, 1871.

COOPER, T. T. Travels of a Pioneer of Commerce in Pigtail and Petticoats; or An Overland Journey from China towards India. Map and plate. 8vo. London, 1871.

GARNIER, F. Voyage lointain aux Royaumes de Cambodge et Laouwen par les Néerlandais et ce qui s'y est passé jusqu'en 1644. (Bulletin de la Société de Géographie, Paris, 1871(2), pp. 249–289.) 8vo. Map.

MARCO POLO. The Book of Ser Marco Polo, the Venetian, concerning the Kingdoms and Marvels of the East. Newly translated and edited, with Notes, etc., by Colonel Henry Yule. 2 vols. Maps and plates. 8vo. London, 1871.

———— Ditto. Third edition, revised throughout in the light of recent discoveries, by Henri Cordier (of Paris). With a Memoir of Henry Yule by his daughter, Amy Frances Yule. 2 vols. London, 1903.

SLADEN, SIR E. B. Copy of Major Sladen's Report on the Bhamo Route: Official Narrative of the Expedition to explore the Trade Routes to China *viâ* Bhamo, under the guidance of Major E. B. Sladen, Political Agent, Mandalay; with connected papers. Map. (Parliamentary Report.) Folio. London, 1871.

SLADEN, MAJOR E. B. Expedition from Burma, *viâ* the Irrawaddy and Bhamo, to South-Western China. (Journal of the Royal Geographical Society, Vol. 41, pp. 257–281.) Map. 8vo. London, 1871.

PEAL, S. E. Notes on a Visit to the Tribes inhabiting the Hills South of Sibsagar, Assam. (Journal of the Asiatic Society of Bengal, Vol. 41, pt. I, 9.) 8vo. Calcutta, 1872.

BAYFIELD, G. T. Narrative of a Journey from Ava to the Frontiers of Assam, and back, performed between December, 1836, and May, 1837. (Selections of Papers regarding the Hill

Tracts between Assam and Burmah, and on the Upper Brahmaputra, Vol. 5.) Large 8vo. Calcutta, 1873.

COOPER, T. T. The Mishmee Hills: An Account of a Journey made in an Attempt to Penetrate Thibet from Assam to open new routes for Commerce. Map and plates. 12mo. London, 1873.

GARNIER, F. Voyage d'Exploration en Indo-Chine, effectué pendant les années 1866, 1867, et 1868, etc. 2 vols. Maps and plates, and Atlas folio. 4to. Paris, 1873.

GRIFFITH, W. Journey from Upper Assam towards Hookhoom, Ava, and Rangoon. (Selections of Papers regarding the Hill Tracts between Assam and Burmah, and on the Upper Brahmaputra, Vol. 4.) Large 8vo. Calcutta, 1873.

JENKINS, H. L. Notes on a Trip across the Patkoi Range from Assam to the Hookoong Valley, in 1869–70. (Selections of Papers regarding the Hill Tracts between Assam and Burmah, etc., Vol. 6.) Large 8vo. Calcutta, 1873.

JENKINS, H. L. Notes on the Burmese Route from Assam to Hookoong Valley. (Selections of Papers regarding the Hill Tracts between Assam and Burmah, etc., Vol. 7.) Large 8vo. Map. Calcutta, 1873.

SELECTIONS OF PAPERS REGARDING THE HILL TRACTS BETWEEN ASSAM AND BURMAH, AND ON THE UPPER BRAHMAPUTRA. Large 8vo. Calcutta, 1873.

THE FIRST VOYAGE ROUND THE WORLD, by Magellan. Translated from the Accounts of Pigafetta and other contemporary writers, accompanied by Original Documents, with Notes and an Introduction, by Lord Stanley of Alderley. (Hakluyt Society's publications, Vol. 52.) Portrait, map, etc. 8vo. London, 1874.

McMAHON, LIEUT.-COL. A. P. On Our Prospects of Opening a Route to South-Western China, and Explorations of the French in Tonquin and Cambodia. (Proceedings of the

Royal Geographical Society, Vol. 18, pp. 463–467.) 8vo. London, 1874.

THE COMMENTARIES OF THE GREAT AFONSO DALBOQUERQUE, SECOND VICEROY OF INDIA. Translated from the Portuguese edition of 1774, with Notes and an Introduction, by Walter de Gray Birch. 4 vols. (Hakluyt Society's publications, Vols. 53, 55, 62, 69.) Maps and plates. 8vo. London, 1875, 1877, 1880, 1884.

CORYTON, J. Trade Routes between British Burmah and Western China. (Journal of the Royal Geographical Society, Vol. 45, pp. 229–249.) Map. 8vo. London, 1875.

MARGARY, A. R. Extracts of Letters from Mr. Margary. (Proceedings of the Royal Geographical Society, Vol. 19, pp. 288–291.) 8vo. London, 1875.

THOMSON, JOHN. The Straits of Malacca, Indo-China, and China; or, Ten Years' Travels, Adventures, and Residence abroad. Plates. 8vo. London, 1875.

ANDERSON, JOHN. Mandalay to Momein: A Narrative of the Two Expeditions to Western China of 1868 and 1875, under Colonel Edward B. Sladen and Colonel Horace Browne. Maps and plans. 8vo. London, 1876.

DESGODINS, L'ABBÉ. Le cours supérieur des fleuves de l'Indo-Chine. (Bulletin Société de Géographie (6 S.), T. 12, pp. 202–205.) 8vo. Paris, 1876.

DESGODINS, L'ABBÉ. Pays frontières du Thibet, de la Birmanie et du Yun-nan. (Bulletin Société de Géographie (6 S.), T. 12, pp. 401–412.) 8vo. Paris, 1876.

DESGODINS, L'ABBÉ. Notes géologiques sur la route de Yerkato à Pa-tang. (Bulletin Société de Géographie (6 S.), T. 12, pp. 492–508.) 8vo. Paris, 1876.

HARMAND, DR. —— Voyage au Cambodge. (Bulletin Société de Géographie (6 S.), T. 12, pp. 337–367.) Map. 8vo. Paris, 1876.

MARGARY, A. R. The Journey of, from Shanghai to Bhamo, and back to Manwyne . . . with Concluding Chapter by Sir Rutherford Alcock. Map and portrait. 8vo. London, 1876.

MARGARY, A. R. Extracts from the Diary of the late Mr. Margary, from Hankow to Tali-fu [and Extracts from his subsequent Letters]. (Proceedings of the Royal Geographical Society, Vol. 20, pp. 184–215.) 8vo. London, 1876.

PAPERS CONNECTED WITH THE DEVELOPMENT OF TRADE BETWEEN BRITISH BURMAH AND WESTERN CHINA, AND WITH THE MISSION TO YUNNAN OF 1874–75. Folio. London, 1876.

DESGODINS, L'ABBÉ. Territoire de Bathang. Notes. (Bulletin Société de Géographie (6 S.), T. 12, pp. 614–625.) 8vo, Paris, 1876.

COTTAM, H. Overland Route to China, viâ Assam, Tenga Pani River, Khamti, and Singphoo Country, across the Irrawaddi River into Yunan. (Proceedings of the Royal Geographical Society, Vol. 21, pp. 590–595.) 8vo. London, 1877.

DUPUIS, J. Voyage au Yûn-nân. (Bulletin Société de Géographie (6 S.), T. 14, pp. 5–57, 151–185, map.) 8vo. Paris, 1877.

HARMAND, DR. J. Les iles re Poulo-Condor, le haut Don-naï et ses habitants. Rapport adressé au président de la Société. (Bulletin Société de Géographie (6 S.), T. 13, pp. 523–534.) 8vo. Paris, 1877.

HARMAND, DR. J. Notes sur les provinces du bassin méridional du Se Moun (Laos et Cambodge Siamois). (Bulletin Société de Géographie (6 S.), T. 14, pp. 225–238. Map.) 8vo. Paris, 1877.

HARMAND, DR. J. Excursion de Bassac à Attopen. (Bulletin Société de Géographie (6 S.), T. 14, pp. 239–247.) 8vo. Paris, 1877.

MIKLOUKHO-MAKLAI, ——. Voyage de, dans la Presqu'ile de Malaisie. Lettre au Secrétaire de la Société russe de géogra-

362 APPENDIX

phie. (Bulletin Société de Géographie (6 S.), T. 13, pp. 424-427, map.) 8vo. Paris, 1877.

THE VOYAGES OF SIR JAMES LANCASTER, KT., TO THE EAST INDIES, with Abstracts of Journals of Voyages to the East Indies during the Seventeenth Century, preserved in the India Office; and the voyage of Capt. John Knight (1606) to seek the North-West Passage. Edited by Clements R. Markham. (Hakluyt Society's publications, Vol. 56.) 8vo. London, 1877.

FYTCHE, COLONEL A. Burma, Past and Present, with Personal Reminiscences of the Country. 2 vols. Map and plates. 8vo. London, 1878.

MACLAY, N. VON MIKLUHO. Ethnological Excursions in the Malay Peninsula. (Journal of the Straits British Royal Asiatic Society, No. 2, pp. 205-221.) 8vo. Singapore, 1878.

SKINNER, A. M. Geography of the Malay Peninsula. Part I. (Journal of the Straits British Royal Asiatic Society, No. 1, pp. 52-62.) 8vo. Singapore, 1878.

BUNBURY, SIR E. H. A History of Ancient Geography Among the Greeks and Romans, from the Earliest Ages till the Fall of the Roman Empire. 2 vols. Maps. 8vo. London, 1879.

DUPUIS, J. L'Ouverture du Fleuve Rouge au Commerce et les Evénements du Tong-Kin, 1872-73: Journal de Voyage et d'Expédition. Map and portrait. 4to. Paris, 1879.

GORDON, ROBERT. Report on the Irrawaddy River. Maps. Folio. Rangoon, 1879-80.

HARMAND, DR. J. Rapport sur une mission en Indo-Chine, de Bassac à Hué (16 Avril—14 Août, 1877). (Archives des Missions Scientifiques et Littéraires (3 S.), 5, 247-281.) 8vo. Paris, 1879.

HORNADAY, A. J. Account of a Naturalist's Visit to Selangor. (Journal of the Straits British Royal Asiatic Society, No. 3, pp. 124-131.) 8vo. Singapore, 1879.

PEAL, S. E. Note on the old Burmese Route over Patkai *via* Nongyang (viewed as the most feasible and direct route from India to China). (Journal of the Asiatic Society of Bengal, Vol. 48, pt. II, 69.) 8vo. Calcutta, 1879.

QUATREFAGES, A. DE. Rapport sur le voyage d'exploration fait par le docteur Harmand dans les provinces de Mulu-Prey, Toulé-Repan et Compong-Soaï; sur la rive droite du Mé-Kong. (Archives des Missions Scientifiques et Littéraires (3 S.), 5, pp. 9-17.) 8vo. Paris, 1879.

COCHINCHINE FRANÇAISE. Excursions et Reconnaissances. Tome 2 (Nos. 5, 6), 3-14 and 15 (No. 33). Maps, etc. Roy. 8vo. Saigon, 1880-89.

DELAPORTE, L. Voyage au Cambodge: L'Architecture Khmer. Maps and plates. 8vo. Paris, 1880.

LEECH, H. W. C. About Kinta. —— About Slim and Bernam. (Journal of the Straits British Royal Asiatic Society, No. 4, pp. 21-45.) 8vo. Singapore, 1880.

SWETTENHAM, F. A. From Pêrak to Slim and down the Slim and Bernam Rivers. (Journal of the Straits British Royal Asiatic Society, No. 5, pp. 51-68a.) 8vo. Singapore, 1880.

DE LA CROIX, J. ERRINGTON. Some Account of the Mining Districts of Lower Pêrak. (Journal of the Straits British Royal Asiatic Society, No. 7, pp. 1-10.) Map and Section. 8vo. Singapore, 1881.

PEAL, S. E. Report on a Visit to the Nongyang Lake, on the Burmese Frontier, February, 1879. (Journal of the Asiatic Society of Bengal, Vol. 50, pt. II, 1.) 8vo. Calcutta, 1881.

SWETTENHAM, F. A. Some Account of the Independent Native States of the Malay Peninsula, Part I. (Journal of the Straits British Royal Asiatic Society, No. 6, pp. 161-202.) Map 8vo. Singapore, 1881.

MAXWELL, W. E. Journey on Foot to the Patani Frontier in 1876. (Journal of the Straits British Royal Asiatic Society, No. 9, pp. 1-67.) 8vo. Singapore, 1882.

CAMERON, W. On the Patani. (Journal of the Straits British Royal Asiatic Society, No. 11, pp. 123–142.) 8vo. Singapore, 1883.

COLQUHOUN, A. R. Across Chrysê: being the Narrative of a Journey of Exploration through the South China Border Lands from Canton to Mandalay. 2 vols. Maps and illustrations. 8vo. London, 1883.

MOURA, J. Le Royaume du Cambodge. 2 vols. Maps, plans, and illustrations. Large 8vo. Paris, 1883.

PEAL, S. E. Notes of a Trip up the Dihing basin to Dapha Pani, etc., January and February, 1882. (Journal of the Asiatic Society of Bengal, Vol. 52, pt. II, 7.) 8vo. Calcutta, 1883.

COLQUHOUN, A. R., and HOLT S. HALLETT. Report on the Railway Connexion of Burmah and China; with Account of Exploration-Survey, by Holt S. Hallett, accompanied by Surveys, Vocabularies, and Appendices. Maps and illustrations. Folio. London, 1884.

THE VOYAGE OF JOHN HUYGHEN VAN LINSCHOTEN TO THE EAST INDIES. From the Old English Translation of 1598. The First Book, containing his Description of the East. Edited, the first volume by the late A. C. Burnell, Ph.D.; the second volume by Mr. P. A. Tiele. 2 vols. (Hakluyt Society's publications, Vols. 70 and 71.) Frontispiece. 8vo. London, 1885.

BOÜINAIS, A., and A. PAULUS. L'Indo-Chine Française Contemporaine. Cochinchine. 2e édition. Cambodge, Tonkin, Annam. 2 vols. Maps and illustrations. Large 8vo. Paris, 1885.

A MISSIONARY'S JOURNEY THROUGH LAOS FROM BANGKOK TO UBON. Contributed by the Rev. N. J. Couvreur. (Journal of the Straits British Royal Asiatic Society, No. 15, pp. 103–117.) 8vo. Singapore, 1885.

COLQUHOUN, A. R. Amongst the Shans; with upwards of fifty

whole-page Illustrations, and a Historical Sketch of the Shans, by Holt S. Hallett: preceded by an Introduction on the Cradle of the Shan Race, by Terrien de Lacouperie. Map. 8vo. London, 1885.

PETIT, E. Francis Garnier, sa Vie, ses Voyages, ses Œuvres. Paris, 1885.

SCOTT, J. G. (Shway Yoe). France and Tonking: a Narrative of the Campaign of 1884 and the Occupation of Further India. Map and plans. 8vo. London, 1885.

SWETTENHAM, F. A. Journal kept during a journey across the Malay Peninsula. (Journal of the Straits British Royal Asiatic Society, No. 15, pp. 1–37.) Map. 8vo. Singapore, 1885.

BRYCE, J. A. Burma: the Country and People. (Proceedings of the Royal Geographical Society (N. S.), Vol. 8, pp. 481–501.) Map. Large 8vo. London, 1886.

HALLETT, HOLT S. Exploration Survey for a Railway Connection between India, Siam, and China. (Proceedings of the Royal Geographical Society, Vol. 8 (N. S.), pp. 1–20.) Map. Large 8vo. London, 1886.

SCOTT, J. G. (Shway Yoe). Burma as it was, as it is, and as it will be. Sm. 8vo. London, 1886.

THE VOYAGE OF FRANÇOIS PYRARD OF LAVAL TO THE EAST INDIES, THE MALDIVES, THE MOLUCCAS, AND BRAZIL. Translated into English from the Third French Edition of 1619, and edited, with Notes, by Albert Gray, assisted by H. C. P. Bell. (Hakluyt Society's publications, Vols. 76, 77, 80.) Vol. 1. Map and illustrations. 8vo. London, 1887. Vol. 2, Part 1. Illustrations. 8vo. London, 1888. Vol. 2, Part 2. Charts and plates. 8vo. London, 1890.

DEW, A. T. Exploring Expedition from Selama Perak, to Pong, Patani. (Journal of the Straits British Royal Asiatic Society, No. 19, pp. 105–123.) 8vo. Singapore, 1887.

BROWNE, LIEUT.-COL. E. C. The Coming of the Great Queen: a Narrative of the Acquisition of Burma. Maps and illustrations. 8vo. London, 1888.

McCARTHY, J. Siam. (Proceedings of the Royal Geographical Society (N. S.), Vol. 10, pp. 117–134.) Map. Large 8vo. London, 1888.

STRINGER, C. E. W. Report of a Journey to the Laos State of Nan, Siam. Map. Folio. London, 1888.

COLQUHOUN, A. R. Exploration in Southern and South-Western China. (R. G. S. Supplementary Papers, Vol. 2.) Maps. Large 8vo. London, 1889.

PARIS, C. Voyage d'Exploration de Hué en Cochinchine par la Route Mandarine. Maps and illustrations. 8vo. Paris, 1889.

WOODTHORPE, COL. R. G. Explorations on the Chindwin River, Upper Burma. (Proceedings of the Royal Geographical Society (N. S.), Vol. 11, pp. 197–216.) Map. Large 8vo. London, 1889.

HALLETT, HOLT S. A Thousand Miles on an Elephant in the Shan States. Maps and illustrations. 8vo. London, 1890.

KEITH, A. An Account of a Journey across the Malay Peninsula from Koh Lak to Mergui. (Journal of the Straits British Royal Asiatic Society, No. 24, pp. 31–41.) 8vo. Singapore, 1891.

KEITH, A. Notes on the Siamese Provinces of Koowi, Bangtaphan, Pateeo and Champoon. (Journal of the Straits British Royal Asiatic Society, No. 24, pp. 63–78.) Map. 8vo. Singapore, 1891.

ELIOTT, LT. Expeditions among the Kachin Tribes on the North-east Frontier of Upper Burma. Compiled from the Reports of Lieutenant Eliott by Gen. J. T. Walker. (Proceedings of the Royal Geographical Society (N. S.), Vol. 14, pp. 161–173.) Map. Large 8vo. London, 1892.

ORLÉANS, PRINCE H. D'. Autour du Tonkin. Maps and illustrations. 8vo. Paris, 1894. Around Tonkin and Siam.

Translation by C. B. Pitman. Map and illustrations. 8vo. London, 1894.

FOURNEREAU, L. Le Siam Ancien, Archéologie, Epigraphie, Géographie. Première Partie. (Annales de Musée Guirnet. T. 27.) Plates and fac-simile maps. Sm. 4to. Paris, 1895.

SMYTH, H. W. Notes of a Journey on the Upper Mekong, Siam. Map and illustrations. 8vo. London [Royal Geographical Society], 1895.

ORLÉANS, PRINCE H. D'. Du Tonkin aux Indes, Janvier, 1895—Janvier, 1896. Maps and illustrations. Large 8vo. Paris, 1898. From Tonkin to India by the Sources of the Irawadi, January, '95, January, '96. Translation by Hawley Bent. Map and illustrations. Large 8vo. London, 1898.

PAVIE, A. Mission Pavie Indo-Chine, 1879-1895. 5 vols. Maps and illustrations. 4to. Paris, 1898–1902.

SMYTH, H. WARINGTON. Five Years in Siam, from 1891 to 1896. 2 vols. Maps and illustrations. 8vo. London, 1898.

AYMONIER, E. Le Cambodge. 2 vols. Maps and illustrations. Sm. folio. Paris, 1900–1901.

DUBOIS, ROBERT. Le Tonkin en 1900. Map and illustrations. 4to. Paris, 1900.

LAGRILLIÈRE-BEAUCLERC, E. A Travers l'Indo-Chine, Cochinchine, Cambodge, Annam, Tonkin, Laos. Map and illustrations. 8vo. Paris, 1900.

McCARTHY, J. Surveying and Exploring in Siam. Map, chart and illustrations. 8vo. London [Royal Geographical Society], 1900.

GERVAIS-COURTELLEMONT, ——, and others. Empire Colonial de la France, L'Indo-Chine, Cochinchine, Cambodge, Laos, Annam, Tonkin. Map and illustrations. 4to. Paris [n. d.].

REINACH, L. DE. Le Laos. 2 vols. Maps and illustrations. 4to. Paris [n. d.].

GENERAL REPORTS OF THE OPERATIONS OF THE SURVEY OF INDIA DEPARTMENT. Annual. Folio. Calcutta.

INDEX